THE JOHN HARVARD LIBRARY

Howard Mumford Jones
Editor-in-Chief

THE
GOSPEL OF WEALTH

And Other Timely Essays

By
ANDREW CARNEGIE

Edited by Edward C. Kirkland

THE BELKNAP PRESS OF
HARVARD UNIVERSITY PRESS
Cambridge, Massachusetts
1 9 6 2

CONTENTS

Editor's Introduction

Few men wanted more intensely to win than Andrew Carnegie; none was more certain his destiny was success. In 1868, at the age of thirty-three, he wrote in a famous introspective note a sentence of self-analysis: "Whatever I engage in I must push inordinately." Thirty years later he was trumpeting his triumphs in golf. "I am beating my friends at golf so all goes well. I played eighteen holes today with Taylor. Beat him! Beat Murray Butler Saturday. Beat Franks the day before."

Though he occasionally expressed a misgiving about success in business, his most genuine, his greatest achievement was as a businessman. The autobiographical fragment, hereafter published as the first essay, is correct in describing the Carnegie family's migration from Scotland when Andrew was young and his start in this country at the bottom of the industrial ladder. Later he found employment on the Pennsylvania Railroad and rose from telegrapher to a divisional superintendent. Meanwhile he was acquiring a fortune by saving and borrowing money and investing it in railroads and in firms supplying railroad equipment, in petroleum, and in various iron works. By 1868, when he penned the note already cited, he could expect an annual income of $50,000. Still pushing "inordinately," he transferred in the seventies his abilities and wealth to metallurgy. A business principle guided him: "Put all your eggs in one basket, and then watch that basket," and the financial strains of the panic of 1873 compelled him to concentrate his funds if he were to complete and operate The Edgar Thomson Steel Works near Pittsburgh. The plant made steel in Bessemer converters.

Though Carnegie was not the leader who introduced this revolutionary process to America, he was among the first to employ it on a large scale. In the years which followed he acquired coal and iron-ore properties and built mills to manufacture finished steel products. By the nineties Carnegie's was the most advanced and the most powerful unit in the American steel and iron industry. At the end of the century he sold out to the financiers and industrialists who were putting together the United States Steel Corporation. In 1901 after the sale he had a fortune of about $300,000,000.

Though he retired from business, he did not disown it. Instead of being its apologist, at a time when critics and reformers were detecting and exposing its flaws, he remained its celebrant. As he informed the undergraduates of Cornell University, "I can confidently recommend to you the business career as one in which there is abundant room for the exercise of man's highest power, and of every good quality in human nature. I believe the career of the great merchant, or banker, or captain of industry, to be favourable to the development of the powers of the mind, and to the ripening of the judgment upon a wide range of general subjects; to freedom from prejudice, and to the keeping of an open mind. . . . If without sound, all-round judgment, he must fail. The business career is thus a stern school of all the virtues. . . ." Commendation of this sort was, however, reserved for businessmen of a certain definition. "A man to be in business must be at least part owner of the enterprise which he manages," and be "chiefly dependent for his revenues . . . upon its profits." "The business man, pure and simple plunges into and tosses upon the waves of human affairs without a life-preserver in the shape of salary; he risks all. . . . The business man pursues fortune." This attitude set Carnegie a little apart from the business currents of his period. At a time when business was increasingly professionalized and bureaucratized, he excluded from the ranks of businessmen all salary receivers; when businessmen were consolidating their organizations into trusts, holding companies, and corporations, Carnegie remained the anarchic individualist, a reluctant participator in pools and agreements and a man who held his big business within the confines of the partnership form of organization until the nineties. But these anachronisms, if such they were, delighted Carnegie. In so far as they made him unique, they tickled his vanity.

Carnegie was fundamentally different, too, in his realization that there were in the world other values than those of a business culture and other goals than that of business success. His background mostly explained this. Radicals who admired the French Revolution and eloquently cursed social inequality and the unjust operation of the economy clustered along both sides of Carnegie's family tree. Indeed one of Andrew's uncles had been arrested for sedition after delivering a lecture on Chartism. For by this time the family's reforming impulse had channelized into supporting the political reform program which the working class had stated in the People's Charter. This document demanded universal manhood suffrage, voting by ballot, abolition of property qualifications for membership in Parliament and salaries for members, annual Parliaments, and equal electoral districts. Chartism, however, had fizzled out in 1848. But the circumstances which drove Andrew's immediate family to migrate to this country in that year were economic rather than political.

Whether defeated or not, a career of agitation developed in the Carnegies an ability at exposition, discussion, argument, public address, and newspaper writing. They were devoted to books. One ancestor, indeed, was nicknamed "Professor," and Carnegie's father was "an awfu' man to read." Carnegie never shook off this inheritance. Perhaps the Scottish admiration for the things of the mind and of the spirit reinforced the family's learned tradition. Nonetheless he was not sure later that the professions had as desirable an effect upon their practitioners as did business. The professional mind, preoccupied with fame rather than dollar getting, was "clear but narrow."

Yet it would be a mistake to ascribe Carnegie's non-business interests and concerns solely to a family or national background. Carnegie liked to be different. In business he loved to depart from the traditional paths of the ironmasters, "Fathers-in-Israel," as he derisively christened them. One of his favorite exhortations to young men was "Attract attention." He followed his own advice. At a time when such businessmen as John D. Rockefeller and Elbert H. Gary (1846–1927) were supposed to be without an intellectual attainment larger than the ability to lead a Sunday-school class, he was the friend of literary men, those characteristically successful like Mark Twain and Richard Watson Gilder (1844–1909) of the *Century*, who acted as a recruiter of the "gods" of the literary world that attended Carnegie's "literary dinners" at his home on upper Fifth Avenue. Carnegie loved to drop names — "My dear friend, Matthew Arnold," — and hobnob with college presidents and statesmen, particularly if British. In one mail he received letters from Gladstone, Spencer, and John Morley. "I am quite set up as no other can say this." There was a strong streak of the show-off in Carnegie; he sought to startle and perplex. This trait, combined with the fact that his attitudes were often formulated for an occasion, prevented his thought from attaining system or consistency. It was often contradictory and impish.

Nonetheless, the essays in this volume reveal certain underlying patterns of thought. The details, of course, were not all Carnegie's own. In the post-Civil War years books rather than preachers frequently converted American businessmen and made the tangle and perplexity of this world literally clear to them. Edward Atkinson (1827–1905), New England cotton manufacturer, insurance man and publicist, one of the most perceptive commentators on America's economic structure in the post-Civil War era, owed his intellectual emancipation to Carlyle's *Sartor Resartus*. Charles Francis Adams, Jr. (1835–1915), later President of the Union Pacific Railroad, found his road to Damascus in England when in 1865 he read John Stuart Mill's essay on Auguste Comte, which "revolutionized in a single morning my whole mental attitude." Andrew Carnegie records in his *Autobiography* how he chanced to read Darwin and certain works of Herbert Spencer. "I remember that light came as in a flood and all was clear. Not only had I got rid of theology and the supernatural, but I had found the truth of evolution. 'All is well since all grows better' became my motto, my true source of comfort." Carnegie became one of Spencer's greatest American friends and through a lifetime of association showered him with kindnesses and admiration. Over the years in book and essay Spencer wrote on many topics; whether Carnegie was acquainted with the whole body of Spencer's work or was influenced by it at every point it is quite impossible to tell. A discussion in the second of these essays, "The Problem of Wealth," uses Spencerian-Darwinian phrases and concepts to justify the regime of competition. But long before the "survival of the fittest" gained fashionable currency in the vocabulary of business and other men, it was believed that the race and its prizes belonged to the swift. Carnegie was as apt to quote the biblical parable of the talents as a justification for wealth as to cite evolution, and it is notable that his original acknowledgment of Spencerian influence was in religious and theological matters. Actually his secularism and skepticism, uncharacteristic of his business generation, owed quite as much to the beliefs of his immediate forebears as they did to natural and social science.

With his family background of Chartist reform it was not surprising that Carnegie was a passionate believer in democracy. Almost as soon as he reached the United States he was writing back to the homeland that he had found the fulfillment of his dreams — no royal family, no aristocracy, no established church. "We have the Charter which you have been fighting for for years as the Panacea for all Britain's woes." In 1886 he wrote *Triumphant Democracy*, as extravagant an example of booster or promotional literature as was ever penned by a public relations expert. In words which are touching for their sincerity and simplicity he dedicated the volume "To the Beloved Republic, under whose Equal Laws I am made the peer of any man, although denied political equality by my native land." Like his definition of the businessman, this statement is as remarkable for its emphasis as for its omissions. Its stress is social and political; its "equality" is political equality. On another occasion he defined democracy as not meaning "equality of conditions, physical or mental, or equality as to property. It does mean political equality and the equality of opportunity."

On nearly every count this was exactly the creed of American business in the decades of the late nineteenth century. Though there were doubters among them, American businessmen, even sophisticated ones, accepted the open-ended character of American society and its institutions — universal manhood suffrage, the free public school, the right of the laborer to choose his occupation and of the receiver of income, whether of salary, wages, or profits, to spend it as he chose. These were the cornerstones of the faith of a generation which, like Carnegie, was exceptionally sanguine, self-reliant and masculine. In some respects Carnegie carried the creed to more logical and more extreme positions than his business contemporaries. Most of them would hardly have seconded his approval of labor organization as an expression of self-reliance and as commendable striving by associated individuals for self-betterment. Carnegie here spoke for himself and a powerful minority of businessmen. If it had not been for these dissenters among employers, the task of labor unions would have been even more onerous.

Triumphant Democracy was more than an effusive love letter to the United States; it recommended a good example which England might well imitate. For one of Carnegie's boyhood dreams had been "to grow up to kill a king" and, more soberly, to transform Britain into a republic. In the early eighties he purchased a string of newspapers in Great Britain and through them and in other ways began to push his campaign. By the middle of the decade his movement petered out, failing to topple the House of Lords or abolish the monarchy and other traces of political privilege. *Triumphant Democracy* was therefore not an opening salvo but a valedictory. The theme of transforming Britain remained, however, a persistent one — if only wistfully. In 1890 Carnegie was writing to William Ewart Gladstone about the comforts and conveniences of the Pennsylvania Limited — "all of them free of charge" — between Chicago and New York. He concluded his letter, "What a quickening of the British mind we may get when the British Republic comes."

Though turned back from ultimate objectives, Carnegie maintained a deep interest in the course of British domestic politics, as the last four essays in this volume demonstrate. He was on friendly terms with English statesmen and did not refrain from lecturing or instructing them — and frequently baffling them. The body of British political doctrine that most appealed to him was Gladstonian liberalism. Its evangelical overtones must have left him cold, but in the later part of his career Gladstone at least supported the broadening of the suffrage and a series of measures culminating in Home Rule to allay or remove the age-old bitterness between Ireland and England. Of course the Carnegie-Gladstone relationship was not based solely upon the mutuality of political outlook. Gladstone was a success, a person who counted; for him Carnegie's admiration approached the idolatrous. When Gladstone commented in print on *The Gospel of Wealth*, the happy author wrote, "It seems like a dream that you who was to the little Scotch lad, something beyond human — should be attracted by anything he has promulgated and that he should really know you in the flesh. Always with reverence, Andrew Carnegie." Other leading

British exponents of liberalism, Lord Rosebery (1847–1929), for example, he tried to turn in a Gladstonian direction.

With a "native land" on one side of the Atlantic and an "adopted country" on the other, Carnegie perforce went beyond mere nationalism. He reinforced this dualism by taking long annual vacations in England and Scotland, the "fairyland," either in coach-and-four or on Scottish estates. Eventually he became the owner of Skibo, an estate of 30,000 acres and a castle with American improvements. At its flagstaff flew "the United flag . . . the Stars and Stripes and the Union Jack sewn together — the first of that kind of flag ever seen." Carnegie was naturally the apostle of a federation of England and the United States (in which the more numerous American inhabitants would outvote their transatlantic cousins), and of the annexation of Canada.

"I tell you," he wrote in 1898, "that *race* is the potent factor." His letters are replete with references to "The Race" or "Our Race." If he wanted a rationalization for the Anglo-Saxon supremacy which was largely instinctive with him, the context of his times would have provided it. The pastor and the professor alike were bursting from their studies to proclaim the glad tidings that the Teutonic or Anglo-Saxon races were "the political nations *par excellence*" and were authorized "in the economy of the world to assume the leadership in the establishment and administration of states." Of such moonshine the logical corollary was imperialism, and Admiral Alfred Thayer Mahan (1840–1914) in his discussions of sea power and historical greatness (*The Influence of Sea Power upon History*, 1890) became its spokesman. But Carnegie had too much common sense; he pulled back. Though the Spanish-American War gave the possibility of realizing imperial visions, such a program appalled Carnegie as a defiance of American principles. Two essays, "Distant Possessions" and "Americanism versus Imperialism," state his reservations to racism thus operating. He joined with other Americans to forestall a peace treaty consummating this betrayal, he helped finance the Anti-Imperialist League, and he tried to influence public men with such zeal as to elicit from one of them the observation that "Andrew Carnegie seems to be off his head." In 1900, however, he refused to finance a third party movement against William McKinley. The ineptitude of this proposal is perhaps enough to justify Carnegie's decision, but his withdrawal cannot but raise the question whether, as in his campaign for a British Republic, he was genuinely interested in following through reforms which were not a success in the short run.

Of course he could elevate a specific issue to a broader basis. He could take comfort for the failure of his British campaign in the thought of an Anglo-Saxon, English-speaking federation and the consequent democratic political changes forced upon his native land. For the failure of federation to materialize and for the collapse of true Americanism, perhaps a campaign for world peace through other devices could be some counterweight. Soon after his arrival as a youth in this country he wrote an essay against the Crimean War in which he maintained that the machines of war deserve the execration given to the scaffold or guillotine. Later he was drawn into the Peace Society of Great Britain, and he dates from the late eighties his preoccupation with the abolition of war. At first he was apparently sanguine enough to believe a hatred of war was enough to abolish it; later he saw in arbitration an alternative to conflict. Eventually Carnegie financed the construction at The Hague of a "Temple of Peace — the most holy building in the world because it has the holiest end in view. I do not even except St. Peter's, or any other building erected to the Glory of God. . . ." And in 1910 he gave $10,000,000 for the Carnegie Endowment for International Peace. Carnegie's commitment to the peace movement had the incidental advantages of personal association with statesmen and scholars at international conferences to which he was frequently appointed a delegate and of the award of foreign decorations.

In the area of war and peace Carnegie was not a deviant from the accepted canon of business thought. In the writings of the business press and of businessmen few themes are more frequent and more persistent than the realization that America's position and policy by conducing to peace gave the nation an immense competitive advantage. It avoided the wasteful expenditure of public funds on armament and the crushing burden of high taxes; it directed our manpower to production rather than military purposes. On the contrary, our European competitors had to shoulder these burdens — much to our advantage. War upset the rationality and order which business was trying to introduce into economic operations.

As I have indicated, it is impossible to treat Carnegie's non-business interests without mentioning his benefactions. The most significant essays in this volume are those which contribute its title. The philosophy there set forth had been succinctly anticipated in 1868 in Carnegie's famous memorandum to himself: "Beyond this [$50,000 a year] never earn — make no effort to increase fortune, but spend the surplus each year for benevolent purposes. . . . Man must have an idol — the amassing of wealth is one of the worst species of idolatry — no idol more debasing than the worship of money. . . . To continue much longer . . . with most of my thoughts wholly upon the way to make more money in the shortest possible time, must degrade me beyond hopes of permanent recovery." As a declaration of personal allegiance to a program this avowal and the later "Gospel of Wealth" are revealing. But historically they have little novelty. For centuries Christianity had exalted and consecrated individual generosity and benevolence; charity was a Christian virtue, and Christ had answered the rich young man's question, "What shall I do to inherit eternal life?" by the directive, "Sell all that thou hast and distribute unto the poor." Through the ages men and women had followed an ideal of the Christian stewardship of wealth.

That Carnegie should take this path was startling, for his tone had been secular, and he believed there was truth in all religions. Since clerics have a keen scent for heresy and a sharp eye for danger, the hostility or moderation with which they greeted Carnegie's "Gospel of Wealth" had significance. While granting that his statement was "interesting," they generally went on to celebrate the virtues and achievements of Christian charity or wandered off into irrelevancies like the tariff. One eminent Methodist divine in England chose to discuss the "Gospel of Wealth" as a therapy for social ills — Carnegie had certainly invited discussion on this level — and concluded that a millionaire of the Carnegie class was "an anti-christian phenomenon, a social monstrosity, and a grave political peril!" To grant that Carnegie contributed a secular tone to giving is not to assert that he was a pioneer in this respect. In America the note goes back at least to Franklin; and Stephen Girard, another Philadelphian, had in his endowment for Girard College expressly stipulated that "no ecclesiastic, missionary, or minister of any sort whatever, shall ever hold or exercise any station or duty whatever in the said College; nor shall any such person ever be admitted for any purpose, or as a visitor, within the premises appropriated to the purposes of the said College."

While it has been demonstrated that American public opinion expected rich men to give at least part of their fortunes for public purposes, it did not follow that such generosity was a path to popularity. Carnegie did not find it so. When he first offered Pittsburgh $250,000 for a library building, the City Council rejected it. Later, when the City changed its mind, Carnegie gave $1,000,000 and went on to give, as well as a library, an art museum and music hall. Smaller places showed the same reluctance to accept a Carnegie gift. It was said he insisted that the building bear his name; this was untrue. Others apparently suspected that acceptance was an endorsement of the methods by which Carnegie had acquired his fortune. A more important and concrete objection was Carnegie's insistence that communities appropriate an amount, usually a percentage of his gift, for the support of the buildings he gave them; communities bristled at dictation from the steel king. Nor did Carnegie find it easy to dispense his fortune wisely. Begging letters poured in by the thousands. For his benefactions Carnegie sought out expert advisors; in the field of education the presidents of Cornell and Johns Hopkins played this role. In cases he handled on his own he often exhibited extraordinary sensitivity and patience. Anyone who reads the interchange of letters about the purchase of Lord Acton's library — the terms stipulated that Acton could continue without embarrassment to use it — will be impressed by the delicacy and tact of the philanthropist. Nonetheless, the evolving forms in the administration of his bequests reflected Carnegie's experiences as a giver and his fatigue as a merely personal administrator.

In the last analysis Carnegie's achievement as a philanthropist lay in doing what he wrote he ought to do; or, phrased in another way, he had an intellectual rather than a purely impulsive formula for his giving. This always overimpresses intellectuals. Be that as it may, he built 2,507 libraries — the free public library was to his mind the people's university. In the more formal educational field he financed technical training at the Carnegie Institute of Technology, encouraged research in basic science by the Carnegie Institution of Washington, and through the Carnegie Foundation for the Advancement of Teaching established a pension fund for college teachers. Only institutions without denominational connections could apply for inclusion. Finally in 1911 he created the Carnegie Corporation of New York, a separate foundation as large as all his other trusts combined. In simplified spelling, the Corporation was enjoined "to promote the advancement and diffusion of knowledge and understanding among the people of the United States, by aiding technical schools, institutions of higher lerning, libraries, scientific reserch, hero funds, useful publications, and by such other agencies and means as shall from time to time be found appropriate therefor." Before his death in 1919 he gave away $311,000,000.

It does not impugn the noble integrity of this achievement to point out that Carnegie's program of philanthropy ministered to his exhibitionism. Though he modestly forbade the specific memorialization of his name, the essay, "Gospel of Wealth," enabled him to be a distinctive rich man, to select among his "dear fellow millionaries" — past and present — those he could commend or, by inference, censure. As he roamed about cracking heads or dispensing bouquets, he could play the congenial role of the maverick, a role J. P. Morgan found so disturbing in him. He could startle. On the stage of attention and influence, where he loved to stride, he could toss about once again the "Fathers-in Israel."

For some reason literateness in businessmen arouses popular and occasionally scholarly suspicion. They are thought not to possess the brains to think abstractly and summon thought or the ability to write the works to which their names are signed. Although Carnegie lived before the days when ghost-writing was standard operating procedure for businessmen and politicians (and occasionally candidates for the Ph.D.), he has not escaped the stigma. In the folklore of possible authorship the most common name given to the "faceless one" is that of James Howard Bridge. Carnegie once referred to him as "my clever secretary." Undoubtedly Bridge was of great assistance in the compilation of *Triumphant Democracy*, and he wrote a book on his own to prove that Carnegie had little to do with the accumulation of his fortune — this was the work of others. An examination of the private papers of Carnegie in the Library of Congress is enough to refute the notion that Carnegie could not express himself. The essays in this volume are authentic Carnegie.

Nor was he the only literate or articulate man of business in a notable business generation. John D. Rockefeller collected in a volume his *Random Reminiscences of Men and Events* (1909); in spite of later scholarship, the volume retains a usefulness. Of business essayists contemporary with Carnegie, Edward Atkinson, the economist David A. Wells (1828–1898), the railroad journalist and economist Henry Varnum Poor (1812–1905), to mention no others, were all penetrating observers. Like Carnegie, they felt writing was a way to influence, and they sought quite consciously so to write and so to publish as to shape public opinion and policy. When due attention has been given to these business writers and to the media in which their work appeared, the business literature of the age will compare favorably in bulk and in force with that of reformists and critics.

Carnegie wrote of events of course as he saw them in his own time, and it is scarcely to his discredit that he could not foresee the ironies subsequent events of twentieth-century history have produced — the two world wars despite his "Temple of Peace" at the Hague; revolution in Cuba and alignment with a foreign power despite the Monroe Doctrine; decline of empire and emergence of new nations on the African continent, then the arena of fierce new imperialistic rivalries; the vast American commitments all over the world; permanent conscription; continuing frustrations of international "co-operation"; the rise in power of Soviet Russia, no longer "one of our best friends." Nevertheless, typical spokesman of business as Carnegie was, he remains unique in the variety of his interests, the fecundity of his writing, and, in my estimation, in the impression he made. The re-publication of these essays should remove once and for all the commonplace notion that the whole business generation was one of "robber barons" and that its members were all either crooks or clowns, dunces or hypocrites.

A Note on the Text

The first edition of THE GOSPEL OF WEALTH *And Other Timely Essays* came out in 1900, when the Century Company adapted and assembled in one volume twelve articles of topical interest written by Carnegie between 1886 and 1899. Acknowledgement of the original sources was made in the following statement: "The various articles in this volume are reprinted by permission of the publishers of the periodicals in which they originally appeared. The autobiographical fragment which precedes the essays proper was written for the 'Youth's Companion'; the other papers were first published in the 'Century Magazine,' the 'North American Review,' the 'Forum,' the 'Contemporary Review,' the 'Fortnightly Review,' and 'Nineteenth Century,' and the 'Scottish Leader.'" Curiously enough, although the edition carefully identified each essay by periodical and year, none is attributed to the *Fortnightly Review*. The present text follows that of 1900. A subsequent edition (1906) includes an additional essay entitled "British Pessimism," which had appeared in the *Nineteenth Century and After* in 1901.

Chronology of Carnegie's Life

1835   Born November 25 at Dunfermline, Scotland, son of Margaret (Morrison) and William Carnegie.

1848   Brought to the United States. Family settled in Allegheny, Pennsylvania. Began work immediately as bobbin-boy in cotton factory.

1849   First messenger, then operator at Pittsburgh telegraph office.

1853   Position with Pennsylvania Railroad.

1861   Accompanied Scott to Washington at outbreak of Civil War.

1865   Resigned from railroad to organize own firm, Keystone Bridge Company.

1873   Travel to Europe and association with British steel makers, especially Bessemer. Began concentration on steel here.

1882   Joined forces with Henry Clay Frick, acquiring vast coke properties.

1883   Published *An American Four-in-Hand* in Britain. Began contributions to magazines, notably *North American Review* and *Nineteenth Century*.

1886   Published *Triumphant Democracy*.

1887   Married Louise Whitfield.

1889   "Wealth" published in *North American Review*.

1892   Break with Frick; Homestead Strike.

1901   Sold out to United States Steel. Gave $5,000,000 to employees for pension and benefit fund. Began major philanthropies.

1907   Built Peace Palace at The Hague.

1919   August 11, died at "Shadowbrook," in Massachusetts.

THE
GOSPEL OF WEALTH

And Other Timely Essays

By
ANDREW CARNEGIE

· I ·

Introduction: How I Served My Apprenticeship [1]

It is a great pleasure to tell how I served my apprenticeship as a business man. But there seems to be a question preceding this: Why did I become a business man? I am sure that I should never have selected a business career if I had been permitted to choose.

The eldest son of parents who were themselves poor, I had, fortunately, to begin to perform some useful work in the world while still very young in order to earn an honest livelihood, and was thus shown even in early boyhood that my duty was to assist my parents and, like them, become, as soon as possible, a bread-winner in the family. What I could get to do, not what I desired, was the question.

When I was born my father was a well-to-do master weaver in Dunfermline, Scotland. He owned no less than four damask-looms and employed apprentices. This was before the days of steam-factories for the manufacture of linen. A few large merchants took orders, and employed master weavers, such as my father, to weave the cloth, the merchants supplying the materials.

As the factory system developed hand-loom weaving naturally declined, and my father was one of the sufferers by the change. The first serious lesson of my life came to me one day when he had taken in the last of his work to the merchant, and returned to our little home greatly distressed because there was no more work for him to do. I was then just about

[1] Published in the *Youth's Companion*, April 23, 1896.

ten years of age, but the lesson burned into my heart, and I resolved then that the wolf of poverty should be driven from our door some day, if I could do it.

The question of selling the old looms and starting for the United States came up in the family council, and I heard it discussed from day to day. It was finally resolved to take the plunge and join relatives already in Pittsburg. I well remember that neither father nor mother thought the change would be otherwise than a great sacrifice for them, but that "it would be better for the two boys."

In after life, if you can look back as I do and wonder at the complete surrender of their own desires which parents make for the good of their children, you must reverence their memories with feelings akin to worship.

On arriving in Allegheny City (there were four of us: father, mother, my younger brother, and myself), my father entered a cotton factory. I soon followed, and served as a "bobbin-boy," and this is how I began my preparation for subsequent apprenticeship as a business man. I received one dollar and twenty cents a week, and was then just about twelve years old.

I cannot tell you how proud I was when I received my first week's own earnings. One dollar and twenty cents made by myself and given to me because I had been of some use in the world! No longer entirely dependent upon my parents, but at last admitted to the family partnership as a contributing member and able to help them! I think this makes a man out of a boy sooner than almost anything else, and a real man, too, if there be any germ of true manhood in him. It is everything to feel that you are useful.

I have had to deal with great sums. Many millions of dollars have since passed through my hands. But the genuine satisfaction I had from that one dollar and twenty cents outweighs any subsequent pleasure in money-getting. It was the direct reward of honest, manual labor; it represented a week of very hard work — so hard that, but for the aim and end which sanctified it, slavery might not be much too strong a term to describe it.

For a lad of twelve to rise and breakfast every morning, except the blessed Sunday morning, and go into the streets and find his way to the factory and begin to work while it was still dark outside, and not be released until after darkness came again in the evening, forty minutes' interval only being allowed at noon, was a terrible task.

But I was young and had my dreams, and something within always told me that this would not, could not, should not last — I should some day get into a better position. Besides this, I felt myself no longer a mere boy, but quite a little man, and this made me happy.

A change soon came, for a kind old Scotsman, who knew some of our relatives, made bobbins, and took me into his factory before I was thirteen. But here for a time it was even worse than in the cotton factory, because I was set to fire a boiler in the cellar, and actually to run the small steam-engine which drove the machinery. The firing of the boiler was all right, for fortunately we did not use coal, but the refuse wooden chips; and I always liked to work in wood. But the responsibility of keeping the water right and of running the engine, and the danger of my making a mistake and blowing the whole factory to pieces, caused too great a strain, and I often awoke and found myself sitting up in bed through the night, trying the steam-gauges. But I never told them at home that I was having a hard tussle. No, no! everything must be bright to them.

This was a point of honor, for every member of the family was working hard, except, of course, my little brother, who was then a child, and we were telling each other only all the bright things. Besides this, no man would whine and give up — he would die first.

There was no servant in our family, and several dollars per

week were earned by the mother by binding shoes after her daily work was done! Father was also hard at work in the factory. And could I complain?

My kind employer, John Hay, — peace to his ashes! — soon relieved me of the undue strain, for he needed some one to make out bills and keep his accounts, and finding that I could write a plain school-boy hand and could "cipher," he made me his only clerk. But still I had to work hard upstairs in the factory, for the clerking took but little time.

You know how people moan about poverty as being a great evil, and it seems to be accepted that if people had only plenty of money and were rich, they would be happy and more useful, and get more out of life.

As a rule, there is more genuine satisfaction, a truer life, and more obtained from life in the humble cottages of the poor than in the palaces of the rich. I always pity the sons and daughters of rich men, who are attended by servants, and have governesses at a later age, but am glad to remember that they do not know what they have missed.

They have kind fathers and mothers, too, and think that they enjoy the sweetness of these blessings to the fullest: but this they cannot do; for the poor boy who has in his father his constant companion, tutor, and model, and in his mother — holy name! — his nurse, teacher, guardian angel, saint, all in one, has a richer, more precious fortune in life than any rich man's son who is not so favored can possibly know, and compared with which all other fortunes count for little.

It is because I know how sweet and happy and pure the home of honest poverty is, how free from perplexing care, from social envies and emulations, how loving and how united its members may be in the common interest of supporting the family, that I sympathize with the rich man's boy and congratulate the poor man's boy; and it is for these reasons that from the ranks of the poor so many strong, eminent, self-reliant men have always sprung and always must spring.

If you will read the list of the immortals who "were not born to die," you will find that most of them have been born to the precious heritage of poverty.

It seems, nowadays, a matter of universal desire that poverty should be abolished. We should be quite willing to abolish luxury, but to abolish honest, industrious, self-denying poverty would be to destroy the soil upon which mankind produces the virtues which enable our race to reach a still higher civilization than it now possesses.

I come now to the third step in my apprenticeship, for I had already taken two, as you see — the cotton factory and then the bobbin factory; and with the third — the third time is the chance, you know — deliverance came. I obtained a situation as messenger boy in the telegraph office of Pittsburg when I was fourteen. Here I entered a new world.

Amid books, newspapers, pencils, pens and ink and writing-pads, and a clean office, bright windows, and the literary atmosphere, I was the happiest boy alive.

My only dread was that I should some day be dismissed because I did not know the city; for it is necessary that a messenger boy should know all the firms and addresses of men who are in the habit of receiving telegrams. But I was a stranger in Pittsburg. However, I made up my mind that I would learn to repeat successively each business house in the principal streets, and was soon able to shut my eyes and begin at one side of Wood Street, and call every firm successively to the top, then pass to the other side and call every firm to the bottom. Before long I was able to do this with the business streets generally. My mind was then at rest upon that point.

Of course every messenger boy wants to become an operator, and before the operators arrive in the early mornings the boys slipped up to the instruments and practised. This I did, and was soon able to talk to the boys in the other offices along the line, who were also practising.

One morning I heard Philadelphia calling Pittsburg and giving the signal, "Death message." Great attention was then paid to "death messages," and I thought I ought to try to take this one. I answered and did so, and went off and delivered it before the operator came. After that the operators sometimes used to ask me to work for them.

Having a sensitive ear for sound, I soon learned to take messages by the ear, which was then very uncommon — I think only two persons in the United States could then do it. Now every operator takes by ear, so easy it is to follow and do what any other boy can — if you only have to. This brought me into notice, and finally I became an operator, and received the, to me, enormous recompense of twenty-five dollars per month — three hundred dollars a year!

This was a fortune — the very sum that I had fixed when I was a factory-worker as the fortune I wished to possess, because the family could live on three hundred dollars a year and be almost or quite independent. Here it was at last! But I was soon to be in receipt of extra compensation for extra work.

The six newspapers of Pittsburg received telegraphic news in common. Six copies of each despatch were made by a gentleman who received six dollars per week for the work, and he offered me a gold dollar every week if I would do it, of which I was very glad indeed, because I always liked to work with news and scribble for newspapers.

The reporters came to a room every evening for the news which I had prepared, and this brought me into most pleasant intercourse with these clever fellows, and besides, I got a dollar a week as pocket-money, for this was not considered family revenue by me.

I think this last step of doing something beyond one's task is fully entitled to be considered "business." The other revenue, you see, was just salary obtained for regular work;

but here was a little business operation upon my own account, and I was very proud indeed of my gold dollar every week.

The Pennsylvania Railroad shortly after this was completed to Pittsburg, and that genius, Thomas A. Scott,[2] was its superintendent. He often came to the telegraph office to talk to his chief, the general superintendent, at Altoona, and I became known to him in this way.

When that great railway system put up a wire of its own, he asked me to be his clerk and operator; so I left the telegraph office — in which there is great danger that a young man may be permanently buried, as it were — and became connected with the railways.

The new appointment was accompanied by what was, to me, a tremendous increase of salary. It jumped from twenty-five to thirty-five dollars per month. Mr. Scott was then receiving one hundred and twenty-five dollars per month, and I used to wonder what on earth he could do with so much money.

I remained for thirteen years in the service of the Pennsylvania Railroad Company, and was at last superintendent of the Pittsburg division of the road, successor to Mr. Scott, who had in the meantime risen to the office of vice-president of the company.

One day Mr. Scott, who was the kindest of men, and had taken a great fancy to me, asked if I had or could find five hundred dollars to invest.

Here the business instinct came into play. I felt that as the door was opened for a business investment with my chief, it would be wilful flying in the face of providence if I did not jump at it; so I answered promptly:

"Yes, sir; I think I can."

"Very well," he said, "get it; a man has just died who owns

---

[2] Scott (1823–1881) was the railroad executive who warned Lincoln not to proceed directly to Washington for his inauguration and who served the Union cause significantly during the Civil War as supervisor and adviser on problems of transportation of men and supplies.

ten shares in the Adams Express Company which I want you to buy. It will cost you fifty dollars per share, and I can help you with a little balance if you cannot raise it all."

Here was a queer position. The available assets of the whole family were not five hundred dollars. But there was one member of the family whose ability, pluck, and resource never failed us, and I felt sure the money could be raised somehow or other by my mother.

Indeed, had Mr. Scott known our position he would have advanced it himself; but the last thing in the world the proud Scot will do is to reveal his poverty and rely upon others. The family had managed by this time to purchase a small house and pay for it in order to save rent. My recollection is that it was worth eight hundred dollars.

The matter was laid before the council of three that night, and the oracle spoke: "Must be done. Mortgage our house. I will take the steamer in the morning for Ohio, and see uncle, and ask him to arrange it. I am sure he can." This was done. Of course her visit was successful — where did she ever fail?

The money was procured, paid over; ten shares of Adams Express Company stock was mine; but no one knew our little home had been mortgaged "to give our boy a start."

Adams Express stock then paid monthly dividends of one per cent, and the first check for five dollars arrived. I can see it now, and I well remember the signature of "J. C. Babcock, Cashier," who wrote a big "John Hancock" hand.

The next day being Sunday, we boys — myself and my ever-constant companions — took our usual Sunday afternoon stroll in the country, and sitting down in the woods, I showed them this check, saying, "Eureka! We have found it."

Here was something new to all of us, for none of us had ever received anything but from toil. A return from capital was something strange and new.

How money could make money, how, without any attention from me, this mysterious golden visitor should come, led to much speculation upon the part of the young fellows, and I was for the first time hailed as a "capitalist."

You see, I was beginning to serve my apprenticeship as a business man in a satisfactory manner.

A very important incident in my life occurred when, one day in a train, a nice, farmer-looking gentleman approached me, saying that the conductor had told him I was connected with the Pennsylvania Railroad, and he would like to show me something. He pulled from a small green bag the model of the first sleeping-car. This was Mr. Woodruff, the inventor.[3]

Its value struck me like a flash. I asked him to come to Altoona the following week, and he did so. Mr. Scott, with his usual quickness, grasped the idea. A contract was made with Mr. Woodruff to put two trial cars on the Pennsylvania Railroad. Before leaving Altoona Mr. Woodruff came and offered me an interest in the venture, which I promptly accepted. But how I was to make my payments rather troubled me, for the cars were to be paid for in monthly instalments after delivery, and my first monthly payment was to be two hundred and seventeen dollars and a half.

I had not the money, and I did not see any way of getting it. But I finally decided to visit the local banker and ask him for a loan, pledging myself to repay at the rate of fifteen dollars per month. He promptly granted it. Never shall I forget his putting his arm over my shoulder, saying, "Oh, yes, Andy; you are all right!"

I then and there signed my first note. Proud day this; and surely now no one will dispute that I was becoming a "business man." I had signed my first note, and, most important of all, — for any fellow can sign a note, — I had found a banker willing to take it as "good."

My subsequent payments were made by the receipts from the sleeping-cars, and I really made my first considerable

[3] Theodore Tuttle Woodruff (1811–1892), whose idea for sleeping cars dated from as early as 1830, produced his first model in 1857.

sum from this investment in the Woodruff Sleeping-car Company, which was afterward absorbed by Mr. Pullman — a remarkable man whose name is now known over all the world.

Shortly after this I was appointed superintendent of the Pittsburg division, and returned to my dear old home, smoky Pittsburg. Wooden bridges were then used exclusively upon the railways, and the Pennsylvania Railroad was experimenting with a bridge built of cast-iron. I saw that wooden bridges would not do for the future, and organized a company in Pittsburg to build iron bridges.

Here again I had recourse to the bank, because my share of the capital was twelve hundred and fifty dollars, and I had not the money; but the bank lent it to me, and we began the Keystone Bridge Works, which proved a great success. This company built the first great bridge over the Ohio River, three hundred feet span, and has built many of the most important structures since.

This was my beginning in manufacturing; and from that start all our other works have grown, the profits of one building the other. My "apprenticeship" as a business man soon ended, for I resigned my position as an officer of the Pennsylvania Railroad Company to give exclusive attention to business.

I was no longer merely an official working for others upon a salary, but a full-fledged business man working upon my own account.

I never was quite reconciled to working for other people. At the most, the railway officer has to look forward to the enjoyment of a stated salary, and he has a great many people to please; even if he gets to be president, he has sometimes a board of directors who cannot know what is best to be done; and even if this board be satisfied, he has a board of stockholders to criticize him, and as the property is not his own he cannot manage it as he pleases.

I always liked the idea of being my own master, of manufacturing something and giving employment to many men. There is only one thing to think of manufacturing if you are a Pittsburger, for Pittsburg even then had asserted her supremacy as the "Iron City," the leading iron-and-steel-manufacturing city in America.

So my indispensable and clever partners, who had been my boy companions, I am delighted to say, — some of the very boys who had met in the grove to wonder at the five-dollar check, — began business, and still continue extending it to meet the ever-growing and ever-changing wants of our most progressive country, year after year.

Always we are hoping that we need expand no farther; yet ever we are finding that to stop expanding would be to fall behind; and even to-day the successive improvements and inventions follow each other so rapidly that we see just as much yet to be done as ever.

When the manufacturer of steel ceases to grow he begins to decay, so we must keep on extending. The result of all these developments is that three pounds of finished steel are now bought in Pittsburg for two cents, which is cheaper than anywhere else on the earth, and that our country has become the greatest producer of iron in the world.

And so ends the story of my apprenticeship and graduation as a business man.

· II ·

The Gospel of Wealth [1]

I

THE problem of our age is the proper administration of wealth, that the ties of brotherhood may still bind together the rich and poor in harmonious relationship. The conditions of human life have not only been changed, but revolutionized, within the past few hundred years. In former days there was little difference between the dwelling, dress, food, and environment of the chief and those of his retainers. The Indians are to-day where civilized man then was. When visiting the Sioux, I was led to the wigwam of the chief. It was like the others in external appearance, and even within the difference was trifling between it and those of the poorest of his braves. The contrast between the palace of the millionaire and the cottage of the laborer with us to-day measures the change which has come with civilization. This

[1] Published originally in the *North American Review*, CXLVIII (June 1889), 653–664, and CXLIX (December 1889), 682–698. Carnegie did not devise the appropriate and fetching title this essay now bears. He called it "Wealth." William T. Stead, editor of the *Pall Mall Gazette*, supplied the heading "The Gospel of Wealth." The personally dramatic circumstances under which the editor of the *North American Review* accepted the original article highly appealed to Carnegie's vanity and bent for personal excitement. He reported the circumstances in the first two paragraphs of his second periodical article, "The Best Fields for Philanthropy," which appeared in the *Review* in December 1889. As the latter article is here reprinted, Carnegie omitted this episode and began with the third paragraph of the original. There were also other minor changes from the original essay.

change, however, is not to be deplored, but welcomed as highly beneficial. It is well, nay, essential, for the progress of the race that the houses of some should be homes for all that is highest and best in literature and the arts, and for all the refinements of civilization, rather than that none should be so. Much better this great irregularity than universal squalor. Without wealth there can be no Mæcenas. The "good old times" were not good old times. Neither master nor servant was as well situated then as to-day. A relapse to old conditions would be disastrous to both — not the least so to him who serves — and would sweep away civilization with it. But whether the change be for good or ill, it is upon us, beyond our power to alter, and, therefore, to be accepted and made the best of. It is a waste of time to criticize the inevitable.

It is easy to see how the change has come. One illustration will serve for almost every phase of the cause. In the manufacture of products we have the whole story. It applies to all combinations of human industry, as stimulated and enlarged by the inventions of this scientific age. Formerly, articles were manufactured at the domestic hearth, or in small shops which formed part of the household. The master and his apprentices worked side by side, the latter living with the master, and therefore subject to the same conditions. When these apprentices rose to be masters, there was little or no change in their mode of life, and they, in turn, educated succeeding apprentices in the same routine. There was, substantially, social equality, and even political equality, for those engaged in industrial pursuits had then little or no voice in the State.

The inevitable result of such a mode of manufacture was crude articles at high prices. To-day the world obtains commodities of excellent quality at prices which even the preceding generation would have deemed incredible. In the commercial world similar causes have produced similar results, and the race is benefited thereby. The poor enjoy what the rich could not before afford. What were the luxuries have become the necessaries of life. The laborer has now more comforts than the farmer had a few generations ago. The farmer has more luxuries than the landlord had, and is more richly clad and better housed. The landlord has books and pictures rarer and appointments more artistic than the king could then obtain.

The price we pay for this salutary change is, no doubt, great. We assemble thousands of operatives in the factory, and in the mine, of whom the employer can know little or nothing, and to whom he is little better than a myth. All intercourse between them is at an end. Rigid castes are formed, and, as usual, mutual ignorance breeds mutual distrust. Each caste is without sympathy with the other, and ready to credit anything disparaging in regard to it. Under the law of competition, the employer of thousands is forced into the strictest economies, among which the rates paid to labor figure prominently, and often there is friction between the employer and the employed, between capital and labor, between rich and poor. Human society loses homogeneity.

The price which society pays for the law of competition, like the price it pays for cheap comforts and luxuries, is also great; but the advantages of this law are also greater still than its cost — for it is to this law that we owe our wonderful material development, which brings improved conditions in its train. But, whether the law be benign or not, we must say of it, as we say of the change in the conditions of men to which we have referred: It is here; we cannot evade it; no substitutes for it have been found; and while the law may be sometimes hard for the individual, it is best for the race, because it insures the survival of the fittest in every department. We accept and welcome, therefore, as conditions to which we must accommodate ourselves, great inequality of environment; the concentration of business, industrial and commercial, in the hands of a few; and the law of competition between these, as being not only beneficial, but essential to the future progress of the race. Having accepted these, it follows that there must be great scope for the exercise of special ability in the merchant and in the manufacturer who has to conduct affairs upon a great scale. That this talent for organization and management is rare among men is proved by the fact that it invariably secures enormous rewards for its possessor, no matter where or under what laws or conditions. The experienced in affairs always rate the MAN whose services can be obtained as a partner as not only the first consideration, but such as render the question of his capital scarcely worth considering: for able men soon create capital; in the hands of those without the special talent required, capital soon takes wings. Such men become interested in firms or corporations using millions; and, estimating only simple interest to be made upon the capital invested, it is inevitable that their income must exceed their expenditure and that they must, therefore, accumulate wealth. Nor is there any middle ground which such men can occupy, because the great manufacturing or commercial concern which does not earn at least interest upon its capital soon becomes bankrupt. It must either go forward or fall behind; to stand still is impossible. It is a condition essential to its successful operation that it should be thus far profitable, and even that, in addition to interest on capital, it should make profit. It is a law, as certain as any of the others named, that men possessed of this peculiar talent for affairs, under the free play of economic forces must, of necessity, soon be in receipt of more revenue than can be judiciously expended upon themselves; and this law is as beneficial for the race as the others.

Objections to the foundations upon which society is based are not in order, because the condition of the race is better with these than it has been with any other which has been tried. Of the effect of any new substitutes proposed we cannot be sure. The Socialist or Anarchist who seeks to overturn present conditions is to be regarded as attacking the foundation upon which civilization itself rests, for civilization took its start from the day when the capable, industrious workman said to his incompetent and lazy fellow, "If thou dost not sow, thou shalt not reap," and thus ended primitive Communism by separating the drones from the bees. One who studies this subject will soon be brought face to face with the conclusion that upon the sacredness of property civilization itself depends — the right of the laborer to his hundred dollars in the savings-bank, and equally the legal right of the millionaire to his millions. Every man must be allowed "to sit under his own vine and fig-tree, with none to make afraid," if human society is to advance, or even to remain so far advanced as it is. To those who propose to substitute Communism for this intense Individualism, the answer therefore is: The race has tried that. All progress from that barbarous day to the present time has resulted from its displacement. Not evil, but good, has come to the race from the accumulation of wealth by those who have had the ability and energy to produce it. But even if we admit for a moment that it might be better for the race to discard its present foundation, Individualism, — that it is a nobler ideal that man should labor, not for himself alone, but in and for a brotherhood of his fellows, and share with them all in common, realizing Swedenborg's idea of heaven,[2] where, as he says, the angels derive their happiness, not from laboring for self, but for each other, — even admit all this, and a sufficient answer is, This is not evolution, but revolution. It necessitates the changing of human nature itself — a work of eons, even if it were good to change it, which we cannot know.

It is not practicable in our day or in our age. Even if desirable theoretically, it belongs to another and long-succeeding sociological stratum. Our duty is with what is practicable now — with the next step possible in our day and generation. It is criminal to waste our energies in endeavoring to uproot,

---

[2] Carnegie is referring to Emanuel Swedenborg's (1688–1772) mystic theology expressed in his work *Heaven and Hell*.

when all we can profitably accomplish is to bend the universal tree of humanity a little in the direction most favorable to the production of good fruit under existing circumstances. We might as well urge the destruction of the highest existing type of man because he failed to reach our ideal as to favor the destruction of Individualism, Private Property, the Law of Accumulation of Wealth, and the Law of Competition; for these are the highest result of human experience, the soil in which society, so far, has produced the best fruit. Unequally or unjustly, perhaps, as these laws sometimes operate, and imperfect as they appear to the Idealist, they are, nevertheless, like the highest type of man, the best and most valuable of all that humanity has yet accomplished.

We start, then, with a condition of affairs under which the best interests of the race are promoted, but which inevitably gives wealth to the few. Thus far, accepting conditions as they exist, the situation can be surveyed and pronounced good. The question then arises, — and if the foregoing be correct, it is the only question with which we have to deal, — What is the proper mode of administering wealth after the laws upon which civilization is founded have thrown it into the hands of the few? And it is of this great question that I believe I offer the true solution. It will be understood that fortunes are here spoken of, not moderate sums saved by many years of effort, the returns from which are required for the comfortable maintenance and education of families. This is not wealth, but only competence, which it should be the aim of all to acquire, and which it is for the best interests of society should be acquired.

There are but three modes in which surplus wealth can be disposed of. It can be left to the families of the decedents; or it can be bequeathed for public purposes; or, finally, it can be administered by its possessors during their lives. Under the first and second modes most of the wealth of the world that has reached the few has hitherto been applied. Let us in turn consider each of these modes. The first is the most injudicious. In monarchical countries, the estates and the greatest portion of the wealth are left to the first son, that the vanity of the parent may be gratified by the thought that his name and title are to descend unimpaired to succeeding generations. The condition of this class in Europe to-day teaches the failure of such hopes or ambitions. The successors have become impoverished through their follies, or from the fall in the value of land. Even in Great Britain the strict law of entail has been found inadequate to maintain an hereditary class. Its soil is rapidly passing into the hands of the stranger. Under republican institutions the division of property among the children is much fairer; but the question which forces itself upon thoughtful men in all lands is, Why should men leave great fortunes to their children? If this is done from affection, is it not misguided affection? Observation teaches that, generally speaking, it is not well for the children that they should be so burdened. Neither is it well for the State. Beyond providing for the wife and daughters moderate sources of income, and very moderate allowances indeed, if any, for the sons, men may well hesitate; for it is no longer questionable that great sums bequeathed often work more for the injury than for the good of the recipients. Wise men will soon conclude that, for the best interests of the members of their families, and of the State, such bequests are an improper use of their means.

It is not suggested that men who have failed to educate their sons to earn a livelihood shall cast them adrift in poverty. If any man has seen fit to rear his sons with a view to their living idle lives, or, what is highly commendable, has instilled in them the sentiment that they are in a position to labor for public ends without reference to pecuniary considerations, then, of course, the duty of the parent is to see that such are provided for in moderation. There are instances of millionaires' sons unspoiled by wealth, who, being rich, still perform great services to the community. Such are the very salt of the earth, as valuable as, unfortunately, they are rare. It is not the exception, however, but the rule, that men must regard; and, looking at the usual result of enormous sums conferred upon legatees, the thoughtful man must shortly say, "I would as soon leave to my son a curse as the almighty dollar," and admit to himself that it is not the welfare of the children, but family pride, which inspires these legacies.

As to the second mode, that of leaving wealth at death for public uses, it may be said that this is only a means for the disposal of wealth, provided a man is content to wait until he is dead before he becomes of much good in the world. Knowledge of the results of legacies bequeathed is not calculated to inspire the brightest hopes of much posthumous good being accomplished by them. The cases are not few in which the real object sought by the testator is not attained, nor are they few in which his real wishes are thwarted. In many cases the bequests are so used as to become only monuments of his folly. It is well to remember that it requires the exercise of not less ability than that which acquires it, to use wealth so as to be really beneficial to the community. Besides this, it may fairly be said that no man is to be extolled for doing what he cannot help doing, nor is he to be thanked by the community to which he only leaves wealth at death. Men who leave vast sums in this way may fairly be thought men who would not have left it at all had they been able to take it with them. The memories of such cannot be held in grateful remembrance, for there is no grace in their gifts. It is not to be wondered at that such bequests seem so generally to lack the blessing.

The growing disposition to tax more and more heavily large estates left at death is a cheering indication of the growth of a salutary change in public opinion. The State of Pennsylvania now takes — subject to some exceptions — one tenth of the property left by its citizens. The budget presented in the British Parliament the other day proposes to increase the death duties; and, most significant of all, the new tax is to be a graduated one. Of all forms of taxation this seems the wisest.[3] Men who continue hoarding great sums all their lives, the proper use of which for public ends would work good to the community from which it chiefly came, should be made to feel that the community, in the form of the State, cannot thus be deprived of its proper share. By taxing estates heavily at death the State marks its condemnation of the selfish millionaire's unworthy life.

It is desirable that nations should go much further in this direction. Indeed, it is difficult to set bounds to the share of a rich man's estate which should go at his death to the public through the agency of the State, and by all means such taxes should be graduated, beginning at nothing upon moderate sums to dependents, and increasing rapidly as the amounts swell, until of the millionaire's hoard, as of Shylock's, at least

> The other half
> Comes to the privy coffer of the State.[4]

This policy would work powerfully to induce the rich man to attend to the administration of wealth during his life, which is the end that society should always have in view, as being by far the most fruitful for the people. Nor need it be feared that this policy would sap the root of enterprise and render men less anxious to accumulate, for, to the class whose ambition it is to leave great fortunes and to be talked about after their death, it will attract even more attention, and, indeed, be a somewhat nobler ambition, to have enormous sums paid over to the State from their fortunes.

[3] Inheritance taxes have historically taken many forms. They may be progressively heavier depending on the size of the transferred estate; they may vary with the relationship of the beneficiary to the testator; they may be levied upon different kinds of property. By the late eighties England had carried the system of "death duties," purportedly a Gladstonian designation, farther than any other nation. By 1890 only six American states levied taxes of one sort or another on inheritances; and federal resort to inheritance taxation had been generally a temporary feature of emergency war financing. By 1900 twenty-one states had inheritance taxes.

[4] Portia's judgment in *Merchant of Venice*, Act IV, scene 1.

There remains, then, only one mode of using great fortunes; but in this we have the true antidote for the temporary unequal distribution of wealth, the reconciliation of the rich and the poor — a reign of harmony, another ideal, differing, indeed, from that of the Communist in requiring only the further evolution of existing conditions, not the total overthrow of our civilization. It is founded upon the present most intense Individualism, and the race is prepared to put it in practice by degrees whenever it pleases. Under its sway we shall have an ideal State, in which the surplus wealth of the few will become, in the best sense, the property of the many, because administered for the common good; and this wealth, passing through the hands of the few, can be made a much more potent force for the elevation of our race than if distributed in small sums to the people themselves. Even the poorest can be made to see this, and to agree that great sums gathered by some of their fellow-citizens and spent for public purposes, from which the masses reap the principal benefit, are more valuable to them than if scattered among themselves in trifling amounts through the course of many years.

If we consider the results which flow from the Cooper Institute, for instance, to the best portion of the race in New York not possessed of means, and compare these with those which would have ensued for the good of the masses from an equal sum distributed by Mr. Cooper in his lifetime in the form of wages, which is the highest form of distribution, being for work done and not for charity, we can form some estimate of the possibilities for the improvement of the race which lie embedded in the present law of the accumulation of wealth. Much of this sum, if distributed in small quantities among the people, would have been wasted in the indulgence of appetite, some of it in excess, and it may be doubted whether even the part put to the best use, that of adding to the comforts of the home, would have yielded results for the race, as a race, at all comparable to those which are flowing and are to flow from the Cooper Institute from generation to generation.[5] Let the advocate of violent or radical change ponder well this thought.

We might even go so far as to take another instance — that of Mr. Tilden's bequest of five millions of dollars for a free library in the city of New York; but in referring to this one cannot help saying involuntarily: How much better if Mr. Tilden had devoted the last years of his own life to the proper administration of this immense sum; in which case neither legal contest nor any other cause of delay could have interfered with his aims. But let us assume that Mr. Tilden's millions finally become the means of giving to this city a noble public library, where the treasures of the world contained in books will be open to all forever, without money and without price.[6] Considering the good of that part of the race which congregates in and around Manhattan Island, would its permanent benefit have been better promoted had these millions been allowed to circulate in small sums through the hands of the masses? Even the most strenuous advocate of Communism must entertain a doubt upon this subject.

[5] Cooper Union, which celebrated in 1959 the centenary of its opening, was the chief philanthropic undertaking of Peter Cooper (1791–1883). A resident of New York, whose main iron mills were in New Jersey, Cooper was moved to establish an institution providing for those of little means an education in pure and applied science. The Union, though its activities soon embraced a wide variety of intellectual interests, stressed contributions "to the useful purposes of life" and adult education. The Union's building at 3rd Avenue and 7th Street appropriately embodied many structural innovations. Before his death Cooper had given the Union upwards of $900,000. In 1902 Carnegie gave $600,000 to its endowment.

[6] Samuel J. Tilden (1814–1886), New Yorker, able corporation lawyer, loser of the disputed presidential election of 1876, bequeathed a considerable share of his large estate "to establish and maintain a free public library and reading room in the City of New York." To accomplish this end his executors were to incorporate a Tilden Trust. Family heirs contested the will, and in a series of decisions — possibly animated by political considerations — various New York courts upset the testator's instructions. Though the Tilden Trust was incorporated in 1887 and the executors settled with the heirs in 1892, the estate was formally in the hands of executors until 1930. With about $2,250,000 in hand for a library, the Tilden Trust amalgamated in 1901 with the Astor and Lenox Libraries to form the New York Public Library. The present classical building on Fifth Avenue, housing the library, was the fruit of this settlement.

Most of those who think will probably entertain no doubt whatever.

Poor and restricted are our opportunities in this life, narrow our horizon, our best work most imperfect; but rich men should be thankful for one inestimable boon. They have it in their power during their lives to busy themselves in organizing benefactions from which the masses of their fellows will derive lasting advantage, and thus dignify their own lives. The highest life is probably to be reached, not by such imitation of the life of Christ as Count Tolstoi gives us, but, while animated by Christ's spirit, by recognizing the changed conditions of this age, and adopting modes of expressing this spirit suitable to the changed conditions under which we live, still laboring for the good of our fellows, which was the essence of his life and teaching, but laboring in a different manner.

This, then, is held to be the duty of the man of wealth: To set an example of modest, unostentatious living, shunning display or extravagance; to provide moderately for the legitimate wants of those dependent upon him; and, after doing so, to consider all surplus revenues which come to him simply as trust funds, which he is called upon to administer, and strictly bound as a matter of duty to administer in the manner which, in his judgment, is best calculated to produce the most beneficial results for the community — the man of wealth thus becoming the mere trustee and agent for his poorer brethren, bringing to their service his superior wisdom, experience, and ability to administer, doing for them better than they would or could do for themselves.

We are met here with the difficulty of determining what are moderate sums to leave to members of the family; what is modest, unostentatious living; what is the test of extravagance. There must be different standards for different conditions. The answer is that it is as impossible to name exact amounts or actions as it is to define good manners, good taste, or the rules of propriety; but, nevertheless, these are verities, well known, although indefinable. Public sentiment is quick to know and to feel what offends these. So in the case of wealth. The rule in regard to good taste in dress of men or women applies here. Whatever makes one conspicuous offends the canon. If any family be chiefly known for display, for extravagance in home, table, or equipage, for enormous sums ostentatiously spent in any form upon itself — if these be its chief distinctions, we have no difficulty in estimating its nature or culture. So likewise in regard to the use or abuse of its surplus wealth, or to generous, free-handed coöperation in good public uses, or to unabated efforts to accumulate and hoard to the last, or whether they administer or bequeath. The verdict rests with the best and most enlightened public sentiment. The community will surely judge, and its judgments will not often be wrong.

The best uses to which surplus wealth can be put have already been indicated. Those who would administer wisely must, indeed, be wise; for one of the serious obstacles to the improvement of our race is indiscriminate charity. It were better for mankind that the millions of the rich were thrown into the sea than so spent as to encourage the slothful, the drunken, the unworthy. Of every thousand dollars spent in so-called charity to-day, it is probable that nine hundred and fifty dollars is unwisely spent — so spent, indeed, as to produce the very evils which it hopes to mitigate or cure. A well-known writer of philosophic books admitted the other day that he had given a quarter of a dollar to a man who approached him as he was coming to visit the house of his friend. He knew nothing of the habits of this beggar, knew not the use that would be made of this money, although he had every reason to suspect that it would be spent improperly. This man professed to be a disciple of Herbert Spencer; yet the quarter-dollar given that night will probably work more injury than all the money will do good which its thoughtless donor will ever be able to give in true charity. He only gratified his own feelings, saved himself from annoyance — and this was probably one of the most selfish and very worst actions of his life, for in all respects he is most worthy.

In bestowing charity, the main consideration should be to help those who will help themselves; to provide part of the means by which those who desire to improve may do so; to give those who desire to rise the aids by which they may rise; to assist, but rarely or never to do all. Neither the individual nor the race is improved by almsgiving. Those worthy of assistance, except in rare cases, seldom require assistance. The really valuable men of the race never do, except in case of accident or sudden change. Every one has, of course, cases of individuals brought to his own knowledge where temporary assistance can do genuine good, and these he will not overlook. But the amount which can be wisely given by the individual for individuals is necessarily limited by his lack of knowledge of the circumstances connected with each. He is the only true reformer who is as careful and as anxious not to aid the unworthy as he is to aid the worthy, and, perhaps, even more so, for in almsgiving more injury is probably done by rewarding vice than by relieving virtue.

The rich man is thus almost restricted to following the examples of Peter Cooper, Enoch Pratt of Baltimore, Mr. Pratt of Brooklyn, Senator Stanford,[7] and others, who know

[7] Of this cluster of philanthropists, Enoch Pratt (1808–1896) was a New Englander who moved to Baltimore and accumulated a fortune as a merchant of iron products and as a general investor. In the eighties he constructed a library building and gave it along with an endowment of over $800,000 to the City of Baltimore. Carnegie once hailed Pratt as "my pioneer." Charles Pratt (1830–1891), also a New Englander, moved to New York and established a firm to deal in paints and oils. Sensing in the sixties the importance of petroleum, he was one of the founders of Charles Pratt and Company; the concern refined oil on Long Island. When the Rockefeller interests acquired this business in 1874, Pratt became a member of the high command in Standard Oil. In 1887 his funds and educational acumen led to the opening of the Pratt Institute in Brooklyn, a secondary school for training in the trades. He also established the Pratt Institute Free Library, "the first free public library in either Brooklyn or New York." Leland Stanford (1824–1893), a New Yorker, moved to California, prospered as a wholesale merchant in Sacramento, was Civil War Governor of the State, and one of the "Big Four" associated in promoting, organizing,

that the best means of benefiting the community is to place within its reach the ladders upon which the aspiring can rise — free libraries, parks, and means of recreation, by which men are helped in body and mind; works of art, certain to give pleasure and improve the public taste; and public institutions of various kinds, which will improve the general condition of the people; in this manner returning their surplus wealth to the mass of their fellows in the forms best calculated to do them lasting good.

Thus is the problem of rich and poor to be solved. The laws of accumulation will be left free, the laws of distribution free. Individualism will continue, but the millionaire will be but a trustee for the poor, intrusted for a season with a great part of the increased wealth of the community, but administering it for the community far better than it could or would have done for itself. The best minds will thus have reached a stage in the development of the race in which it is clearly seen that there is no mode of disposing of surplus wealth creditable to thoughtful and earnest men into whose hands it flows, save by using it year by year for the general good. This day already dawns. Men may die without incurring the pity of their fellows, still sharers in great business enterprises from which their capital cannot be or has not been withdrawn, and which is left chiefly at death for public uses; yet the day is not far distant when the man who dies leaving behind him millions of available wealth, which was free to him to administer during life, will pass away "unwept, unhonored, and unsung," no matter to what uses he leaves the dross which he cannot take with him. Of such as these

financing, and building the Central Pacific, the western link of the first transcontinental railroad. Subsequently he became a pioneer in the Southern Pacific Railroad and a United States Senator. In 1884 the death of an only son at the age of fifteen shattered Stanford and his wife. After personal reflection and after seeking advice among educators, the parents founded Leland Stanford Junior University on their Palo Alto "farm." The new institution charged no tuition and emphasized preparation for the practical affairs of life. For many years the Stanfords concerned themselves with the details of university administration, whether in the architecture of the buildings or the character of appointments.

the public verdict will then be: "The man who dies thus rich dies disgraced."

Such, in my opinion is the true gospel concerning wealth, obedience to which is destined some day to solve the problem of the rich and the poor, and to bring "Peace on earth, among men good will."

II

THE BEST FIELDS FOR PHILANTHROPY

While "The Gospel of Wealth" has met a cordial reception upon this side of the Atlantic, it is natural that in the motherland it should have attracted more attention, because the older civilization is at present brought more clearly face to face with socialistic questions. The contrast between the classes and the masses, between rich and poor, is not yet quite so sharp in this vast, fertile, and developing continent, with less than twenty persons per square mile, as in crowded little Britain, with fifteen times that number and no territory unoccupied. Perhaps the "Pall Mall Gazette" in its issue of September 5 puts most pithily the objections that have been raised to what the English have been pleased to call "The Gospel of Wealth." I quote: "Great fortunes, says Mr. Carnegie, are great blessings to a community, because such and such things may be done with them. Well, but they are also a great curse, for such and such things are done with them. Mr. Carnegie's preaching, in other words, is altogether vitiated by Mr. Benzon's practice.[8] The gospel of wealth is killed by the acts."

To this the reply seems obvious: the gospel of Christianity is also killed by the acts. The same objection that is urged against the gospel of wealth lies against the commandment,

[8] Ernest Benzon, commonly known as the "Jubilee plunger," was an English rogue of the fin-de-siècle variety. His career apparently came to grief on the Riviera when he was brought into court for forgery or obtaining money under false pretenses.

"Thou shalt not steal." It is no argument against a gospel that it is not lived up to; indeed, it is an argument in its favor, for a gospel must be higher than the prevailing standard. It is no argument against a law that it is broken: in that disobedience lies the reason for making and maintaining the law; the law which is never to be broken is never required.

Undoubtedly the most notable incident in regard to "The Gospel of Wealth" is that it was fortunate enough to attract the attention of Mr. Gladstone, and bring forth the following note from him: "I have asked Mr. Lloyd Bryce [9] [*North American Review*] kindly to allow the republication in this country of the extremely interesting article on 'Wealth' by Mr. Andrew Carnegie, which has just appeared in America." This resulted in the publication of the article in several newspapers and periodicals, and an enterprising publisher issued it in pamphlet form, dedicated by permission to Mr. Gladstone.

All this is most encouraging, proving as it does that society is alive to the great issue involved, and is in a receptive mood. Your request, Mr. Editor, that I should continue the subject and point out the best fields for the use of surplus wealth, may be taken as further proof that whether the ideas promulgated are to be received or rejected, they are at least certain to obtain a hearing.

The first article held that there is but one right mode of using enormous fortunes — namely, that the possessors from time to time during their own lives should so administer these as to promote the permanent good of the communities from which they were gathered. It was held that public sentiment would soon say of one who died possessed of available wealth which he was free to administer: "The man who dies thus rich dies disgraced."

[9] Lloyd Stephens Bryce (1851–1917) was owner and editor of the *North American Review* beginning in 1889. He combined the diverse talents of man of wealth, bon vivant, merchant, and member of Congress.

The purpose of this paper is to present some of the best methods of performing this duty of administering surplus wealth for the good of the people. The first requisite for a really good use of wealth by the millionaire who has accepted the gospel which proclaims him only a trustee of the surplus that comes to him, is to take care that the purposes for which he spends it shall not have a degrading, pauperizing tendency upon its recipients, but that his trust shall be so administered as to stimulate the best and most aspiring poor of the community to further efforts for their own improvement. It is not the irreclaimably destitute, shiftless, and worthless which it is truly beneficial or truly benevolent for the individual to attempt to reach and improve. For these there exists the refuge provided by the city or the State, where they can be sheltered, fed, clothed, and kept in comfortable existence, and — most important of all — where they can be isolated from the well-doing and industrious poor, who are liable to be demoralized by contact with these unfortunates. One man or women who succeeds in living comfortably by begging is more dangerous to society, and a greater obstacle to the progress of humanity, than a score of wordy Socialists. The individual administrator of surplus wealth has as his charge the industrious and ambitious; not those who need everything done for them, but those who, being most anxious and able to help themselves, deserve and will be benefited by help from others and by the extension of their opportunities by the aid of the philanthropic rich.

It is ever to be remembered that one of the chief obstacles which the philanthropist meets in his efforts to do real and permanent good in this world, is the practice of indiscriminate giving; and the duty of the millionaire is to resolve to cease giving to objects that are not clearly proved to his satisfaction to be deserving. He must remember Mr. Rice's [10] belief, that nine hundred and fifty out of every thousand dol-

---

[10] Charles Allen Thorndike Rice (1851–1889), publisher of the *North American Review*, 1886–1889.

lars bestowed to-day upon so-called charity had better be thrown into the sea. As far as my experience of the wealthy extends, it is unnecessary to urge them to give of their super-abundance in charity so called. Greater good for the race is to be achieved by inducing them to cease impulsive and injurious giving. As a rule, the sins of millionaires in this respect are not those of omission, but of commission, because they do not take time to think, and chiefly because it is much easier to give than to refuse. Those who have surplus wealth give millions every year which produce more evil than good, and really retard the progress of the people, because most of the forms in vogue to-day for benefiting mankind only tend to spread among the poor a spirit of dependence upon alms, when what is essential for progress is that they should be inspired to depend upon their own exertions. The miser millionaire who hoards his wealth does less injury to society than the careless millionaire who squanders his unwisely, even if he does so under cover of the mantle of sacred charity. The man who gives to the individual beggar commits a grave offense, but there are many societies and institutions soliciting alms, to aid which is none the less injurious to the community. These are as corrupting as individual beggars. Plutarch's "Morals" contains this lesson: "A beggar asking an alms of a Lacedæmonian, he said: 'Well, should I give thee anything, thou wilt be the greater beggar, for he that first gave thee money made thee idle, and is the cause of this base and dishonorable way of living.'" As I know them, there are few millionaires, very few indeed, who are clear of the sin of having made beggars.

Bearing in mind these considerations, let us endeavor to present some of the best uses to which a millionaire can devote the surplus of which he should regard himself as only the trustee.

First. Standing apart by itself there is the founding of a university by men enormously rich, such men as must necessarily be few in any country. Perhaps the greatest sum ever given by an individual for any purpose is the gift of Senator Stanford, who undertakes to establish a complete university upon the Pacific coast, where he amassed his enormous fortune, which is said to involve the expenditure of ten millions of dollars, and upon which he may be expected to bestow twenty millions of his surplus. He is to be envied. A thousand years hence some orator, speaking his praise upon the then crowded shores of the Pacific, may thus adapt Griffith's eulogy of Wolsey:

> In bestowing, madam,
> He was most princely. Ever witness for him
> This seat of learning, . . .
> though unfinished, yet so famous.
> So excellent in art, and still so rising,
> That Christendom shall ever speak his virtue.[11]

Here is a noble use of wealth. We have many such institutions, — Johns Hopkins, Cornell, Packer, and others,[12] — but most of these have only been bequeathed, and it is impossible to extol any man greatly for simply leaving what he cannot take with him. Cooper and Pratt and Stanford, and others of this class, deserve credit and admiration as much for the time and attention given during their lives as for their expenditure upon their respective monuments.

We cannot think of the Pacific coast without recalling another important work of a different character which has recently been established there — the Lick Observatory.[13]

[11] Quoted inaccurately from *Henry VIII,* Act IV, scene 2, lines 51 ff.

[12] In the founding of universities by private wealth in the post-Civil War era, the names of institutions perpetuate the donations and other assistance of Johns Hopkins (1795–1873), a Baltimore philanthropist, and Ezra Cornell (1807–1874), an upstate New Yorker who built a fortune from the telegraph. Asa Packer (1805–1879), a New England youth who emigrated to Pennsylvania, acquired his fortune from transporting and mining coal in the anthracite region. He was a judge and a politician. After the Civil War Packer donated money and land to a new institution, Lehigh University. He originally had in mind a technical institution, but when the school was opened in 1885 its scheme was more traditional. The total of Packer's donations in his lifetime gifts and bequests was over $3,800,000.

[13] James Lick (1796–1876), an eccentric who made a fortune from investments in San Francisco real estate and California land, was with

If any millionaire be interested in the ennobling study of astronomy, — and there should be and would be such if they but gave the subject the slightest attention, — here is an example which could well be followed, for the progress made in astronomical instruments and appliances is so great and continuous that every few years a new telescope might be judiciously given to one of the observatories upon this continent, the last being always the largest and the best, and certain to carry further and further the knowledge of the universe and of our relation to it here upon the earth. As one among many of the good deeds of the late Mr. Thaw of Pittsburg, his constant support of the observatory there may be mentioned. This observatory enabled Professor Langley to make his wonderful discoveries. He is now at the head of the Smithsonian Institution, a worthy successor to Professor Henry. Connected with him was Mr. Braeshier of Pittsburg, whose instruments are in most of the principal observatories of the world. He was a common millwright, but Mr. Thaw recognized his genius and was his main support through trying days. This common workman has been made a professor by one of the foremost scientific bodies of the world. In applying part of his surplus in aiding these two now famous men, the millionaire Thaw did a noble work. Their joint labors have brought great credit, and are destined to bring still greater credit, upon their country in every scientific center throughout the world.[14]

---

difficulty guided by careful advisers to give $700,000 for a telescope "superior to and more powerful than any telescope ever made." Previous to this decision he had never seen a telescope or looked through one and had not even an amateur's acquaintance with astronomy. Eventually the managers of the gift located the Lick observatory on Mt. Hamilton, a wilderness peak in Santa Clara County, and contracted for a 36-inch lens, the largest feasible under the technology of the eighties. The regents of the University of California became the trustees of the Lick observatory.

[14] Pittsburgh immediately after the Civil War became a center of astronomical activity and scholarship. A popular subscription had raised funds to build in 1860 the old Allegheny observatory, and five years later it was transferred to the Western University of Pennsylvania (since 1908 the University of Pittsburgh). In 1867 Samuel P. Langley (1834–1906), a man

It is reserved for very few to found universities, and, indeed, the use for many, or perhaps, any, new universities does not exist. More good is henceforth to be accomplished by adding to and extending those in existence. But in this department a wide field remains for the millionaire as distinguished from the Croesus among millionaires. The gifts to Yale University have been many, but there is plenty of room for others. The School of Fine Arts, founded by Mr. Street, the Sheffield Scientific School, endowed by Mr. Sheffield, and Professor Loomis's fund for the observatory, are fine examples. Mrs. C. J. Osborne's building for reading and recitation is to be regarded with especial pleasure as being the wise gift of a woman.[15] Harvard University has not been forgotten; the Peabody Museum and the halls of Wells, Matthews, and Thayer may be cited. Sever Hall is worthy of special mention, as showing what a genius like Richardson could do with the small sum of a hundred thousand dollars.[16]

---

of immense erudition and scientific originality, became director of the observatory and professor of physics and astronomy. Twenty years later Langley became the third secretary of the Smithsonian Institution. Meanwhile, John Alfred Brashear (1840–1920) — one of many variant spellings — a Pittsburgh machinist who in his youth had been inspired by his maternal grandfather with a love of the stars, had built his own telescope and had attracted the attention of Langley. William Thaw, who had acquired wealth as a freight forwarder and Pennsylvania Railroad official and investor, was a director of Western University. He financed Langley's researches — the observatory incidentally provided correct time for the railroad — and enabled Brashear to set up in business as a maker of precision instruments and telescopes. Carnegie later selected him as one of three men to draw up plans for the Carnegie Institute of Technology founded in 1905.

[15] A series of gifts enlarged the physical facilities and instructional offerings of Yale College. Just before the Civil War Joseph E. Sheffield (1793–1882), a Connecticut man who had made a fortune as a railroad contractor in the West and, out of personal and civic pride, spent some of it financing a needless New England railroad, gave the first of his donations to the Yale Scientific School, renamed the Sheffield Scientific School in 1861. After the War, Augustus R. Street (1791–1866), a New Haven-born Yale graduate, and his wife, a woman of wealth, financed a building for the Yale School of Fine Arts and endowed instruction in a number of areas at Yale. In the late eighties Elias Loomis (1811–1889), who had made a fortune as author of books in the field of natural science, bequeathed $300,000 to Yale. Mrs. Miriam A. (C.J.) Osborn gave in the eighties a sum for a building for history. Its construction "resulted in the removal of the Fence."

[16] Mr. Carnegie's stroll through Harvard produced some inaccurate

The Vanderbilt University, at Nashville, Tennessee, may be mentioned as a true product of the gospel of wealth. It was established by the members of the Vanderbilt family [17] during their lives — mark this vital feature, during their lives; for nothing counts for much that is left by a man at his death. Such funds are torn from him, not given by him. If any millionaire be at a loss to know how to accomplish great and indisputable good with his surplus, here is a field which can never be fully occupied, for the wants of our universities increase with the development of the country.

Second. The result of my own study of the question, What is the best gift which can be given to a community? is that a free library occupies the first place, provided the community will accept and maintain it as a public institution, as much a part of the city property as its public schools, and, indeed, an adjunct to these. It is, no doubt, possible that my own personal experience may have led me to value a free library beyond all other forms of beneficence. When I was a working-boy in Pittsburg, Colonel Anderson of Allegheny — a name I can never speak without feelings of devotional gratitude — opened his little library of four hundred books to boys. Every Saturday afternoon he was in attendance at his house to exchange books. No one but he who has felt it

observations. George Peabody (1795–1869), an American banker in London, donated in 1866, at the suggestion of a Yale nephew, $150,000 for a "Museum and Professorship of American Archaeology and Ethnology." But there is not and never was a Wells Hall. This is a mistake for Weld Hall, given in 1872 by W. F. Weld, a Boston financier, in memory of his brother. Like Weld, the other "halls" were domitories. Matthews Hall was the gift in 1872 of Nathan Matthews (1854–1927), a Boston merchant; Thayer Hall, of Nathanial Thayer (1808–1883), a member of a Boston investment banking house, in memory of his brother. Colonel James W. Sever, a shoeman in southeastern Massachusetts, bequeathed $100,000 for a hall to be named for the family. Sever Hall is a classroom building.

[17] The first Vanderbilt gift to the Central University of the Methodist Episcopal Church of the South at Nashville came from Cornelius ("The Commodore") Vanderbilt (1794–1877), veteran steamship tycoon and virtually a synonym for the New York Central Railroad. Since the Commodore became Vanderbilt's benefactor in a decidedly offhand manner, Carnegie's note of admiration is surprising. In time the Commodore's descendants generously supplemented his original benefaction.

can ever know the intense longing with which the arrival of Saturday was awaited, that a new book might be had. My brother and Mr. Phipps,[18] who have been my principal business partners through life, shared with me Colonel Anderson's precious generosity, and it was when reveling in the treasures which he opened to us that I resolved, if ever wealth came to me, that it should be used to establish free libraries, that other poor boys might receive opportunities similar to those for which we were indebted to that noble man.

Great Britain has been foremost in appreciating the value of free libraries for its people. Parliament passed an act permitting towns and cities to establish and maintain these as municipal institutions; whenever the people of any town or city voted to accept the provisions of the act, the authorities were authorized to tax the community to the extent of one penny in the pound valuation. Most of the towns already have free libraries under this act. Many of these are the gifts of rich men, whose funds have been used for the building, and in some cases for the books also, the communities being required to maintain and to develop the libraries. And to this feature I attribute most of their usefulness. An endowed institution is liable to become the prey of a clique. The public ceases to take interest in it, or rather, never acquires interest in it. The rule has been violated which requires the recipients to help themselves. Everything has been done for the community instead of its being only helped to help itself, and good results rarely ensue.

Many free libraries have been established in our country, but none that I know of with such wisdom as the Pratt Library in Baltimore. Mr. Pratt built and presented the library

[18] Thomas M. Carnegie (1843–1886), a younger brother of Andrew, followed a somewhat similar career. Henry Phipps, Jr. (1839–1930), was a boyhood neighbor and chum of Andrew. Tom Carnegie and Phipps early entered the iron business. Tom died in 1886; Phipps stayed with the Carnegie firm until its acquisition by United States Steel in 1901. His money supported a wide variety of philanthropic undertakings from public baths to psychiatric institutes.

to the city of Baltimore, with the balance of cash handed over; the total cost was one million dollars, upon which he required the city to pay five per cent, per annum, fifty thousand dollars per year, to trustees for the maintenance and development of the library and its branches. During 1888 430,217 books were distributed; 37,196 people of Baltimore are registered upon the books as readers. And it is safe to say that 37,000 frequenters of the Pratt Library are of more value to Baltimore, to the State, and to the country, than all the inert, lazy, and hopelessly poor in the whole nation. And it may further be safely said that, by placing books within the reach of 37,000 aspiring people which they were anxious to obtain, Mr. Pratt has done more for the genuine progress of the people than has been done by all the contributions of all the millionaires and rich people to help those who cannot or will not help themselves. The one wise administrator of his surplus has poured a fertilizing stream upon soil that was ready to receive it and return a hundredfold. The many squanderers have not only poured their streams into sieves which can never be filled — they have done worse; they have poured them into stagnant sewers that breed the diseases which most afflict the body politic. And this is not all. The million dollars of which Mr. Pratt has made so grand a use are something, but there is something greater still. When the fifth branch library was opened in Baltimore, the speaker said:

Whatever may have been done in these four years, it is my pleasure to acknowledge that much, very much, is due to the earnest interest, the wise counsels, and the practical suggestions of Mr. Pratt. He never seemed to feel that the mere donation of great wealth for the benefit of his fellow-citizens was all that would be asked of him, but he wisely labored to make its application as comprehensive and effective as possible. Thus he constantly lightened burdens that were, at times, very heavy, brought good cheer and bright sunshine when clouds flitted across the sky, and made every officer and employee feel that good work was appreciated, and loyal devotion to duty would receive hearty commendation.

This is the finest picture I have ever seen of any of the millionaire class. As here depicted, Mr. Pratt is the ideal disciple of the gospel of wealth. We need have no fear that the mass of toilers will fail to recognize in such as he their best leaders and their most invaluable allies; for the problem of poverty and wealth, of employer and employed, will be practically solved whenever the time of the few is given, and their wealth is administered during their lives, for the best good of that portion of the community which has not been burdened with the responsibilities which attend the possession of wealth. We shall have no antagonism between classes when that day comes, for the high and the low, the rich and the poor, shall then indeed be brothers.

No millionaire will go far wrong in his search for one of the best forms for the use of his surplus who chooses to establish a free library in any community that is willing to maintain and develop it. John Bright's [19] words should ring in his ear: "It is impossible for any man to bestow a greater benefit upon a young man than to give him access to books in a free library." Closely allied to the library, and, where possible, attached to it, there should be rooms for an art-gallery and museum, and a hall for such lectures and instruction as are provided in the Cooper Union. The traveler upon the Continent is surprised to find that every town of importance has its art-gallery and museum; these may be large or small, but each has a receptacle for the treasures of the locality, in which are constantly being placed valuable gifts and bequests. The Free Library and Art Gallery of Birmingham are remarkable among such institutions, and every now and then a rich man adds to their value by presenting books, fine pictures, or other works of art. All that our cities require, to begin with, is a proper fire-proof building. Their citizens who travel will send to it rare and costly things from every quarter of the globe they visit, while those who remain at

[19] The noted British liberal statesman, reformer, and orator (1811–1889), who believed strongly in self-education.

home will give or bequeath to it of their treasures. In this way collections will grow until our cities will ultimately be able to boast of permanent exhibitions from which their own citizens will derive incalculable benefit, and which they will be proud to show to visitors. In the Metropolitan Museum of Art in New York we have made an excellent beginning. Here is another avenue for the proper use of surplus wealth.

Third. We have another most important department in which great sums can be worthily used — the founding or extension of hospitals, medical colleges, laboratories, and other institutions connected with the alleviation of human suffering, and especially with the prevention rather than with the cure of human ills. There is no danger of pauperizing a community in giving for such purposes, because such institutions relieve temporary ailments or shelter only those who are hopeless invalids. What better gift than a hospital can be given to a community that is without one? — the gift being conditioned upon its proper maintenance by the community in its corporate capacity. If hospital accommodation already exists, no better method for using surplus wealth can be found than in making additions to it. The late Mr. Vanderbilt's gift of half a million dollars to the Medical Department of Columbia College for a chemical laboratory was one of the wisest possible uses of wealth.[20] It strikes at the prevention of disease by penetrating into its causes. Several others have established such laboratories, but the need for them is still great.

If there be a millionaire in the land who is at a loss what to do with the surplus that has been committed to him as trustee, let him investigate the good that is flowing from these chemical laboratories. No medical college is complete

[20] Gifts from the Vanderbilts enabled Columbia's College of Physicians and Surgeons in the eighties to move to a new location and plant on West 59th Street. W. H. Vanderbilt (1821–1885), the son of the Commodore and an exceedingly able business man in his own right, was for the moment the chief of the Vanderbilt givers.

without its laboratory. As with universities, so with medical colleges: it is not new institutions that are required, but additional means for the more thorough equipment of those that exist. The forms that benefactions to these may wisely take are numerous, but probably none is more useful than that adopted by Mr. Osborne when he built a school for training female nurses at Bellevue College.[21] If from all gifts there flows one half of the good that comes from this wise use of a millionaire's surplus, the most exacting may well be satisfied. Only those who have passed through a lingering and dangerous illness can rate at their true value the care, skill, and attendance of trained female nurses. Their employment as nurses has enlarged the sphere and influence of woman. It is not to be wondered at that a senator of the United States, and a physician distinguished in this country for having received the highest distinctions abroad, should recently have found their wives in this class.

Fourth. In the very front rank of benefactions public parks should be placed, always provided that the community undertakes to maintain, beautify, and preserve them inviolate. No more useful or more beautiful monument can be left by any man than a park for the city in which he was born or in which he has long lived, nor can the community pay a more graceful tribute to the citizen who presents it than to give his name to the gift. Mrs. Schenley's gift last month of a large park to the city of Pittsburg deserves to be noted. This lady, although born in Pittsburg, married an English gentleman while yet in her teens. It is forty years and more since she took up her residence in London among the titled and the wealthy of the world's metropolis, but still she turns to the home of her childhood and by means of Schenley Park links her name with it forever.[22] A noble use this of great

---

[21] William Henry Osborn (1820–1894), reorganizer and financial savior of the Illinois Central Railroad, after his retirement in 1882 became interested in aiding medical institutions, among which was the Bellevue Training School for Nurses in New York City.

[22] Pittsburgh advocates of parks induced Mrs. Mary E. Schenley to

wealth by one who thus becomes her own administrator. If a park be already provided, there is still room for many judicious gifts in connection with it. Mr. Phipps of Allegheny has given conservatories to the park there, which are visited by many every day of the week, and crowded by thousands of working-people every Sunday; for, with rare wisdom, he has stipulated as a condition of the gift that the conservatories shall be open on Sundays. The result of his experiment has been so gratifying that he finds himself justified in adding to them from his surplus, as he is doing largely this year. To lovers of flowers among the wealthy I commend a study of what is possible for them to do in the line of Mr. Phipps's example; and may they please note that Mr. Phipps is a wise as well as a liberal giver, for he requires the city to maintain these conservatories, and thus secures for them forever the public ownership, the public interest, and the public criticism of their management. Had he undertaken to manage and maintain them, it is probable that popular interest in the gift would never have been awakened.

The parks and pleasure-grounds of small towns throughout Europe are not less surprising than their libraries, museums, and art-galleries. I saw nothing more pleasing during my recent travels than the hill at Bergen, in Norway. It has been converted into one of the most picturesque of pleasure-grounds; fountains, cascades, waterfalls, delightful arbors, fine terraces, and statues adorn what was before a barren mountain-side. Here is a field worthy of study by the millionaire who would confer a lasting benefit upon his fellows. Another beautiful instance of the right use of wealth in the direction of making cities more and more attractive is to be found in Dresden. The owner of the leading paper there bequeathed its revenues forever to the city, to be used in beauti-

---

donate 300 acreas for a park and the city purchased for $200,000 an additional acreage. In addition to facilities for sports and beauty, Schenley Park was the site of the Phipps conservatories, the first Carnegie Pittsburgh Library, and the Carnegie Institute.

fying it. An art committee decides, from time to time, what new artistic feature is to be introduced, or what hideous feature is to be changed, and as the revenues accrue, they are expended in this direction. Thus, through the gift of this patriotic newspaper proprietor his native city of Dresden is fast becoming one of the most artistic places of residence in the whole world. A work having been completed, it devolves upon the city to maintain it forever. May I be excused if I commend to our millionaire newspaper proprietors the example of their colleague in the capital of Saxony?

Scarcely a city of any magnitude in the older countries is without many structures and features of great beauty. Much has been spent upon ornament, decoration, and architectural effect. We are still far behind in these things upon this side of the Atlantic. Our Republic is great in some things — in material development unrivaled; but let us always remember that in art and in the finer touches we have scarcely yet taken a place. Had the exquisite Memorial Arch recently erected temporarily in New York been shown in Dresden, the art committee there would probably have been enabled, from the revenue of the newspaper given by its owner for just such purposes, to order its permanent erection to adorn the city forever.*

While the bestowal of a park upon a community will be universally approved as one of the best uses for surplus wealth, in embracing such additions to it as conservatories, or in advocating the building of memorial arches and works of adornment, it is probable that many will think I go too far, and consider these somewhat fanciful. The material good to flow from them may not be so directly visible; but let not any practical mind, intent only upon material good, depreciate the value of wealth given for these or for kindred esthetic purposes as being useless as far as the mass

* Popular subscriptions have accomplished this result in the case referred to (the Washington Monument), and two other memorial arches have been designed and are to be erected here. — ED. [Note in original edition.]

of the people and their needs are concerned. As with libraries and museums, so with these more distinctively artistic works: they perform their great use when they reach the best of the masses of the people. It is better to reach and touch the sentiment for beauty in the naturally bright minds of this class than to pander to those incapable of being so touched. For what the improver of the race must endeavor is to reach those who have the divine spark ever so feebly developed, that it may be strengthened and grow. For my part, I think Mr. Phipps put his money to better use in giving the working-men of Allegheny conservatories filled with beautiful flowers, orchids, and aquatic plants, which they, with their wives and children, can enjoy in their spare hours, and upon which they can feed their love for the beautiful, than if he had given his surplus money to furnish them with bread; for those in health who cannot earn their bread are scarcely worth considering by the individual giver, the care of such being the duty of the State. The man who erects in a city a conservatory or a truly artistic arch, statue, or fountain, makes a wise use of his surplus. "Man does not live by bread alone."

Fifth. We have another good use for surplus wealth in providing our cities with halls suitable for meetings of all kinds, and for concerts of elevating music. Our cities are rarely possessed of halls for these purposes, being in this respect also very far behind European cities. Springer Hall, in Cincinnati, a valuable addition to the city, was largely the gift of Mr. Springer, who was not content to bequeath funds from his estate at death, but gave during his life, and, in addition, gave — what was equally important — his time and business ability to insure the successful results which have been achieved.[23] The gift of a hall to any city lacking one is an

[23] Reuben R. Springer (1800–1884), a successful investor in real estate and railroads, gave the major share of the money for the erection of the Cincinnati Music Hall. Opened in 1878, this red brick, semi-Gothic building housed the Cincinnati Music Festival and later the Cincinnati Symphony Orchestra. Perhaps inspired by this example, Andrew Carnegie in 1892

excellent use for surplus wealth for the good of a community. The reason why the people have only one instructive and elevating, or even amusing, entertainment when a dozen would be highly beneficial, is that the rent of a hall, even when a suitable hall exists, which is rare, is so great as to prevent managers from running the risk of financial failure. If every city in our land owned a hall which could be given or rented for a small sum for such gatherings as a committee or the mayor of the city judged advantageous, the people could be furnished with proper lectures, amusements, and concerts at an exceedingly small cost. The town halls of European cities, many of which have organs, are of inestimable value to the people, utilized as they are in the manner suggested. Let no one underrate the influence of entertainments of an elevating or even of an amusing character, for these do much to make the lives of the people happier and their natures better. If any millionaire born in a small village which has now become a great city is prompted in the day of his success to do something for his birthplace with part of his surplus, his grateful remembrance cannot take a form more useful than that of a public hall with an organ, provided the city agrees to maintain and use it.

Sixth. In another respect we are still much behind Europe. A form of benevolence which is not uncommon there is providing swimming-baths for the people. The donors of these have been wise enough to require the city benefited to maintain them at its own expense, and as proof of the contention that everything should never be done for any one or for any community, but that the recipients should invariably be called upon to do a part, it is significant that it is found essential for the popular success of these healthful establishments to exact a nominal charge for their use. In many cities, however, the school-children are admitted free

---

built the New York Music Hall on 57th Street. Since the latter name repelled European artists, who associated it with vaudeville, it was changed to Carnegie Hall.

at fixed hours upon certain days; different hours being fixed for the boys and the girls to use the great swimming-baths, hours or days being also fixed for the use of these baths by women. In addition to the highly beneficial effect of these institutions upon the public health in inland cities, the young of both sexes are thus taught to swim. Swimming clubs are organized, and matches are frequent, at which medals and prizes are given. The reports published by the various swimming-bath establishments throughout Great Britain are filled with instances of lives saved because those who fortunately escaped shipwreck had been taught to swim in the baths; and not a few instances are given in which the pupils of certain bathing establishments have saved the lives of others. If any disciple of the gospel of wealth gives his favorite city large swimming and private baths, provided the municipality undertakes their management as a city affair, he will never be called to account for an improper use of the funds intrusted to him.

Seventh. Churches as fields for the use of surplus wealth have purposely been reserved for the last, because, these being sectarian, every man will be governed in his action in regard to them by his own attachments; therefore gifts to churches, it may be said, are not, in one sense, gifts to the community at large, but to special classes. Nevertheless, every millionaire may know of a district where the little cheap, uncomfortable, and altogether unworthy wooden structure stands at the cross-roads, in which the whole neighborhood gathers on Sunday, and which, independently of the form of the doctrines taught, is the center of social life and source of neighborly feeling. The administrator of wealth makes a good use of a part of his surplus if he replaces that building with a permanent structure of brick, stone, or granite, up whose sides the honeysuckle and columbine may climb, and from whose tower the sweet-tolling bell may sound. The millionaire should not figure how cheaply this structure can be built, but how perfect it can be made.

If he has the money, it should be made a gem, for the educating influence of a pure and noble specimen of architecture, built, as the pyramids were built, to stand for ages, is not to be measured by dollars. Every farmer's home, heart, and mind in the district will be influenced by the beauty and grandeur of the church; and many a bright boy, gazing enraptured upon its richly colored windows and entranced by the celestial voice of the organ, will there receive his first message from and in spirit be carried away to the beautiful and enchanting realm which lies far from the material and prosaic conditions which surround him in this workaday world — a real world, this new realm, vague and undefined though its boundaries be. Once within its magic circle, its denizens live there an inner life more precious than the external, and all their days and all their ways, their triumphs and their trials, and all they see, and all they hear, and all they think, and all they do, are hallowed by the radiance which shines from afar upon this inner life, glorifying everything, and keeping all right within. But having given the building, the donor should stop there; the support of the church should be upon its own people. There is not much genuine religion in the congregation or much good to come from the church which is not supported at home.

Many other avenues for the wise expenditure of surplus wealth might be indicated. I enumerate but a few — a very few — of the many fields which are open, and only those in which great or considerable sums can be judiciously used. It is not the privilege, however, of millionaires alone to work for or aid measures which are certain to benefit the community. Every one who has but a small surplus above his moderate wants may share this privilege with his richer brothers, and those without surplus can give at least a part of their time, which is usually as important as funds, and often more so.

It is not expected, neither is it desirable, that there should be general concurrence as to the best possible use of surplus wealth. For different men and different localities there are different uses. What commends itself most highly to the judgment of the administrator is the best use for him, for his heart should be in the work. It is as important in administering wealth as it is in any other branch of a man's work that he should be enthusiastically devoted to it and feel that in the field selected his work lies.

Besides this, there is room and need for all kinds of wise benefactions for the common weal. The man who builds a university, library, or laboratory performs no more useful work than he who elects to devote himself and his surplus means to the adornment of a park, the gathering together of a collection of pictures for the public, or the building of a memorial arch. These are all true laborers in the vineyard. The only point required by the gospel of wealth is that the surplus which accrues from time to time in the hands of a man should be administered by him in his own lifetime for that purpose which is seen by him, as trustee, to be best for the good of the people. To leave at death what he cannot take away, and place upon others the burden of the work which it was his own duty to perform, is to do nothing worthy. This requires no sacrifice, nor any sense of duty to his fellows.

Time was when the words concerning the rich man entering the kingdom of heaven were regarded as a hard saying. To-day, when all questions are probed to the bottom and the standards of faith receive the most liberal interpretations, the startling verse has been relegated to the rear, to await the next kindly revision as one of those things which cannot be quite understood, but which, meanwhile, it is carefully to be noted, are not to be understood literally. But is it so very improbable that the next stage of thought is to restore the doctrine in all its pristine purity and force, as being in perfect harmony with sound ideas upon the subject of wealth and poverty, the rich and the poor, and the contrasts everywhere seen and deplored? In Christ's day, it is evident, reformers were against the wealthy. It is none the less evident that we are fast recurring to that position to-day; and there will be nothing to surprise the student of sociological development if society should soon approve the text which has caused so much anxiety: "It is easier for a camel to enter the eye of a needle than for a rich man to enter the kingdom of heaven." Even if the needle were the small casement at the gates, the words betoken serious difficulty for the rich. It will be but a step for the theologian from the doctrine that he who dies rich dies disgraced, to that which brings upon the man punishment or deprivation hereafter.

The gospel of wealth but echoes Christ's words. It calls upon the millionaire to sell all that he hath and give it in the highest and best form to the poor by administering his estate himself for the good of his fellows, before he is called upon to lie down and rest upon the bosom of Mother Earth. So doing, he will approach his end no longer the ignoble hoarder of useless millions; poor, very poor indeed, in money, but rich, very rich, twenty times a millionaire still, in the affection, gratitude, and admiration of his fellow-men, and — sweeter far — soothed and sustained by the still, small voice within, which, whispering, tells him that, because he has lived, perhaps one small part of the great world has been bettered just a little. This much is sure: against such riches as these no bar will be found at the gates of Paradise.

· III ·

The Advantages of Poverty [1]

Two essays from my pen, published in the *North American Review*, have been doubly fortunate in Britain in being reprinted by the *Pall Mall Gazette* under the new and striking title of "The Gospel of Wealth," and in attracting the attention of the one man who, of all others, could bring them most prominently before thinking people. Mr. Gladstone's review and recommendation in the November number of this *Review* gave them the most illustrious of sponsors; he is followed in the December number by others of the highest eminence and authority. The discussion has taken a wide range, but I shall restrict myself to its bearings upon the ideas presented in "The Gospel of Wealth."

Mr. Gladstone first calls attention to the portentous growth of wealth. From every point of view this growth seems to me most beneficial; for we know that, rapid as is the increase of wealth, its distribution among the people in streams more and more numerous is still more rapid, the share of the joint product of capital and labor which has gone to

[1] Published originally in the *Nineteenth Century*, XXIX (March 1891), 367–385; the same journal, XXVIII (November 1890), 677–694, published W. E. Gladstone, "Mr. Carnegie's 'Gospel of Wealth.' A Review and a Recommendation," which characteristically had something good to say about the advantages of inherited wealth. The review was of a pamphlet embodying Carnegie's articles which had received wide circulation here and abroad and had been issued in thousands of copies. A month later comments on "Irresponsible Wealth" (XXVIII, 876–900) appeared by Cardinal Manning (1808–1892); Hermann Adler (1839–1911), chief rabbi of the United Hebrew Congregations of the British Empire (1891–1911); and Hugh Price Hughes (1847–1902), an influential Methodist divine. These three dwelt especially upon religious directives and motives which they thought Carnegie had brushed aside. Hughes was the most severe critic.

labor during this generation being much greater than in any generation preceding, and constantly increasing. Evidences, drawn from many independent sources, converge and prove this beyond question. A few enormous fortunes have been amassed during the present generation in this new and undeveloped continent, but under conditions which no longer exist. In our day, even in the United States, it is much easier to lose a great fortune than to make one, and more are being lost than made. It is rather surprising, therefore, that the Rev. Mr. Hugh Price Hughes should say: "Whatever may be thought of Mr. Henry George's doctrines and deductions, no one can deny that his facts are indisputable, and that Mr. Carnegie's 'progress' is accompanied by the growing 'poverty' of his less fortunate fellow-countrymen." [2]

So far as I have observed, all writers of authority upon social and economic subjects have not only disputed Mr. George's statements, but pronounce their opposites to be the truth. Mr. George's "Progress and Poverty" is founded upon two statements: first, that the rich are growing richer, and the poor poorer; and second, that land is going more and more into the hands of the few. The truth is that the rich are growing poorer, and the poor growing richer, and that land is passing from the hands of the few into the hands of the many. A study of Mulhall's *Fifty Years of National Progress* [3] (pages 23–27) is strongly recommended to those desirous of learning the truth in regard to the distribution of wealth, upon which Mr. Mulhall says: "Nor does this wealth become congested among a small number of people; on the contrary, the rich grow less rich and more numerous every year, the poor fewer in ratio to population."

[2] Hughes's belief that "the rich were getting richer and the poor poorer," was a widely quoted aphorism of this period. It had little factual basis. Henry George (1862–1916), the American economist and author of *Progress and Poverty* (1879), justifying the "single tax," accepted the commonly held notion.

[3] Michael George Mulhall (1836–1900). His book, one of several on economic matters and statistics, appeared in England in 1887.

The same results are shown even in a more remarkable degree in the Republic. In regard to land, the United States census gives the number and average size of farms as follows:

(NUMBER OF FARMS) *			
1850	1860	1870	1880
1,449,073	2,044,077	2,659,985	4,008,907

AVERAGE SIZE OF FARMS (ACRES)			
1850	1860	1870	1880
203	199	153	134

This tendency to more numerous and smaller holdings exists also in Britain, although hampered in its operation by repressive laws.

I rejoice that Mr. Hughes quotes the well-known passage from Herbert Spencer,[4] which, as he says, "exposes the sad delusion that great wealth is a great blessing" — a passage which is throughout profoundly true; but is it possible that Mr. Hughes can be uninformed of the position Mr. George occupies in the wise mind of our mutual teacher? In speaking to me of Mr. George's book, Mr. Spencer said that he had read a few pages, and then thrown it down as "trash." I know of no writer or thinker of recognized authority, except Mr. Hughes, who differs with the philosopher in this judgment.

So far as the reference to myself is concerned, — I understand, of course, it is in nowise personal, but only as the representative of a class, — I beg to assure Mr. Hughes that the indisputable fact I know is that my "progress" has inevitably carried with it not the "growing poverty," but the growing riches of my fellow-countrymen, as the progress of every employer of labor must necessarily carry with it

* In 1890 the number of farms in the United States was 4,564,641 and the average size 136½ acres. — ED. [Note in original edition.]

[4] The passage is from Spencer's *Study of Sociology*, pp. 256–59.

the enrichment of the country and of the laborer. Imagine
one speaking of "growing poverty" in the United States! The
American, more than any other workman, spends his savings
for the purchase of a home. The savings-banks are only one
of several depositories used by him.

Nevertheless, the returns just made for the year 1890, for
all the New England and Middle States (where millionaires
do most abound), comprising a population of 17,300,000 —
more than half the total population of Britain — show that
the deposits are $1,279,000,000 — say £255,000,000, the in-
crease for the year being £13,000,000. The number of de-
positors is 3,520,000, showing that about one out of every
five men, women, and children has a bank-account, equal
practically to one to each family. The amount of savings
invested for homes far exceeds the savings-bank deposits.

The United States census of 1880 shows only 88,665
public paupers in a population of 50,000,000, mainly aged
and superannuated — one third being foreigners. There were
more blind and idiotic people in the public charitable institutions than paupers, and half as many deaf-mutes, although
the percentage of the "defective classes" is less than half
that of Europe. The total number of all "dependent" persons
cared for was less than five per thousand, as compared with
thirty-three per thousand in the United Kingdom. This percentage for Britain is happily only about one fourth of what
it has been, and its steady decrease is most encouraging.
Good and charitable workers among the poor can best
accelerate this decreasing process, until something like the
American figure is reached, by instilling within the working-
classes of Britain those feelings of manly self-respect and
those habits of sobriety and thrift which distinguish their
race here, and keep it almost free, not only from pauperism,
but from want or extreme poverty, except as the necessary
result (accident and sickness excepted) of their own bad
habits.

Mr. Hughes would not give currency knowingly to statements that were the reverse of correct. I earnestly hope, therefore, that he will satisfy himself that every writer of authority is not deceived when he asserts that poverty, want, and pauperism are rapidly diminishing quantities; and most significantly so, not so much through almsgiving, or efforts of the rich, but because of an improvement through education in the habits of the people themselves — the only foundation upon which their continued progress can surely be built. Mr. Hughes can also readily learn another indisputable fact by inquiring at the shipyards of Glasgow, the iron and steel mills of Sheffield, the coal-mines of the Midlands, or at industrial establishments generally — namely, that the working-classes receive much greater compensation for their services than they ever did or now do for any other form of labor, and much greater than they could possibly receive, except for the establishment of great enterprises by men of wealth. In these days of excitement and exaggeration, let it always be borne in mind that at no period in the history of the English-speaking race, wherever that race resides, has it been so easy as it is to-day for the masses not only to earn comfortable livelihoods, but to save and have money in bank for a rainy day. When they fail to do so, the true reformer looks more to their habits than to existing conditions for a satisfactory explanation.

So far from its being a fact that "millionaires at one end of the scale mean paupers at the other," as Mr. Hughes says, the reverse is obviously true. In a country where the millionaire exists there is little excuse for pauperism; the condition of the masses is satisfactory just in proportion as a country is blessed with millionaires. There is not a great millionaire among the whole four hundred millions of China, nor one in Japan, nor in India; one or two perhaps in the whole of Russia; there are two or three in Germany, and not more than four or five in the whole of France, monarchs and hereditary nobles excepted. There are more millionaires upon the favored little isle of Britain than in the whole of

Europe, and in the United States still more, of recent origin, than in Britain; and the revenues of the masses are just in proportion to the ease with which millionaires grow. The British laborer receives more for one day's handling of the shovel than the blacksmith or carpenter of China, Russia, India, or Japan receives for a whole week's labor, and double that of his Continental fellow-workman. The skilled artisan of America receives more than twice as much as the artisan of Britain. Millionaires can only grow amid general prosperity, and this very prosperity is largely promoted by their exertions. Their wealth is not made, as Mr. Hughes implies, at the expense of their fellow-countrymen. Millionaires make no money when compelled to pay low wages. Their profits accrue in periods when wages are high, and the higher the wages that have to be paid, the higher the revenues of the employer. It is true, and not false, therefore, that capital and labor are allies and not antagonistic forces, and that one cannot prosper when the other does not.

I feel as if I should apologize for taking so much space in stating truisms; but much of the prejudice and hostility which unnecessarily exist between capital and labor arise from such statements as those quoted.

To return to Mr. Gladstone. Would that his adhesion to "The Gospel of Wealth" in its entirety could be obtained! Deeply gratifying is the favor which he accords in general to its scope and aim; but the destructive character of its criticism upon one vital point is important. He is quite right in saying that, "though partial, it is a serious difference." It arises from his fond, clinging affection for the principle of hereditary transmission of position and wealth, and of business, and for magnificence upon the part of those in station. We must meet this serious matter at the threshold.

⌐The fundamental idea of the gospel of wealth is that surplus wealth should be considered as a sacred trust to be administered by those into whose hands it falls, during their lives, for the good of the community. It predicts that the day is at hand when he who dies possessed of enormous sums, which were his and free to administer during his life, will die disgraced, and holds that the aim of the millionaire should be to die poor. It likewise pleads for modesty of private expenditure.⌋

The most serious obstacle to the spread of such a gospel is undoubtedly the prevailing desire of men to accumulate wealth for the express purpose of bequeathing it to their children, or to spend it in ostentatious living. I have therefore endeavored to prove that at the root of the desire to bequeath to children there lay the vanity of the parents, rather than a wise regard for the good of the children. That the parent who leaves his son enormous wealth generally deadens the talents and energies of the son, and tempts him to lead a less useful and less worthy life than he otherwise would, seems to me capable of proof which cannot be gainsaid. It is many years since I wrote in a rich lady's album, "I should as soon leave to my son a curse as the almighty dollar." Exceptions abound to every general rule, but I think not more exceptions to this rule than to others — namely, that "wealth is a curse to young men, and poverty a blessing"; but if these terms seem rather strong, let us state the proposition thus: that wealth left to young men, as a rule, is disadvantageous; that lives of poverty and struggle are advantageous.

Mr. Gladstone asks: "Is it too much to affirm that the hereditary transmission of wealth and position, in conjunction with the calls of occupation and of responsibility, is a good and not an evil thing? I rejoice to see it among our merchants, bankers, publishers; I wish it were commoner among our great manufacturing capitalists." He also says: "Even greater is the subject of hereditary transmission of land — more important and more difficult." Mr. Gladstone does not favor entails of money, but adds: "But is it another matter when in commerce, or in manufacture, or in other forms of enterprise, such for example as the business of a great publishing house, the work of the father is propagated by his descendants?"

These passages imply that the hereditary transmission of wealth and position and of business are not detrimental — as I think them — but desirable: a good and not an evil thing. Let us take the first form, that of sons following the occupations of their fathers. Little, I think, does one know, who is not in the whirl of business affairs, of the rarity of the combined qualities requisite for conducting the business enterprises of to-day. The time has passed when business once established can be considered almost permanently secure. Business methods have changed; good will counts for less and less. Success in business is held by the same tenure, nowadays, as the Premiership of Britain — at the cost of a perpetual challenge to all comers. The fond parent who invests his son with imaginary business qualifications, and places him in charge of affairs — upon the successful management of which the incomes of thousands depend — incurs a grave responsibility. Most of the disastrous failures of the day arise from this very cause. It is as unjust to the son as to the community. Out of seven serious failures during a panic in New York, five were traced to this root. One of these sons is an exile to escape punishment for breaking a law which he did not clearly understand. I have joined with others in asking the President to pardon him — a step I have never taken before on behalf of any law-breaker, but in this case I consider the father, not the son, the guilty party. The duty of the head of a great enterprise is to interest capable assistants who are without capital, but who have shown aptitude for affairs, and raise these to membership and management. The banker who hands over his business to sons, because they are sons, is guilty of a great offense. The transmission of wealth and rank, without regard to merit or qualifications, may pass from one peer to another, not without much, but without serious injury, since the duties are a matter of routine, seldom involving the welfare or means of others; but the management of business, never.

But assuming that business enterprises can be handed over properly in deference to hereditary claims, is it wise or desirable that they should be? I think not. The millionaire business man rates his vocation higher than I, who sees in it the best or highest, or even a desirable career for his sons. The sons of the wealthy have a right instinct which tells them that to engage in work where the primary object is gain is unworthy of those who, relieved from the necessity of earning a livelihood, are in a position to devote themselves to any of the hundred pursuits in which their time and knowledge can be employed primarily for the good of the community. The sons of the millionaire are to be regarded with approval who cannot be induced to take the absorbing and incessant interest in their father's business which is necessary to save it from ruin. The day is over when even the richest can play at business, as rich men's sons almost invariably do. There are exceptions where the son shows tastes and decided ability which render him the natural successor; but these are rare, far too rare to take into account in estimating the value of a custom. This ability, moreover, should be proved in some other establishment than that of the father.

When we come to the hereditary transmission of land, Mr. Gladstone's words are most touching. He paints a lovely picture of the "wonderful diversity and closeness of the ties by which, when rightly used, the office of the landed proprietor binds together the whole structure of rural society, ... that cohesion, interdependence, and affection of the gens which is in its turn a fast-compacting bond of societies at large." But is this a picture of to-day? Has not that day passed also, except in a few instances such as that furnished by the late lamented Lord Tollemache,[5] and upon

[5] Lord Tollemache (1805-1890) was the landlord of two estates, totaling

a smaller scale by Mr. Gladstone himself, in that earthly
Paradise, Hawarden? [6]

The cultivation of land is now a business conducted upon
a commercial basis by independent men, whom the landed
proprietor no longer leads, and who most fortunately can
lead themselves. The American citizen, who is himself landlord, factor, tenant, and laborer, requiring from the land he
owns and tills only the support of himself and family, has
rendered impossible the maintenance of more than one class
from the product of agricultural land anywhere in the world.
Knowing the kind of citizen which this condition creates,
and knowing also the character of the Scotch farmer, as
evolved through the operation of long leases which make
him practically independent, — although in his case the
magic power of ownership, which counts for so much, is
still lacking, — and estimating these classes as men and as
citizens, I have no doubt that the balance of advantage,
both to the individual and to the State, is largely in favor of
the change. Should the abolition of primogeniture and entail
come with the changes democracy is expected to inaugurate,
large estates in Britain would probably be divided into
farms and owned by the people. The history of Denmark in
this particular might then be that of Britain; and the temptation which now exists to leave territorial domains to eldest
sons would thus be removed, and with it one great obstacle
to the adoption of the gospel of wealth — the desire, futile
as vain, to found or maintain hereditary families.

Mr. Gladstone instances the Marquis of Salisbury [7] suc-

33,000 acres, in Suffolk and Cheshire. He contributed a phrase and a practice
to land reform by giving each of his 250 cottage tenants "three acres and a
cow," from the returns of which they could supplement their wages on neighboring farms. At the same time he divided his own estates into farms of 200
acres as the most profitable unit of cultivation. He had the most advanced
ideas about a landlord's responsibility and knew every tenant and his capa-
bilities. On his death in 1890 the *Times* characterized him "as the finest
practical agriculturist in the country."

[6] Gladstone's large private estate in Wales, site of an ancient castle.

[7] Lord Salisbury was a Cecil. The family, one of the most distinguished
in English history, attained eminence at least as early as the reign of Queen

ceeding to the office of Prime Minister, which office ten generations ago was filled by one of his ancestors, and asks: "Is not this tie of lineage a link binding him to honor and to public virtue?" Is not Mr. Gladstone unfortunate in naming Lord Salisbury in support of his views? I have always regarded him as a striking instance of the advantage of not being born to hereditary wealth and position. Like the great founder of the Cecils, Lord Salisbury himself was born a commoner — a younger son with a younger son's portion; and with the promptings of decided ability within him, he did everything in his power to prevent being narrowed and restricted by the smothering robes of rank and wealth. The laws of his country forced him to sink his individuality in a peerage, but for which English history might have told of a first and a second Cecil, as it tells of a first and a second Pitt — men too great to be obliterated as men by any title. It is a sad descent in historical rank from "Cecil" to the "Marquis" of anything. The highest title which a man can write upon the page of history is his own name. Mr. Gladstone's will be there; Gladstone he is, Gladstone he will remain, even if he tried to make future generations lose his commanding personality in the "Dukedom of Clydesdale," or any title whatever. But who among his contemporaries in public life is to stand this supreme test of masterdom? There is room for one only in each generation. It is safe to predict that, whoever he be, he will resemble "Gladstone" in one essential feature: he will be of the people, free from the dis-

Elizabeth. Robert Cecil, the first Earl of Salisbury, younger son of William Lord Burghley, was Queen Elizabeth's famous Lord Treasurer. A lineal descendant, Robert Arthur Talbot Gascoyne-Cecil, third Marquis of Salisbury, was born in 1830. His father, disapproving of the young man's marriage, gave him only a limited income. Thereupon he became a contributor to magazines, notably Bentley's *Quarterly Review* and the *Saturday Review*. On the death of an older brother in 1865 he became his father's heir. Meanwhile in the Commons he had made a reputation as a conservative and a foe of Gladstone. After serving as Secretary of State for Foreign Affairs and in other positions, he became in 1885 prime minister for the first time. Through the next fifteen years he recurrently held this office as well as that for foreign affairs. He left office for the last time in 1902 and died the following year.

advantage of hereditary wealth and position, and stamp his name and personality upon the glittering scroll. "Disraeli" promised well for a time, but he fades rapidly into Beaconsfield [8] — a shadow of a name. The title proves greater than the man.

As a "Saturday Reviewer," Robert Talbot Cecil (what a glorious name to lose!) had proved himself a power: it is a hundred to one that, had he been born to the hereditary title, he would have remained an obscure commonplace Marquis, resembling in this respect the many generations of Marquises of Salisbury which had followed each other, and whose noble history is comprised — and fully comprised — in "Burke's Peerage" in the three letters, b, m, d. The only man of his family from whom he can derive inspiration "binding him to honor and to public virtue," is the great original Cecil, and the founder of his own branch of the house, who, like himself, was a younger son, and had neither wealth nor rank. He did not even reach knighthood till late in his career. The great Cecil sprang from the people, and had none of the advantages which Mr. Gladstone, as I think wrongly, attributes to hereditary wealth and position. Lineage is, indeed, most important, but only the lineage of the immediate parents; for in each generation one half of the strain is changed. Fortunately for the high-placed ones of the earth, it is unnecessary for them to scrutinize the characters of their ancestors beyond the preceding generation. Happy for the royal children of Britain that they can dwell upon the virtues of father and mother, and stop there. Lord Salisbury, like many able men, perhaps, owes his commanding qualities to his mother, who was the daughter of a country gentleman — a commoner, secure from the disadvantages of the hereditary transmission of wealth and rank. It is curious that the present ruler of the other branch of the English race, our President, has the same good fortune Mr. Gladstone claims for the

[8] Benjamin Disraeli (1804–1881) became Earl of Beaconsfield in 1876 but did not exactly "fade" as statesman until 1880.

Marquis of Salisbury, his grandfather having been President.[9] But it is safe to say that the American ruler would never have occupied that high office had he received fortune and position from his grandfather, or had he himself acquired riches. No party is so foolish as to nominate for the Presidency a rich man, much less a millionaire. Democracy elects poor men. The man must have worked for his bread to be an available candidate; and if, like Lincoln, he has been so fortunate as to be compelled to split rails, or, like Garfield,[10] to drive mules upon a canal, and subsequently to clean the rooms and light the fires of the school in part payment for his tuition, or, like Blaine,[11] to teach school, so much more successfully does he appeal to the people. This applies not only to the Presidency: one of the strongest aspirants for that office lost his renomination to the Senate because a house that he erected in Washington was taken as an indication of tastes incompatible with republican simplicity of life.

Nothing is more fatal to the prospects of a public man in America than wealth, or the display of wealth. The dangers of a plutocracy that his Eminence Cardinal Manning fears are, I assure him, purely imaginary. There is no country in which wealth counts for so little as in the Republic. The current is all the other way. Is the influence of lineage less upon the republican President, in binding him to honor and public virtue, because neither hereditary rank nor wealth was transmitted? Because he is poor and a commoner, is he less sensitive to the promptings of honor and virtue? I think it will be found that the best and greatest of Britain do not differ from the greatest and best of other lands. These have had a lineage which linked them to honor and to public virtue, but almost

---

[9] Benjamin Harrison (1833–1901), twenty-third President of the United States, was the grandson of William Henry Harrison, the ninth.

[10] James A. Garfield (1831–1881) reputedly was the last president to be born in a log cabin.

[11] James G. Blaine (1830–1893), Secretary of State in Garfield's administration (1880–81) and again in 1889–1902, taught school at Western Military Institute, Georgetown, Kentucky, and at an institution for the blind in Philadelphia.

without exception the lineage of honest poverty — of labori-
ous, wage-receiving parents, leading lives of virtuous priva-
tion, sacrificing comforts that their sons might be kept at
school — lineage from the cottage of poverty, not the palace
of hereditary rank and position.

Mr. Gladstone himself has a lineage. Does it bind him less
than Lord Salisbury is bound by his to honor and public
virtue? His ancestors were Scotch farmers without wealth or
rank, yet I doubt not that Mr. Gladstone's career has been as
strongly and as nobly influenced by his knowledge or rec-
ollections of the poor and virtuous lives lived by his fore-
fathers as that of any hereditary monarch or noble who ever
lived could be by thoughts of his ancestors; and of one thing
I am absolutely sure: he has reason to be much prouder of
his lineage than nobles or monarchs in general can possibly
be of theirs. Among many advantages arising, not from the
transmission of hereditary wealth and position, but from the
transmission of hereditary "poverty and health," there is one
which, to my mind, overweighs all the others combined. It is
not permitted the children of king, millionaire, or noble to
have father and mother in the close and realizing sense of
these sacred terms. The name of father, and the holier name
of mother, are but names to the child of the rich and the
noble. To the poor boy these are the words he conjures with
— his guides, the anchors of his soul, the objects of his adora-
tion. Neither nurse, servant, governess, nor tutor has come
between him and his parents. In his father he has had tutor,
companion, counselor, and judge. It is not given to the born
millionaire, noble, or prince to dwell upon such a heritage as
is his who has had in his mother nurse, seamstress, teacher,
inspirer, saint — his all in all.

Hereditary wealth and position tend to rob father and
mother of their children, and the children of father and
mother. It cannot be long ere their disadvantages are felt
more and more, and the advantages of plain and simple
living more clearly seen.

Poor boys reared thus directly by their parents possess such advantages over those watched and taught by hired strangers, and exposed to the temptations of wealth and position, that it is not surprising they become the leaders in every branch of human action. They appear upon the stage, athletes trained for the contest, with sinews braced, indomitable wills, resolved to do or die. Such boys always have marched, and always will march, straight to the front and lead the world; they are the epoch-makers. Let one select the three or four foremost names, the supremely great in every field of human triumph, and note how small is the contribution of hereditary rank and wealth to the short list of immortals who have lifted and advanced the race. It will, I think, be seen that the possession of these is almost fatal to greatness and goodness, and that the greatest and best of our race have necessarily been nurtured in the bracing school of poverty — the only school capable of producing the supremely great, the genius.

Upon the plea made by "The Gospel of Wealth" for modesty of private expenditure, Mr. Gladstone says: "Among those whose station excuses or even requires magnificence, there are abundant opportunities, and there are also beautiful and graceful examples of personal simplicity and restraint." This seems to me a branch from the upas-tree of hereditary transmission of wealth and position. Is it true that station requires magnificence, or true that true dignity of station is enhanced by simplicity?

Here are some words of President Cleveland in his message to Congress upon this point: "We should never be ashamed of the simplicity and prudential economies which are best suited to the operation of a republican form of government and most compatible with the mission of the American people. Those who are selected for a limited time to manage public affairs are still of the people, and may do much by their example to encourage, consistently with the dignity of their official functions, that plain way of life which among their fellow-citizens aids integrity and promotes thrift and prosperity."

President Cleveland only follows the teachings and examples of every American President, and of all others in official station. There are no pecuniary prizes in the Republic for judge, bishop, or President; neither any pensions,[12] except that judges are retired upon half-pay at seventy years of age. The very moderate salaries given to all officials enforce modest expenditure, and the influence of this upon the nation is as powerful as salutary. Were some future King of Britain to announce that the serious consideration of the subject of wealth and poverty had led him to resolve to live as the President of the United States and his family live, upon ten thousand pounds a year, and to return to the nation, or devote to public uses, the hundreds of thousands of pounds spent for magnificence, and were he to live in accordance with this resolve, would it lessen or enhance the true dignity of his life and station? Would it lessen or enhance his influence? Is it reasonable to estimate that all the good that monarch could possibly do in his restricted position would equal that which would flow from setting the example of living a quiet, unostentatious, modest life — administering his surplus not upon himself, but for others? The only objection that might be raised against such action is that it would render the king a personage far too powerful for the system of constitutional monarchy, which requires "king" to be but a word meaning the will of the Cabinet. The man capable of taking such action would be not only titular "king," but a power in the State. The Right Hon. John Morley,[13] replying to a question asked by a constituent at a meeting in Newcastle, some time ago, bearing upon this very point of expend-

---

[12] On the other hand, Carnegie, pained by the ingratitude of republics, bequeathed in his will an income of $10,000 a year to ex-President Taft and $5,000 a year each to Mrs. Grover Cleveland and Mrs. Theodore Roosevelt.

[13] English statesman and author (1838–1923), Secretary of Ireland under Gladstone and Secretary for India, 1905–1910.

iture and magnificence in the State, gave expression to the hope that the highly placed might learn that the truest dignity consisted in quiet and simple living. I do not quote his words but the sense of his reply. Mr. Gladstone himself will leave behind him many titles to the affection, gratitude, and admiration of his countrymen; but when the future eulogist says of him — as he will truly be able to say — what is said of Pitt upon his monument in G[u]ildhall, he will pay him the greatest of all tributes. These words are: "Dispensing for many years the favours of his sovereign, he lived without ostentation, and died poor." If we cannot have Mr. Gladstone preaching in favor of modest living upon the part of those in station, we rejoice that none excels him in the practice of that virtue. It is seldom we are permitted to extol the example beyond the precept of the sage.

Upon this subject I thank Mr. Hughes for the words he has written. He says: "The real question is not how much we ought to give away, but how much we dare retain for our own gratification." These words strike home to every man of wealth and station: "How much *dare we retain* for our own gratification?" This is a troublesome question which will not "down." Giving the one tenth — the tithe — is easy. The true disciple of the gospel of wealth has to pass far beyond that stage. His conscience may be quieted by arguing that he and his family are entitled to enjoy in moderation the best that the world affords. The earnest disciple can easily discover the efficacy of running in debt, as it were, by anticipating his expected surplus, and engaging in works for the general good before the cash is in hand, to an extent which really keeps him without available surplus, and even entails the necessity of figuring how to meet engagements. He can, when so situated, consider himself poor, and he will certainly feel himself so. The personal expenditure of the very rich forms so small a part of their income, provided the rule is obeyed which forbids such extravagance as would render them conspicuous, that they can, perhaps, also find refuge from self-questioning in the thought of the much greater portion of their means which is being spent upon others. But I do not profess that this is entirely satisfactory, and I am glad to agree with Mr. Hughes in the very low estimate he places upon this partial treatment of the serious question he has raised: "How much *dare we retain* for our own gratification?"

Upon the subject of giving, Mr. Gladstone thinks that I am severe in my judgment of private charity when I estimate that of every thousand dollars spent in so-called charity nine hundred and fifty of them had better be thrown into the sea. The history of the Charity Organization Society of New York is here most instructive.[14] Its confidential monthly bulletin recently gave the names of twenty-three bogus organizations which were soliciting contributions, many of them, unfortunately, with success. These have their printed annual reports, lists of distinguished contributors, — in many cases, alas! these are genuine, — their lady collectors, and all the other details. When the various charitable societies first combined and compared lists of those receiving aid, it was found that many names were upon seven or eight of the lists. Did my space permit, a story could be told that would impress upon every wealthy person that his duty is not to resolve to give, but to withhold until certain that his aid will not increase the area of what is called, in the stirring language of the day, the "hell of want and misery," which he longs to remove. The towns of Connecticut have recently been getting light upon almsgiving. A morning paper says: "The experience of Hartford with well-to-do public beggars may be duplicated in almost every town in Connecticut. A year or two ago, in Norwich, a town agent investigated the condition

[14] The Charity Organization Society of New York was established in 1881 to correlate the efforts and grants of the many private charity organizations "engaged in teaching and relieving the poor of the city in their own homes." It was an example of a general movement in the late nineteenth century to introduce more efficiency and less duplication in the bestowal of private charity.

of the numerous persons who were receiving town aid. In forty instances he found that the applicants for charity had from five hundred to three thousand dollars in the savings-bank; in one case, that of a woman who had been drawing 'town money' for years, it was found she had nearly twenty thousand dollars in a local bank."

This is the least deplorable side of the matter, for the money given to prudent, saving people, even if they may not need it, cannot produce the serious consequences of that given to the much more numerous class who use it for the gratification of vice, and to enable them to live in idleness. Unless the individual giver knows the person or family in misfortune, their habits, conduct, and cause of distress, and knows that help given will aid them to help themselves, he cannot act properly; and if he does act to save his own feelings — which one is very apt to do — he will increase rather than diminish the distress which appeals to him. There is really no true charity except that which will help others to help themselves, and place within the reach of the aspiring the means to climb.

I notice a prevalent disposition to think only of the unfortunate wretches into whom the virtues necessary for improvement cannot be instilled. Common humanity impels us to provide for the actual wants of human beings — to see, through our poor laws, that none die of starvation, and to provide comfortable shelter, clothing, and instruction, which should, however, always be dependent upon work performed; but in doing this our thoughts should also turn to the benefits that are to accrue to those who are yet sound and industrious and seeking through labor the means of betterment, by removing from their midst and placing under care of the State in workhouses the social lepers. Every drunken vagabond or lazy idler supported by alms bestowed by wealthy people is a source of moral infection to a neighborhood. It will not do to teach the hard-working, industrious man that there is an easier path by which his wants can be supplied.

The earnest reformer will think as much, if not more, of the preservation of the sound and valuable members among the poor, as of any real change which can be effected in those who seem hopelessly lost to temperance, industry, and thrift. He will labor more to prevent than to cure, feeling that it is necessary to remove the spoiled grape from the bunch, the spoiled apple from the barrel, mainly for the sake of the sound fruit that remains. He who would plunge the knife into the social cancer, if any good is to be effected thereby, must needs be a skilled surgeon with steady hand and calm judgment, with the feelings as much under control as possible; the less emotion the better.

One reads or hears everywhere of rash proposals, well-meaning, no doubt, full of the innocence of the dove; but there is no task which more requires the wisdom of the serpent, which seems woefully lacking in these sensational schemes. The following from Rabbi Adler is sound to the core: "Giving, however, is an easy matter; it needs neither special training nor sustained thought. But the purpose and methods of charitable relief cannot be learned without a long and diligent apprenticeship, for which discipline in the painful school of personal experience is alone of any avail."

Sorry as I am to say it, the more attention I give to this subject, the greater the genuine knowledge obtained, the higher I am disposed to raise my estimate of the evil produced by indiscriminate giving.

From the standpoint of "The Gospel of Wealth" Mr. Gladstone's criticisms are, indeed, serious — almost fatal; for it will be readily seen that if the hereditary transmission of wealth and position and of business concerns be not pernicious as a rule, as I hold, but advantageous to the individuals receiving these bequests, and to the nation as well, and if, instead of simplicity, as I think, station requires magnificence, it will be hard indeed, if not impossible, to teach the wealthy that surplus wealth should be regarded as a sacred trust to be administered during their lives for the public good; they will continue to gather and leave fortunes to their families or spend them for magnificence as hitherto. I turn, therefore, for support to the views of the other contributors. His Eminence Cardinal Manning says:

> Mr. Carnegie tells us plainly, first, that the accumulation of stagnant wealth to be bequeathed to heirs is a vainglory in the giver, and may be a ruin to the receiver; secondly, that the bequeathing of wealth for charities when the man is gone out of life is an empty way of making a name for generosity; thirdly, that to *distribute all beyond the reasonable and temperate reserves due to kindred and their welfare, inter vivos, or now in life,* with his own will, judgment, and hand to works of public and private beneficence and ultility, is the highest and noblest use of wealth. This is a gospel, not according to capital, but according to the mind and life of the Founder of the Christian world. It is nothing new. It is no private opinion or exorbitant notion of a morbid prodigality, but the words of soberness and truth. If men so acted they would change the face of the world.

The Rev. Mr. Hughes writes:

> In the long and arduous task of reconstructing society on a Christian basis, with due and careful regard to all legitimate existing interests, it would be an inestimable public service if every one whom Mr. Carnegie represents would follow the example of Mr. Carnegie in getting rid of his money as quickly as possible. Mr. Carnegie's gospel is the very thing for the transition period from social heathenism to social Christianity. If a man is so unfortunate as to have enormous wealth, he cannot do better than act upon Mr. Carnegie's distributive principles.

I cannot but express the hope that further reflection upon the vital points may bring Mr. Gladstone into closer agreement with our colleagues in the discussion. In none of their articles is there a word in support of the advantages of the hereditary transmission of wealth and position, or of the necessity for magnificence upon the part of those in station. Their views seem to be in quite the other direction.

Fortunately, from this point forward we have Mr. Gladstone's powerful and unreserved support. He says: "The accumulation of wealth has had adversaries, but it has been too strong for them all; it is the business of the world." "The Gospel of Wealth" advocates leaving free the operation of laws of accumulation. It accepts this condition as unassailable, and seeks to make the best of it by directing into new and better channels the streams of accumulated and accumulating wealth, which it is found impossible to prevent. But in this, while we have Mr. Gladstone with us, we have regretfully lost Mr. Hughes, who rises in stern opposition and says: "If 'Lay not up for yourselves treasures upon the earth' [15] does not forbid the accumulation of wealth, the New Testament was written on Talleyrand's principle and was intended to 'conceal thoughts.' " [16]

It is quite true, as Mr. Hughes says, "that expositors can prove anything, and that theologians can explain away anything." When applied to a rich man, his view of this very text — only part of which is quoted by Mr. Hughes — was that he strictly complied with the injunction by always placing his treasures in the safety deposit company, where he was quite sure "neither moth nor rust could corrupt, nor thieves break through and steal." Mr. Hughes quotes the parable of the master of the vineyard, whose conduct is cited by Christ with approval. How came he master of a vineyard? Can he have sinned and "accumulated wealth" for the payment of labor? Mr. Hughes says: "Christ distinctly prohibited the accumulation of wealth." But when Christ spoke, the revenues of a leading minister, even if divided among the whole twelve apostles, would have been accounted "wealth." It seems to me we have only to interpret literally, in this manner, a few parts of isolated texts to find warrant for the destruction of civilization. Five words spoken by Christ so interpreted, if strictly obeyed, would at one blow strike down all that distinguishes man from the beast. "Take no thought for to-morrow." [17] There is reason to believe that the

[15] Matt. 6:19.
[16] Also attributed to Voltaire, *Dialogue XIV, Le Chapon et la Poularde* — "Men . . . employ speech only to conceal their thoughts."
[17] Matt. 6:34.

forces of Christianity are not thus to be successfully arrayed against the business of the world — the accumulation of wealth. The parable of the talents [18] bears in the other direction. It was those who had accumulated and even doubled their capital to whom the Lord said: "Well done, thou good and faithful servant: thou has been faithful over a few things, I will make thee ruler over many things: enter thou into the joy of thy Lord."

Those who had "laid up" their treasures and not increased them were reprimanded. Consider the millionaire who continues to use his capital actively in enterprises which give employment and develop the resources of the world. He who manages the ships, the mines, the factories, cannot withdraw his capital, for this is the tool with which he works such beneficent wonders; nor can he restrict his operations, for the cessation of growth and improvement in any industrial undertaking marks the beginning of decay. The demands of the world for new and better things are continuous, and existing establishments must supply these, or lose even the trade they now have. I hope Mr. Hughes will find good ground for an interpretation which justifies the belief that the text has no bearing upon him, but is intended solely for those who hoard realized capital, adding the interest obtained for its use to the principal, and dying with their treasures "laid up," which should have been used as they accrued during the life of the individual for public ends, as the gospel of wealth requires.

Acting in accordance with this advice, it becomes the duty of the millionaire to increase his revenues. The struggle for more is completely freed from selfish or ambitious taint and becomes a noble pursuit. Then he labors not for self, but for others; not to hoard, but to spend. The more he makes, the more the public gets. His whole life is changed from the moment that he resolves to become a disciple of the gospel of wealth, and henceforth he labors to acquire

[18] Matt. 25:14-28.

that he may wisely administer for others' good. His daily labor is a daily virtue. Instead of destroying, impairing, or disposing of the tree which yields such golden fruit, it does not degrade his life nor even his old age to continue guarding the capital from which alone he can obtain the means to do good. He may die leaving a sound business in which his capital remains, but beyond this die poor, possessed of no fortune which was free for him to distribute, and therefore, I submit, not justly chargeable with belonging to the class which "lay up their treasures upon earth."

In this connection I commend to my reverend colleague the sermon of the founder of his church (*The Use of Money*, American edition, vol. i. p. 44, Sermon 50). He says:

> Gain all you can by honest industry. Use all possible diligence in your calling. Lose no time. Gain all you can by common sense, by using in your business all the understanding which God has given you. It is amazing to observe how few do this — how men run on in the same dull track with their forefathers.
>
> Having gained all you can by honest wisdom and unwearied diligence, the second rule of Christian prudence is, "Save all you can." Do not throw it away in idle expenses — to gratify pride, etc. If you desire to be a good and faithful steward, out of that portion of your Lord's goods which he has for the present lodged in your hands, first provide things needful for yourself, food, raiment, etc.
>
> Second, provide these for your wife, your children, your servants, and others who pertain to your household. If then you have an overplus, do good to them that are of the household of faith. If there be still an overplus, do good to all men.[19]

Upon this sermon the gospel of wealth seems founded. Indeed, had I known of its existence before writing upon the subject, I should certainly have quoted it. I shall, therefore, not be shaken, even if a leading disciple of Wesley informs

[19] John Wesley (1703–1791), the "founder" of Methodism, Mr. Hughes's denomination, accumulated about $250,000 by his writings. The quotations, as Carnegie cited them, are from the *Works of John Wesley*. There are several "first" American editions. The earliest to include this sermon, here numbered LIII, was published by J. & J. Harper (New York, 1826–1827), VI, 101. The sermon is numbered L in the *First American Complete and Standard Edition from the Latest London Edition* (New York: Emory & B. Waugh, 1831), I, 444.

us that Mr. Carnegie (as representing the millionaire class, of course) is an "anti-Christian phenomenon," a "social monstrosity," and a "grave political peril," and says that "in a really Christian country — that is, in a country constructed upon a Christian basis — a millionaire would be an economic impossibility." The millionaire class needs no defense, although Mr. Hughes thinks it no longer of use since joint-stock companies provide the means for establishing industries upon the large scale now demanded. It is most significant that the business concerns which have given Britain supremacy are, with few or no exceptions, the creations of the individual millionaire — the Cunards, Ismays, Allens, Elders, Bessemers, Rothschilds, Barings, Clarks, Coatses, Crossleys, the Browns, Siemens, Cammels, Gillotts, Whitworths, the Armstrongs, Listers, the Salts, Bairds, Samuelsons, Howards, Bells,[20] and others. Joint-stock companies have not yet proven themselves equal to managing business properly after such men have created it. Where they have succeeded, it will be found that a very few individuals, and generally but one, have still control of affairs. Joint-stock companies cannot be credited with invention or enterprise. If it were not for the millionaire still in business, leading the way, a serious check would fall upon future improvement, and I believe business men generally will concur in the opinion, which I very firmly hold, that partnership — a very few, not more than two or three men — in any line of business will make full interest upon the capital invested; while a similar concern as a joint-stock company, owned by many in small amounts, will scarcely pay its way and is very likely to fail. Railroads may occur to some as examples of joint-stock management, but the same rule applies to these. America has most of the railroads of the world, and it is found that whenever a few able men control a line and make

[20] These are families who established great 19th century British enterprises — shipping and ship-building, finance, manufacturing, metallurgy, chemicals, textiles, armaments, mining, etc. — and who in many cases promoted philanthropic and educational projects in England.

its management their personal affair, dividends are earned where before there were none. The railways of Britain being monopolies, and charging from two to three times higher rates for similar service than those of America, only manage to pay their shareholders a small return. It would be quite another story if these were the property of one or two able men and managed by them.

The "promotion" of an individual into a joint-stock concern is precisely what the promotion of the individual is from the House of Commons to the House of Lords. The push and masterfulness of the few owners who have created the business are replaced by the limited authority and regulation performance of routine duties by salaried officials, after promotion. While the career of both concern and individual may continue respectable, it is necessarily dull. They are no longer in the race; the great work of both is over. It would not be well for Britain's future if her commercial and manufacturing supremacy depended upon joint-stock companies. It is her individual millionaires who have created this supremacy, and upon them its maintenance still depends. Those who insure steady employment to thousands, at wages not lower than others pay, need not be ashamed of their record; for steady employment is, after all, the one indispensable requisite for the welfare and the progress of the people. Still, I am neither concerned nor disposed to dispute Mr. Hughes's assertion that in a state under really Christian principles a millionaire would be an impossibility. He may be right; it is a far guess ahead. But the millionaire will not lack good company in making his exit; for surely nothing is clearer than that in the ideal day there can be no further use whatever for those of Mr. Hughes's profession. The millionaire and the preacher will alike have to find some other use for their talents, some other work to do that they may honorably earn and eat their daily bread. In this I doubt not both will continue to be eminently successful. The successors of the Rev. Mr. Hughes and myself, arm in arm, will

make a pretty pair out in search of some light work with
heavy pay.

Upon speculations as to the future of the race involving
revolutionary change of existing conditions, it seems unwise
to dwell. I think we have nothing whatever to do with what
may come a thousand or a million years hence, and none of
us can know what will come. Our duties lie with the present
— with our day and generation; and even these are hard
enough to discern. The race toils slowly upward step by
step; it has even to create each successive step before it can
stand upon it, for

> [Yet] Nature is made better by no mean
> But nature makes that mean.[21]

If it attempts to bound over intervening space to any ideal,
it will not rise, but fall to lower depths. I cannot, therefore,
but regard such speculations a waste of time — of valuable
time — which is imperatively required for dealing with the
next step possible in the path upward. And it is in this light
that Mr. Gladstone's suggestion is of the greatest value. It
accepts and builds upon present conditions — accommodates
itself to our present environments. Mr. Gladstone has been
engaged during his long public career in focusing, as it were,
the various wishes of others, and so grouping them for a
common end that practical results might follow. It has
been his mission to restrain extremes, and to unite in common action the advance, the center, and the rear. He shows
his rare constructive skill in suggesting that there should
be formed a brotherhood of those who recognize their duties
to their fellows less favored with this world's goods. This
society will, no doubt, be so wide as to admit all, no limit
being put to the amount of percentage of his surplus which
each can secretly resolve to devote to others, nor any interference attempted with the wide field of its application. We
may expect kindred societies to be formed throughout the

[21] *Winter's Tale*, Act IV, scene 3, line 89.

world, and, at intervals, delegates from these might meet together in one world-wide brotherhood, thereby strengthening each other in the desire and effort to do their best to improve the condition of the masses, and to bring rich and poor into closer union. Those who ask, "not how much we ought to give away, but how much we dare retain," would represent the advanced section. Passing from this through many gradations, those who still fondly plead for the continued hereditary transmission of wealth and position and for magnificence in station would constitute the other great wing of the army. All would be equally welcome, equally necessary, it being enough that members of the brotherhood feel that the duty of the day is that, intrusted as they are with surplus wealth beyond their wants, — as their conscience may determine these wants, — they should regularly set apart and expend all or a proportion, greater or less, of the remainder, for the good of their less fortunate fellows, in the manner which seems to each best calculated to promote their genuine improvement. Should Mr. Gladstone's suggestion find the response which it deserves, he will have added much to the usefulness of his life in a sphere happily far removed from and far above the political; a field in which there can be room neither for strife, jealousy, gain, nor personal ambition; a cause so high, so holy, that all its surroundings must breathe of peace, good will, brotherhood!

Every earnest good man, anxious to leave the world a little better than he found it, will wish Mr. Gladstone Godspeed in his new, inspiring task — a task which is indeed "too great for haste, too high for rivalry."

· IV ·

Popular Illusions About Trusts [1]

THE platforms of both parties in the coming Presidential contest are likely to ring with express or implied denunciation of trusts, in order to minister to the popular outcry against them, many of the people having been led to believe that great aggregations of capital must be inimical to the interests of the masses who have little or none. While this policy may be more or less successful for the moment, from a party point of view, it must be ephemeral, because, as the writer hopes to show, trusts cannot permanently thwart the laws of competition, and hence must prove beneficial agencies for the people.

The world does not spin round any faster in our day than it has for ages past, but undoubtedly new ideas in the world come into view and flash past with a rapidity hitherto unknown. It seems as if, in our time, man were chiefly absorbed in obeying the injunction to try all things. Fortunately, we evolutionists know that in the end he must and will hold fast only to that which is good for the organism known as human society. His attitude hitherto toward new things or new ideas has been one of suspicion and hesitation. We see traces of this yet in the older countries and older civilizations; but the bounding, irrepressible, "cock-sure" spirit of Western civilization seems possessed by an entirely different tendency. It grasps everything new with avidity, and is sanguine beyond measure of its merits, ever ready to discard the old, and to see in any new thing the golden

[1] Published originally in *Century Magazine*, LX (May 1900), 143–149.

bow of promise. The American is the modern magician, ever exchanging old lamps for new. Panaceas for all the ills of life are more numerous than the ills. Not one doctor, but a hundred, arise, competent to cure every defect in the body politic, and none is without patients or — may we write? — dupes. We must all have our toys and our fads. It is natural for man to indulge in the delusions of hope.

The day is not far past when the industrial world saw its millennium in the joint-stock idea. Every department of industry was to be captured by it. Shares in every conceivable enterprise were to be distributed among the people en masse, thus insuring the much-needed redistribution of wealth, where every man was no longer a consumer only, but his own manufacturer, his own transporter, clothier, butcher, baker, and candlestick-maker. There was nothing to prevent him being in one sense his own undertaker through shares in the "Burial Company, Limited," or the "Crematorium Company," thus carrying out to his very end the grand joint-stock corporation panacea. Every employee in mill or factory, in railway or steamship service, was soon to become an owner, with a possible future seat on the board.

Though all these over-sanguine expectations have not been realized through the laws establishing corporations, thus encouraging the massing of the innumerable small savings of the public in general, yet few new forms have been productive of so much benefit to the thrifty and aspiring people with small savings, who are the salt of the working millions and of the country, as the corporate idea.

Another highly important step forward in this domain resulted from the authorization of limited partnerships, by which the undoubted advantages of individual over corporate management could be secured without danger of ruin to the members, whose liability is limited to the amount of the capital stock of the partnership. In the great corporation the shares are generally bought and sold upon the stock exchange, and the real owners are unknown. All depends upon salaried officials, who may or may not have a dollar in the enterprise. In the limited partnership, on the contrary, only shareholders can be members; the shares are not sold to outsiders, and thus is insured the eye of the master over all. With proper, but absolutely necessary, provisions, it is possible, under this system, to create owners from among exceptional but poor employees, from whom no capital is required, the partnership agreeing to permit the profits to pay for the interest given, the capitalistic owners reserving the right to discontinue the partnership by a two-thirds vote, or a three-fourths majority vote, should the new partner not prove desirable. By this plan it is possible for the rise of the poor but able employee, thus neutralizing, to some extent, the acknowledged difficulty of men rising to ownership in our day, because of the enormous amount of capital required for successful operations under present, and probably enduring, conditions. The day of small concerns within the means of many able men seems to be over, never to return. The rise to partnership in vast concerns must come chiefly through such means as these permitted by the laws of limited partnership.

To-day we hear little of the joint-stock corporation, which has settled into its proper sphere and escapes notice. It was succeeded by the "syndicate," a combination of corporations which pulled together for a time, and expected to destroy destructive competition. The word has already almost passed out of use, and now the syndicate has given place to the trust.

We see in all these efforts of men the desire to furnish opportunities to mass capital, to concentrate the small savings of the many and to direct them to one end. The conditions of human society create for this an imperious demand; the concentration of capital is a necessity for meeting the demands of our day, and as such should not be looked at askance, but be encouraged. There is nothing detrimental to human society in it, but much that is, or is bound soon to become, beneficial. It is an evolution from the heterogeneous to the homogeneous,[2] and is clearly another step in the upward path of development.

Abreast of this necessity for massing the wealth of the many in even larger and larger sums for huge enterprises, another law is seen in operation in the invariable tendency from the beginning till now to lower the cost of all articles produced by man. Through the operation of this law the home of the laboring man of our day boasts luxuries which even in the palaces of monarchs as recent as Queen Elizabeth were unknown. It is a trite saying that the comforts of to-day were the luxuries of yesterday, and conveys only a faint impression of the contrast, until one walks through the castles and palaces of older countries, and learns that two or three centuries ago these had for carpets only rushes, small open spaces for windows, glass being little known, and were without gas or water-supply, or any of what we consider to-day the conveniences of life. As for those chief treasures of life, books, there is scarcely a working-man's family which has not at its command, without money and without price, access to libraries to which the palace was recently a stranger.

If there be in human history one truth clearer and more indisputable than another, it is that the cheapening of articles, whether of luxury or of necessity or of those classed as artistic, insures their more general distribution, and is one of the most potent factors in refining and lifting a people, and in adding to its happiness. In no period of human activity has this great agency been so potent or so widespread as in our own. Now, the cheapening of all these

[2] Spencer's Law of Evolution, enunciated in Part 2 of *First Principles* (1862), reads: "an integration of matter and concomitant dissipation of motion, during which the matter passes from an indefinite incoherent homogeneity to a definite coherent heterogeneity." Carnegie, not notably exact in quotation, has here literally reversed the order of "development" — something of a commentary on his subservience to or understanding of the English thinker.

good things, whether it be in the metals, in textiles, or in food, or especially in books and prints, is rendered possible only through the operation of the law, which may be stated thus: cheapness is in proportion to the scale of production. To make ten tons of steel a day would cost many times as much per ton as to make one hundred tons; to make one hundred tons would cost double as much per ton as a thousand; and to make one thousand tons per day would cost greatly more than to make ten thousand tons. Thus, the larger the scale of operation the cheaper the product. The huge steamship of twenty thousand tons burden carries its ton of freight at less cost, it is stated, than the first steamships carried a pound. It is, fortunately, impossible for man to impede, much less to change, this great and beneficent law, from which flow most of his comforts and luxuries, and also most of the best and most improving forces in his life.

In an age noted for its inventions, we see the same law running through these. Inventions facilitate big operations, and in most instances require to be worked upon a great scale. Indeed, as a rule, the great invention which is beneficent in its operation would be useless unless operated to supply a thousand people where ten were supplied before. Every agency in our day labors to scatter the good things of life, both for mind and body, among the toiling millions. Everywhere we look we see the inexorable law ever producing bigger and bigger things. One of the most notable illustrations of this is seen in the railway freight-car. When the writer entered the service of the Pennsylvania Railroad from seven to eight tons were carried upon eight wheels; to-day they carry fifty tons. The locomotive has quadrupled in power. The steamship to-day is ten times bigger, the blast-furnace has seven times more capacity, and the tendency everywhere is still to increase. The contrast between the hand printing-press of old and the elaborate newspaper printing-machine of to-day is even more marked.

We conclude that this overpowering, irresistible tendency

toward aggregation of capital and increase of size in every branch of product cannot be arrested or even greatly impeded, and that, instead of attempting to restrict either, we should hail every increase as something gained, not for the few rich, but for the millions of poor, seeing that the law is salutary, working for good and not for evil. Every enlargement is an improvement, step by step, upon what has preceded. It makes for higher civilization, for the enrichment of human life, not for one, but for all classes of men. It tends to bring to the laborer's cottage the luxuries hitherto enjoyed only by the rich, to remove from the most squalid homes much of their squalor, and to foster the growth of human happiness relatively more in the workman's home than in the millionaire's palace. It does not tend to make the rich poorer, but it does tend to make the poor richer in the possession of better things, and greatly lessens the wide and deplorable gulf between the rich and the poor. Superficial politicians may, for a time, deceive the uninformed, but more and more will all this be clearly seen by those who are now led to regard aggregations as injurious.

In all great movements, even of the highest value, there is cause for criticism, and new dangers arising from new conditions, which must be guarded against. There is no nugget free from more or less impurity, and no good cause without its fringe of scoria. The sun itself has spots, but, as has been wisely said, these are rendered visible only by the light itself sends forth.

The benefits, therefore, which have come to the world through this law of aggregation and increase take several forms, to some of which objection is made.

One form of aggregation is the growth of establishments constantly extending their field of operations, the special form which has been most criticized being the department store. We look back to the time when one petty establishment sold one class of articles. The subdivision of labor is seen in its fullest development throughout the Eastern world, where many servants are required, each restricted to doing one part of many operations required to produce one whole. Traces of this system still linger among us. In dealing with department stores the first question is, Do they provide articles at less cost for the masses? Upon cheapness, indeed, depends the wider distribution of desirable articles among the people, the enjoyment of which is greatly to be desired as inevitably carrying with it elevation to a higher stage of civilization. Increased comfort means increased refinement, and this means a higher standard of life. No one questions the fact that these great stores do furnish more value for the money than it was possible for small separate-selling agencies to do. The increased scale of operations all under one management insures much cheaper distribution. That they are so generally patronized is the best proof that they are beneficial, and, what should not be lost sight of, they are relatively more advantageous for the general public than for the few rich. In like manner it is the masses of the people, not the few, who are most benefited by the growth of huge and all-embracing establishments in every line of production and distribution. It is inevitable that the introduction of a new system should disturb and finally overthrow the older and less desirable system.

The chief complaint made against the department stores is that, while under the old system of small separate establishments there were secured as valuable citizens to the State a hundred independent owners, the department store may have only five. In the writer's opinion, this is a mistake, as experience already demonstrates that the great and successful establishment is dependent upon numerous active members participating directly in the results. It may be accepted as a law that the store which interests the greatest number of assistants, other things being equal, will prove the most successful, and it is a matter of common knowledge even to-day that in these vast establishments it is already the rule for all those in charge of the numerous departments to be directly interested in the profits. In other words, the small, petty master in his little store has given place to the bigger, much more important manager of a department, whose revenues generally exceed those of the petty owner he has supplanted. Nor is this all: the field for the display of exceptional ability is much wider than it could possibly be in the smaller establishment, and will as often win partnership in one of these establishments, or at least an equivalent of partnership, as the owner of the small store achieved success. This bigger system grows bigger men, and it is by the big men that the standard of the race is raised. The race of shopkeepers is bound to be improved, and to become not only better business men, and better men in themselves, but more valuable citizens for the State. Dealing with petty affairs tends to make small men; dealing with larger affairs broadens and strengthens character.

We have taken department stores as the form most under criticism, but what we have said here may be taken as said of all other branches of business, that the larger the scale upon which it can be successfully conducted the better it is for the race as a whole, and in greater degree better for the masses of the race than for the few.

We come now to another phase of aggregation: the consolidation of various works scattered in different parts of the country into one solid company. These consolidations are now classed as trusts.

As far as the consolidation of various plants engaged in one branch of manufacture is concerned, this is only obeying the great law of aggregation, which, we have seen, is beneficial, although the real object of the consolidators may, in some cases, have been the belief that through these consolidations ruinous competition might be ended. Color is given to this belief because it is obvious that the cheapening of product cannot result to so great an extent by combining works in scattered places as when one establishment enlarges itself. On the other hand, something is to be allowed for the claim that each separate work may be utilized to supply the wants of a tributary region, thus saving cost of transportation. The one solid enlarged establishment will, however, probably be able to manufacture its surplus not needed in the region tributary to it at a cost so much less than is possible at the small scattered establishments as to enable it to pay the freight upon what it desires to sell beyond its natural territory. In so far as consolidation of scattered works is intended to save cost of transportation, and thus to produce more cheaply, the consolidation is to be hailed as beneficial for the country; for the foundation upon which we rest is that cheapness of articles leads to their wider distribution among the masses, and is a gain when attained. Reduced cost of production, under the free play of competition, insures reduced prices to the consumer.

The people are aroused against trusts because they are said to aim at securing monopolies in the manufacture and distribution of their products; but the whole question is, Have they succeeded, or can they succeed, in monopolizing products? Let us consider. That the manufacturer of a patented article can maintain a monopoly goes without saying. Our laws expressly give him a monopoly. That it has been wise for the State to give an inventor this for a time will not be seriously questioned. So beneficial has it proved that the nations of the world are one after the other following our patent laws. Our chief industrial rival, Great Britain, has done so as far as possible, and the chairman of the British Patent Commission expressed to me the regret that it was found impracticable, at present, to go further in the same direction.

There are only two conditions other than patents which render it possible to maintain a monopoly. These are when the parties absolutely control the raw material out of which the article is produced, or control territory into which rivals can enter only with extreme difficulty. Such is virtually the case with the Standard Oil Company, and as long as it can maintain a monopoly of raw materials it goes without saying that it can maintain a monopoly in the product. This is a fact that the public must recognize, but what legislation can do to prevent it is difficult to say. Citizens of the United States have a right to buy anything they choose. This right could scarcely be restricted, nor, upon the whole, would it seem wise to restrict it, since that of the Standard Oil is the only case in which monopoly of an article has been secured. It has been rendered possible only by exceptional ability and in circumstances not likely ever to occur again. The price of its continued success is a line of such able men as its originators. Its second source of strength lies in the fact that through its extensive operations it has been enabled to reduce the price of its product to the consumer. It is a unique organization, for there is nothing like it in the world, and therefore it is not to be classed with the ordinary trusts, which are numerous and are constantly increasing.

Within the last few months a wholly new and surprising development of the trust idea has appeared in the railway world — one which reflects much credit upon the brain which conceived it. This is the purchase by the leading trunk-lines of large amounts of the stock of their less prominent competitors. We now see a vice-president of the Pennsylvania Railway Company sitting on the board of the Baltimore and Ohio. The possible outcome of this movement, if pursued, assumes portentous proportions, far surpassing in their effect any previous phase of the trust, and may lead to an extension of the powers of the Interstate Commission, and perhaps to other legislation at present unthought of. The subject is too far-reaching for more than mere mention in this paper. The country must see its future development, which will be waited with deep concern by the thoughtful student of economic problems.

The genesis of trusts is as follows: Manufacturers of most staple articles (especially of iron and steel) are subject to long periods of serious depression, succeeded by short intervals of high profits. Because during depression no increase is made in capacity, and the world's population and wants are constantly growing, one morning it is discovered that demand has overtaken and outrun supply. But the production of an increased supply is no easy matter. It usually means, beginning at the beginning, obtaining the raw materials from mine or soil, passing these through various processes for which the necessary machinery and facilities are wanting, and it is a year or eighteen months, or even two years, before the supply of most articles can be materially increased. Demand becomes imperious and unsatisfied, and prices bound upward. Many new men are induced to build new works. The extensions of the old works supply all demands, and even a shade beyond; then comes the collapse. It is during one of these long periods of depression, when many of the manufacturers are on the verge of bankruptcy, that there arises in the heart a hope, soon crystallized into a belief, that a new way has been found to avoid the natural consequences of the unchanging economic laws. It is soon felt that savage competition should cease between those enduring a common affliction, who should be brother manufacturers, and that the lion and the lamb should lie down together. They forget, in the hour of their misery, that the moralist has expressed the fear lest the one may be found inside the other. First, all kinds of understandings and fair promises are made — alas! only to be broken; and finally the promoter makes his appearance, and our unfortunate manufacturers fall an easy prey. Enormous sums are offered for antiquated plants which may not have been able to do more than pay their way for years. These are tied together, and the new industrial makes its appearance as a trust, under the delusion that if a dozen or twenty invalids be tied together vitality will be infused thereby into the mass. This is not true of all that are classed as trusts; there are exceptions; I speak only generally.

Should these combinations be made upon the eve of a

period of activity, as was the case recently, then there is a triumphant vindication of the new nostrum, the industrial world has found its panacea for all ills, and there is never to be ruinous competition again. The public is alarmed; it hears for a time of the advance of prices in the products of these gigantic concerns which temporarily control the market, and demands legislation against them. Generally speaking, as in the present instance, the advance in prices would have taken place even if no trusts existed, being caused by increased demand. The very name of trust stinks in our nostrils. We believe the public to be needlessly alarmed upon the subject, for the following reasons:

Few trusts have a monopoly through patents or through the supply of raw material or of territory, and what happens is this: For a short time competition is hindered, but rarely, if ever, completely stifled. The profits of the trusts are high, and capital, ever watchful for an opportunity to make unusual gains, seeks its level by a law of its being, and needs only the opportunity to engage in this highly profitable manufacture. A relative of one of the principal officials or one of the chiefs of a department in the trust, knowing its great profits, gets some friend with capital to build new works in cooperation with him, and the result is that we soon see springing up over the country rival works, each of which has the great giant trust more or less at its mercy. A threat to reduce prices, and the trust, to which this may mean millions of dollars of loss, will sooner or later come to an agreement with the little David who threatens to attack the Goliath, and the rival concern is arranged with or purchased. This only whets the appetite of others who see the success of the first innovator, and other works soon spring up. No sooner has the trust purchased one threatened rival than two appear, and the end is disaster. The people may rest assured that neither in one article nor in another is it possible for any trust to exact exorbitant profits without thereby speedily undermining its own foundations. It is not long since trusts first made their appearance, and already many have disappeared. Many still existing are being assailed, the names of which will readily occur to our readers. Only a few survive to-day, and none have secured the coveted monopoly. Most of the metals and many of the staple articles have been formed into trusts, which, although yet living, are rapidly being attacked to their final destruction. The press used to tell every morning of the organization of some trust or other, and even to-day we still hear of proposed additions to the list of these attempted gigantic monopolies, which enjoy an ephemeral existence. Upon most of them can already be written the appropriate epitaph:

> If I was so soon to be done for,
> I wonder what I was begun for.[3]

Every attempt to monopolize the manufacture of any staple article carries within its bosom the seeds of failure. Long before we could legislate with much effect against trusts there would be no necessity for legislation. The past proves this, and the future is to confirm it. There should be nothing but encouragement for these vast aggregations of capital for the manufacture of staple articles. As for the result being an increase of price to the consumer beyond a brief period, there need be no fear. On the contrary, the inevitable result of these aggregations is, finally and permanently, to give to the consumer cheaper articles that would have been otherwise possible to obtain; for capital is stimulated by the high profits of the trust, for a season, to embark against it. The result is very soon a capacity of production beyond the wants of the consumer, and as the new works erected are of the most improved pattern, and capable of producing cheaper than the old works, the vulnerable trusts are compelled to buy and capitalize at two or three times their cost. There is thus no danger ahead to the community from trusts, nor any cause for fear.

[3] The first line should read: "It is so soon that I am done for." An Epitaph "For a Child Aged Three Weeks," Cheltenham Churchyard.

The great natural laws, being the outgrowth of human nature and human needs, keep on their irresistible course. Competition in all departments of human activity is not to be suppressed. The individual manufacturer who is tempted into the unusually profitable business of the trust will take care of the monopoly question and prevent injury to the nation. The trust, so far as aggregation and enlargement go, is one day to be recognized as a grand step toward cheaper products for the people than could have been obtained by any other mode than the aggregation of capital and establishments. Already the ghosts of numerous departed trusts which aimed at monopolies have marched across the stage of human affairs, each pointing to its fatal wound, inflicted by that great corrective, competition. Like the ghosts of Macbeth's victims, the line promises to stretch longer and longer, and also like those phantoms of the brain, they "come like shadows, so depart."

> The earth hath bubbles as the water hath,
> And these are of them.[4]

The masses of the people, the toiling millions, are soon to find in this great law of aggregation of capital and of factories another of those beneficent agencies which in their operation tend to bring to the homes of the poor, in greater degree than ever, more and more of the luxuries of the rich, and into their lives more of sweetness and light. The only people who have reason to fear trusts are those who trust them.

[4] *Macbeth*, Act I, scene 3, line 79.

· V ·

An Employer's View of the Labor Question[1]

T HE struggle in which labor has been engaged during the past three hundred years, first against authority and then against capital, has been a triumphal march. Victory after victory has been achieved. Even so late as in Shakspere's time, remains of villeinage or serfdom still existed in England. Before that, not only the labor but the person of the laborer belonged to the chief. The workers were either slaves or serfs; men and women were sold with the estate upon which they worked, and became the property of the new lord, just as did the timber which grew on the land. In those days we hear nothing of strikes or of trades-unions, or differences of opinion between employer and employed. The fact is, labor had then no right which the chief, or employer, was bound to respect. Even as late as the beginning of this century, the position of the laborer in some departments was such as can scarcely be credited. What do our laboring friends think of this, that down to 1779 the miners of Britain were in a state of serfdom. They "were compelled by law to remain in the pits as long as the owner chose to keep them at work there, and were actually sold as part of the capital invested in the works. If they accepted an engagement elsewhere, their master could always have them fetched back and flogged as thieves for having attempted to rob him of their labor. This law was modified in 1779, but was not repealed till after the acts passed in

[1] From the *Forum*, I (April 1886), 114–125.

1797 and 1799" (*The Trades-Unions of England*, p. 119).[2]
This was only ninety-seven years ago. Men are still living who
were living then. Again, in France, as late as 1806, every
workman had to procure a license; and in Russia, down to
our own days, agricultural laborers were sold with the soil
they tilled.

Consider the change, nay, the revolution! Now the poorest laborer in America or in England, or indeed throughout
the civilized world, who can handle a pick or a shovel, stands
upon equal terms with the purchaser of his labor. He sells
or withholds it as may seem best to him. He negotiates,
and thus rises to the dignity of an independent contractor.
When he has performed the work he bargained to do, he
owes his employer nothing, and is under no obligation to
him. Not only has the laborer conquered his political and
personal freedom: he has achieved industrial freedom as
well, as far as the law can give it, and he now fronts his
master, proclaiming himself his equal under the law.

But, notwithstanding this complete revolution, it is evident that the permanent relations to each other of labor and
capital have not yet evolved. The present adjustment does
not work without friction, and changes must be made before
we can have industrial peace. To-day we find collisions
between these forces, capital and labor, when there should
be combination. The mill hands of an industrial village in
France have just risen against their employers, attacked
the manager's home and killed him. The streets of another
French village are barricaded against the expected forces
of order. The ship-builders of Sunderland, in England, are
at the verge of starvation, owing to a quarrel with their employers; and Leicester has just been the scene of industrial
riots. In our country, labor disputes and strikes were never
so numerous as now.[3] East and West, North and South,

[2] By Louis Philippe Albert d'Orleans, Comte de Paris (1830–1894). His
Les Associations ouvrières en Angleterre was translated and published in
England in 1869 (Thomas Hughes, ed.).
[3] For work stoppages — strikes or boycotts — there are only fragmentary

everywhere, there is unrest, showing that an equilibrium has not yet been reached between employers and employed.

A strike or lockout is, in itself, a ridiculous affair. Whether a failure or a success, it gives no direct proof of its justice or injustice. In this it resembles war between two nations. It is simply a question of strength and endurance between the contestants. The gage of battle, or the duel, is not more senseless, as a means of establishing what is just and fair, than an industrial strike or lockout. It would be folly to conclude that we have reached any permanent adjustment between capital and labor until strikes and lockouts are as much things of the past as the gage of battle or the duel have become in the most advanced communities.

Taking for granted, then, that some further modifications must be made between capital and labor, I propose to consider the various plans that have been suggested by which labor can advance another stage in its development in relation to capital. And, as a preliminary, let it be noted that it is only labor and capital in their greatest masses which it is necessary to consider. It is only in large establishments that the industrial unrest of which I have spoken ominously manifests itself. The farmer who hires a man to assist him, or the gentleman who engages a groom or a butler, is not affected by strikes. The innumerable cases in which a few men only are directly concerned, which comprise in the aggregate the most of labor, present upon the whole a tolerably satisfactory condition of affairs. This clears the ground of much, and leaves us to deal only with the immense mining

---

figures before 1880. Beginning with that date the United States Commissioner of Labor began a more systematic compilation. These statistics bore out Carnegie's contention. Following the depression of 1884–1885 there was a nationwide wave of strikes. In 1885, when Carnegie must have been maturing this essay, an index of strikes and workers involved increased by fifty per cent. The next year, 1886, was to be even more fruitful of labor turbulence. Its full impact came in May, after the publication of this essay, but the rapid growth of labor union membership, the multiplication of new unions, and "the great railroad strike" on the southwest lines of Jay Gould occurred in the early months of that year.

and manufacturing concerns of recent growth, in which capital and labor often array themselves in alarming antagonism.

Among expedients suggested for their better reconciliation, the first place must be assigned to the idea of coöperation, or the plan by which the workers are to become part-owners in enterprises, and share their fortunes.[4] There is no doubt that if this could be effected it would have the same beneficial effect upon the workman which the ownership of land has upon the man who has hitherto tilled the land for another. The sense of ownership would make of him more of a man as regards himself, and hence more of a citizen as regards the commonwealth. But we are here met by a difficulty which I confess I have not yet been able to overcome, and which renders me less sanguine than I should like to be in regard to coöperation. The difficulty is this, and it seems to me inherent in all gigantic manufacturing, mining, and commercial operations. Two men or two combinations of men will erect blast-furnaces, iron-mills, cotton-mills, or piano manufactories adjoining each other, or engage in shipping or commercial business. They will start with equal capital and credit; and to those only superficially acquainted with the personnel of these concerns, success will seem as likely to attend the one as the other. Nevertheless, one will fail after dragging along a lifeless existence, and pass into the hands of its creditors; while the neighboring mill or business will make a fortune for its owners. Now, the successful manufacturer, dividing every month or every year a proportion of his profits among his workmen, either as a bonus or as dividends upon shares

---

[4] Producer's co-operation was of immense interest to organized labor in the post-Civil War era. Aside from harmonizing appealingly with American ideals, it was during depression years a form of unemployment relief. The officers of the Knights of Labor gave the device much verbal, though inconstant, support; it also made a wide appeal to liberal preachers, professors, and editors. Even E. L. Godkin (1831–1902), editor of the *Nation* and generally a conservative spokesman, supported co-operation. In the mid-eighties, the "highest point of the cooperative movement," producers' cooperative ventures numbered 135, chiefly in mining, cooperage, and shoes. Most were very small scale enterprises.

owned by them, will not only have a happy and contented body of operatives, but he will inevitably attract from his rival the very best workmen in every department. His rival, having no profits to divide among his workmen, and paying them only a small assured minimum to enable them to live, finds himself despoiled of foremen and of workmen necessary to carry on his business successfully. His workmen are discontented and, in their own opinion, defrauded of the proper fruits of their skill, through incapacity or inattention of their employers. Thus, unequal business capacity in the management produces unequal results.

It will be precisely the same if one of these manufactories belongs to the workmen themselves; but in this case, in the present stage of development of the workmen, the chances of failure will be enormously increased. It is, indeed, greatly to be doubted whether any body of working-men in the world could to-day organize and successfully carry on a mining or manufacturing or commercial business in competition with concerns owned by men trained to affairs. If any such coöperative organization succeeds, it may be taken for granted that it is principally owing to the exceptional business ability of one of the managers, and only in a very small degree to the efforts of the mass of workmen-owners. This business ability is excessively rare, as is proved by the incredibly large proportion of those who enter upon the stormy sea of business only to fail. I should say that twenty coöperative concerns would fail to every one that would succeed. There are, of course, a few successful establishments, notably two in France and one in England, which are organized upon the coöperative plan, in which the workmen participate in the profits. But these were all created by the present owners, who now generously share the profits with their workmen, and are making the success of their manufactories upon the coöperative plan the proud work of their lives. What these concerns will become when the genius for affairs is no longer with them to guide, is a matter of grave doubt and, to me, of foreboding. I can, of course, picture in my mind a state of civilization in which the most talented business men shall find their most cherished work in carrying on immense concerns, not primarily for their own personal aggrandizement, but for the good of the masses of workers engaged therein, and their families; but this is only a foreshadowing of a dim and distant future. When a class of such men has evolved, the problem of capital and labor will be permanently solved to the entire satisfaction of both. But as this manifestly belongs to a future generation, I cannot consider coöperation, or common ownership, as the next immediate step in advance which it is possible for labor to make in its upward path.

The next suggestion is that peaceful settlement of differences should be reached through arbitration. Here we are upon firmer ground. I would lay it down as a maxim that there is no excuse for a strike or a lockout until arbitration of differences has been offered by one party and refused by the other. No doubt serious trouble attends even arbitration at present, from the difficulty of procuring suitable men to judge intelligently between the disputants. There is a natural disinclination among business men to expose their business to men in whom they have not entire confidence. We lack, so far, in America a retired class of men of affairs. Our vile practice is to keep on accumulating more dollars until we die. If it were the custom here, as it is in England, for men to withdraw from active business after acquiring a fortune, this class would furnish the proper arbitrators. On the other hand, the ex-presidents of trades-unions, such as Mr. Jarrett or Mr. Wihle,[5] after they have retired from active control, would

[5] John Jarrett, an immigrant from Wales, was a mill worker who became President of the Amalgamated Association of Iron and Steel Workers, a consolidation of the various craft unions in the industry. When the Federation of Organized Trades and Labor Unions, a predecessor of the American Federation, was organized in 1881, Jarrett became the first president. William Weihe (the Carnegie misspelling reflects on his acquaintance with the union in his industry), a native American, succeeded Jarrett in the early eighties as President of the Amalgamated Association of Iron and Steel

commend themselves to the manufacturers and to the men as possessed of the necessary technical knowledge, and educated to a point where commercial reasons would not be without their proper weight upon them. I consider that of all the agencies immediately available to prevent wasteful and embittering contests between capital and labor, arbitration is the most powerful and most beneficial.

The influence of trades-unions upon the relations between the employer and employed has been much discussed. Some establishments in America have refused to recognize the right of the men to form themselves into these unions, although I am not aware that any concern in England would dare to take this position. This policy, however, may be regarded as only a temporary phase of the situation. The right of the working-men to combine and to form trades-unions is no less sacred than the right of the manufacturer to enter into associations and conferences with his fellows, and it must sooner or later be conceded. Indeed, it gives one but a poor opinion of the American workman if he permits himself to be deprived of a right which his fellow in England long since conquered for himself. My experience has been that trades-unions, upon the whole, are beneficial both to labor and to capital. They certainly educate the working-men, and give them a truer conception of the relations of capital and labor than they could otherwise form. The ablest and best workmen eventually come to the front in these organizations; and it may be laid down as a rule that the more intelligent the workman the fewer the contests with employers. It is not the intelligent workman, who knows that labor without his brother capital is helpless, but the blatant ignorant man, who regards capital as the natural enemy of labor, who does so much to embitter the relations between employer and

Workers. Ironically, in view of Carnegie's admiration, Weihe was president of the Association in 1892, when at the Homestead Works, one of the Carnegie plants, occurred the classic test of strength between union and management, the latter represented by Henry Clay Frick (1849–1919). The Homestead Strike of 1892 was, of course, subsequent to this essay.

employed; and the power of this ignorant demagogue arises chiefly from the lack of proper organization among the men through which their real voice can be expressed. This voice will always be found in favor of the judicious and intelligent representative. Of course, as men become intelligent more deference must be paid to them personally and to their rights, and even to their opinions and prejudices; and, upon the whole, a greater share of profits must be paid in the day of prosperity to the intelligent than to the ignorant workman. He cannot be imposed upon so readily. On the other hand, he will be found much readier to accept reduced compensation when business is depressed; and it is better in the long run for capital to be served by the highest intelligence, and to be made well aware of the fact that it is dealing with men who know what is due to them, both as to treatment and compensation.

One great source of the trouble between employers and employed arises from the fact that the immense establishments of to-day, in which alone we find serious conflicts between capital and labor, are not managed by their owners, but by salaried officers, who cannot possibly have any permanent interest in the welfare of the working-men. These officials are chiefly anxious to present a satisfactory balance-sheet at the end of the year, that their hundreds of shareholders may receive the usual dividends, and that they may therefore be secure in their positions, and be allowed to manage the business without unpleasant interference either by directors or shareholders. It is notable that bitter strikes seldom occur in small establishments where the owner comes into direct contact with his men, and knows their qualities, their struggles, and their aspirations. It is the chairman, situated hundreds of miles away from his men, who only pays a flying visit to the works and perhaps finds time to walk through the mill or mine once or twice a year, that is chiefly responsible for the disputes which break out at intervals. I have noticed that the manager who confers oftenest with a committee of his leading men has the least trouble with his workmen. Although it may be impracticable for the presidents of these large corporations to know the working-men personally, the manager at the mills, having a committee of his best men to present their suggestions and wishes from time to time, can do much to maintain and strengthen amicable relations, if not interfered with from headquarters. I, therefore, recognize in trades-unions, or, better still, in organizations of the men of each establishment, who select representatives to speak for them, a means, not of further embittering the relations between employer and employed, but of improving them.

It is astonishing how small a sacrifice upon the part of the employer will sometimes greatly benefit the men. I remember that at one of our meetings with a committee, it was incidentally remarked by one speaker that the necessity for obtaining credit at the stores in the neighborhood was a grave tax upon the men. An ordinary workman, he said, could not afford to maintain himself and family for a month, and as he only received his pay monthly, he was compelled to obtain credit and to pay exorbitantly for everything, whereas, if he had the cash, he could buy at twenty-five per cent less. "Well," I said, "why cannot we overcome that by paying every two weeks?" The reply was: "We did not like to ask it, because we have always understood that it would cause much trouble; but if you do that it will be worth an advance of five per cent. in our wages." We have paid semi-monthly since. Another speaker happened to say that although they were in the midst of coal, the price charged for small lots delivered at their houses was a certain sum per bushel. The price named was double what our best coal was costing us. How easy for us to deliver to our men such coal as they required, and charge them cost! This was done without a cent's loss to us, but with much gain to the men. Several other points similar to these have arisen by which their labors might be lightened or products increased, and others suggesting changes in machinery or facilities which, but for the conferences referred to, would have been unthought of by the employer and probably never asked for by the men. For these and other reasons I attribute the greatest importance to an organization of the men, through whose duly elected representatives the managers may be kept informed from time to time of their grievances and suggestions. No matter how able the manager, the clever workman can often show him how beneficial changes can be made in the special branch in which that workman labors. Unless the relations between manager and workmen are not only amicable but friendly, the owners miss much; nor is any man a first-class manager who has not the confidence and respect, and even the admiration, of his workmen. No man is a true gentleman who does not inspire the affection and devotion of his servants. The danger is that such committees may ask conferences too often; three or four meetings per year should be regarded as sufficient.

I come now to the greatest cause of the friction which prevails between capital and labor in the largest establishments, the real essence of the trouble, and the remedy I have to propose.

The trouble is that the men are not paid at any time the compensation proper to that time. All large concerns necessarily keep filled with orders, say for six months in advance, and these orders are taken, of course, at prices prevailing when they are booked. This year's operations furnish perhaps the best illustration of the difficulty. Steel rails at the end of last year for delivery this year were $29 per ton at the works. Of course the mills entered orders freely at this price, and kept on entering them until the demand growing unexpectedly great carried prices up to $35 per ton. Now, the various mills in America are compelled for the next six months or more to run upon orders which do not average $31 per ton at the seaboard and Pittsburg, and pay $34 at Chicago. Transportation, ironstone, and prices of all kinds have advanced upon them in the meantime, and they must therefore run the bulk of the year upon very small margins of profit. But the men, noticing in the papers the "great boom in steel rails," very naturally demand their share of the advance, and, under existing faulty arrangements between capital and labor, they have secured it. The employers, therefore, have grudgingly given what they know under proper arrangements they should not have been required to give, and there has been friction, and still is dissatisfaction upon the part of the employers. Reverse this picture. The steel-rail market falls again. The mills have still six months' work at prices above the prevailing market, and can afford to pay men higher wages than the then existing state of the market would apparently justify. But having just been amerced in extra payments for labor which they should not have paid, they naturally attempt to reduce wages as the market price of rails goes down, and there arises discontent among the men, and we have a repetition of the negotiations and strikes which have characterized the beginning of this year. In other words, when the employer is going down the employee insists on going up, and vice versa. What we must seek is a plan by which the men will receive high wages when their employers are receiving high prices for their product, and hence are making large profits; and, *per contra*, when the employers are receiving low prices for product, and therefore small if any profits, the men will receive low wages.[6] If this plan can be found, employers and employed will be "in the same boat," rejoicing together in their prosperity, and calling into play their fortitude together in adversity. There will be no room for quarrels, and instead of a feeling of antagonism

[6] Methods of paying labor, whereby wages had a fluctuating relation with changes in the market price of the product, were not uncommon at this time in American industry. Wages were lowered when prices fell and vice versa. Attempts to introduce maximum or minimum limits to wage changes were variants of the scheme. Workers of course preferred a fixed rate of wages. Sliding scales existed in coal mining, shipping on the Great Lakes, and in the iron and steel industry. A dispute over this feature of payment was one facet of the Homestead outbreak.

there will be a feeling of partnership between employers and employed.

There is a simple means of producing this result, and to its general introduction both employers and employed should steadily bend their energies. Wages should be based upon a sliding scale, in proportion to the net prices received for product month by month. And I here gladly pay Mr. Potter, president of the North Chicago Rolling Mill Company, the great compliment to say that he has already taken a step in this direction, for to-day he is working his principal mill upon this plan. The result is that he has had no stoppage whatever this year, nor any dissatisfaction. All has gone smoothly along, and this in itself is worth at least as much to the manufacturer and to the men as the difference in wages one way or another which can arise from the new system.

The celebrated Crescent Steel Works of Pittsburg, manufacturers of the highest grades of tool steel, pay their skilled workmen by a sliding scale, based upon prices received for product — an important factor in the eminent success of that firm. The scale adopted by the iron manufacturers and workmen is only an approach to the true sliding scale; nevertheless it is a decided gain both to capital and labor, as it is adopted from year to year, and hence eliminates strikes on account of wages during the year, and limits these interruptions from that cause to the yearly negotiation as to the justice or injustice of the scale. As this scale, however, is not based upon the prices actually received for product, but upon the published list of prices, which should be received in theory, there is not complete mutuality between the parties. In depressed times, such as the iron industry has been passing through in recent years, enormous concessions upon the published card prices have been necessary to effect sales, and in these the workmen have not shared with their employers. If, however, there was added to the scale, even in its present form, a stipulation that all causes of difference which could not be postponed till the end of the year, and then considered with the scale, should be referred to arbitration, and that, in case of failure of the owners and workmen to agree at the yearly conference, arbitration should also be resorted to, strikes and lockouts would be entirely eliminated from the iron business; and if the award of the arbitrators took effect from the date of reference the works could run without a day's interruption.

Dismissing, therefore, for the present all consideration of coöperation as not being within measurable distance, I believe that the next steps in the advance toward permanent, peaceful relations between capital and labor are:

First. That compensation be paid the men based upon a sliding scale in proportion to the prices received for product.

Second. A proper organization of the men of every works to be made, by which the natural leaders, the best men, will eventually come to the front and confer freely with the employers.

Third. Peaceful arbitration to be in all cases resorted to for the settlement of differences which the owners and the mill committee cannot themselves adjust in friendly conference.

Fourth. No interruption ever to occur to the operations of the establishment, since the decision of the arbitrators shall be made to take effect from the date of reference.

If these measures were adopted by an establishment, several important advantages would be gained:

First. The employer and employed would simultaneously share their prosperity or adversity with each other. The scale once settled, the feeling of antagonism would be gone, and a feeling of mutuality would ensue. Capital and labor would be shoulder to shoulder, supporting each other.

Second. There could be neither strike nor lockout, since both parties had agreed to abide by a forthcoming decision of disputed points. Knowing that in the last resort strangers were to be called in to decide what should be a family affair, the cases would, indeed, be few which would not be amicably adjusted by the original parties without calling in others to judge between them.

Whatever the future may have in store for labor, the evolutionist, who sees nothing but certain and steady progress for the race, will never attempt to set bounds to its triumphs, even to its final form of complete and universal industrial coöperation, which I hope is some day to be reached. But I am persuaded that the next step forward is to be in the direction I have here ventured to point out; and as one who is now most anxious to contribute his part toward helping forward the day of amicable relations between the two forces of capital and labor, which are not enemies, but are really auxiliaries who stand or fall together, I ask at the hands of both capital and labor a careful consideration of these views.

· VI ·

Results of the Labor Struggle[1]

W HEN "An Employer's View of the Labor Question" was
written, labor and capital were at peace, each performing its
proper function; capital providing for the wants of labor, and
labor regularly discharging its daily task. But before that
paper reached the public the most serious labor revolt that
ever occurred in this country was upon us. Capital, frightened
almost into panic, began to draw back into its strongholds,
and many leaders of public opinion seemed to lose self-
command. Among the number were not a few of our foremost political economists. These writers of the closet, a small
but important class in this country, removed from personal
contact with every-day affairs, and uninformed of the solid

---

[1] Published originally in the *Forum*, I (August 1886), 538–551. Between
the date of this and the preceding essay, part of organized labor had
launched on May 1, 1886, a movement for the eight-hour day. According
to one contemporary estimate, no fewer than 340,000 men took part, and
190,000 actually struck. Regionally this labor pressure was most uneven.
Chicago was a center of great excitement. There the eight-hour program
got tangled with an existing strike in the McCormick Harvester Works and
with the agitational efforts of a small group of anarchists who displayed the
familiar radical desire to fish in troubled waters. A mass meeting called in
Haymarket Square on May 4th to protest a police attack upon McCormick
workers proved a dull affair, but later in the evening when the police moved
into the Square to disperse the meeting, some unidentified person threw a
bomb which killed a police officer. Eight anarchists were arrested and tried
as accessories to murder; of the seven sentenced to hang, four were executed,
one committed suicide, and two, whose sentences were commuted to life,
along with one sentenced to fifteen years, were pardoned in 1893 by
Governor Altgeld (1847–1902) of Illinois. The Haymarket trial became one
of the most famous illustrations of a miscarriage of justice in American history. Carnegie does not exaggerate the hysteria or terror of the times; few,
including many labor leaders, shared his serenity.

basis of virtue in the wage-receiving class upon which American society rests, necessarily regarded such phenomena from a purely speculative standpoint. Some of them apparently thought that the fundamental institutions upon which peaceful development depends had been, if not completely overthrown, at least gravely endangered, and that civilization itself had received a rude shock from the disturbance. More than one did not hesitate to intimate that the weakness of democratic institutions lay at the foundation of the revolt. Suggestions were made that the suffrage should be confined to the educated; that the masses might be held in stricter bonds. When we hear the cry of these alarmists we are tempted to reverse the rebuke of the sacred Teacher: they are always troubled more by the mote in their own country's eye than by the beam in the eye of other lands. They forget that not sixty days before, monarchical Belgium was convulsed with labor revolts, compared with which ours were insignificant and practically harmless. That country, with its five and a half millions of inhabitants, had more rioters than the United States, with its fifty-six millions; and instead of restoring peace, as this country did, by means of the established forms of order, the Belgian government had to abandon, for a time, all law, and publicly authorize every citizen to wage private war against the insurgents.[2]

Our magazines, reviews, and newspapers have been filled with plans involving radical changes considered necessary by these sciolists for the restoration and maintenance of proper relations between capital and labor. The pulpit has been equally prolific. Thirty days have not elapsed since the excitement was at its height, and yet to-day capital and labor are again coöperating everywhere, as at the date of my first paper, and we are now in position to judge of the extent of the disturbance and to reduce the specter to its real dimensions. It will soon be seen that what occurred was a very

---

[2] In March 1886 there was a riot in Liége, followed by outbreaks in all the industrial districts. They were repressed with much bloodshed.

inadequate cause for the alarm created. The eruption was not, in itself, a very serious matter, either in its extent or in its consequences. Its lesson lay in the indications it gave of the forces underlying it. There are in the United States to-day a total of more than twenty millions of workers who earn their bread by the sweat of their brow; in trade and transportation alone there are more than seven millions. At the very height of the revolt, not more than 250,000 of these had temporarily ceased to labor. This was the estimate given by "Bradstreet's" on the 14th of May. Three days later it was 80,000, and four days after that only 47,000. The remaining millions continued to pursue their usual vocations in peace. It is fair to assume that the number reported on the 14th of May included all those who were dissatisfied and had requested advance of wages or redress of grievances, but were not really strikers at all. A demonstration that shrinks to one fourth its size from the 14th to the 17th of May, and then again to one half its remaining proportions in the next three days, can scarcely be called a contest. The number of those involved in a serious struggle with capital did not, therefore, at any one time exceed 50,000 — not one per cent of the total wage-receiving class, in the branches where labor troubles occurred. How then, one is tempted to ask, did so small an interruption seem so great? Why was it taken for granted that a general revolt of labor had taken place, when not one worker in a hundred had really entered upon a contest? The reason for the delusion is obvious. The omnipresent press, with the electric telegraph at its command, spreads the report of a local disturbance in East St. Louis over the entire three million square miles of the land.[3] It is felt almost as

---

[3] The great railroad strike of 1886 was precipitated on the Gould southwest lines, Texas Pacific, Missouri Pacific, and others, by the Knights of Labor in order to raise the wages of unskilled workers, secure the recognition of the union, and punish Gould for the discharge of union workmen in spite of an understanding concluding a strike in 1885. The outbreak did not involve at first hand engineers, firemen, conductors, or brakemen, who were organized in brotherhoods or craft unions. Shopmen, trackmen, and yardmen contributed the strike's core; telegraphers were sympathetic. About 9,000

distinctly in New Orleans, Boston, and San Francisco as in the city of St. Louis itself, upon the opposite side of the river. The thoughts of men throughout the country concentrate upon this one point of outbreak. Excitable natures fancy the trouble to be general, and even imagine that the very ground trembles under their own feet. In this way the petty, local difficulty upon the Wabash system of railways, which involved only 3700 Knights of Labor, and a strike of a few hundred men on the Third Avenue Railway, New York, together with a few trifling and temporary disputes at other points, were magnified into a general warfare between capital and labor. There were but a few local skirmishes; peace already reigns; and our professors and political economists and the whole school of pessimists who tremble for the safety of human society in general, and of the Republic in particular, and the ministers that have bodily essayed to revolutionize existing conditions, are free to find another subject for their anxious fears and forebodings. The relations between capital and labor which have slowly evolved themselves in the gradual development of the race will not be readily changed. The solid walls with which humanity fortifies itself in each advanced position gained in its toilsome march forward will not fall to the ground at the blast of trumpets. Present conditions have grown up slowly, and can be changed for the better only slowly and by small, successive steps. A short history of the disturbances will, however, furnish many useful and needed lessons.

The trouble grew, as many serious troubles do grow, from a trifle. A leader of the Knights of Labor was dismissed.

---

strikers were involved. The local leader was Martin Irons, a machinist who had emigrated from Scotland as a boy. A Congressional committee stigmatized him as "a dangerous if not pernicious man." In any case he did not act harmoniously with the centralized command of the Knights, notably Terence V. Powderly (1849–1924), Grand Master Workman. The strikers effectively interfered with freight traffic by "killing engines" and other devices, and the strike did great damage to the commerce and prosperity of St. Louis. The "chaos" which the Congressional committee found endemic in East St. Louis erupted in April into a day of violence with gunfire and incendiarism. Early in May the strike petered out; Gould was victorious.

Whether the fact that he was a labor leader influenced his superior to dismiss him will probably never be known; but this much is to be said, that it was very likely to do so. Salaried officials in the service of large corporations are naturally disposed to keep under them only such men as give them no trouble.

On the other hand, the safety of its leaders is the key of labor's position. To surrender that is to surrender everything. Even if the leader in question had not been as regularly at work as other men, even if he had to take days now and then to attend to official duties for his brethren, the superior of that man should have dealt very leniently with him. The men cannot know whether their leader is stricken down for proper cause or not; but, at the same time, they cannot help suspecting. And here I call the attention of impartial minds to the elements of manhood and the high sense of honor and loyalty displayed upon the part of working-men who sacrifice so much and throw themselves in the front of the conflict to secure the safety of their standard-bearers. Everything reasonable can be done with men of this spirit. The loyalty which they show to their leaders can be transferred to their employers by treating them as such men deserve. Society has nothing to fear from men so stanch and loyal to one another. Nor is the loyalty shown in this instance exceptional; it distinguishes working-men as a class. Mr. Irons has said that "one hour's gentlemanly courtesy on the part of the manager would have averted all the disaster." Whether this be true or not, the statement should not be overlooked, for it is true that one hour of courtesy on the part of employers would prevent many strikes. Whether the men ask in proper manner for interviews, or observe all the rules of etiquette, is immaterial. We expect from the presumably better-informed party representing capital much more in this respect than from labor; and it is not asking too much of men intrusted with the management of great properties that they should devote some part of their attention to searching out the causes of disaffection among their employees, and, where any exist, that they should meet the men more than half-way in the endeavor to allay them. There is nothing but good for both parties to be derived from labor teaching the representative of capital the dignity of man, as man. The workingman, becoming more and more intelligent, will hereafter demand the treatment due to an equal.

The strikers at first were excusable, even if mistaken, in imagining that their leader had been stricken down; but, under the excitement of conflict, violence was resorted to; and further, an attempt was made to drag into the quarrel railway lines that had nothing to do with it. The men took up these wrong positions and were deservedly driven from them. And labor here received a salutary lesson — namely, that nothing is to be gained by violence and lawlessness, nor by endeavoring to unjustly punish the innocent for the sins of the guilty. Public sentiment, always disposed to side with labor, was with the men at first, but soon finding itself unable to sanction their doings, it veered to the other side. When the strikers lost that indispensable ally they lost all.

The other branch of the revolt of labor occurred in New York city, where the employees of the Third Avenue Railway struck for fewer hours and better pay. If ever a strike was justifiable this one was. It is simply disgraceful for a corporation to compel its men to work fifteen or sixteen hours a day. Such was the verdict of the public, and the men won a deserved victory. Here again, as at St. Louis, for lack of proper leadership, they went too far; and in their demand for the employment of certain men and the dismissal of others they lost their only sure support — public sentiment. This was compelled to decide against their final demands, and consequently they failed, and deservedly failed. How completely public sentiment, when aroused, compels obedience, as we have seen it did both at St. Louis and in New York city, is further shown by the result of the order, issued June 6, requiring the men of all the city railroads in Brooklyn and New York to stop work until the striking employees of the Third Avenue line were reinstated. The edict was disregarded by the men themselves, who found that compliance would not be approved by the community, and that, therefore, the attempt would fail. It was an attempt that the worst foe of labor might have instigated.

These were the two chief strikes from which came the epidemic of demands and strikes throughout the country.

None of these ebullitions proved of much moment. A rash had broken out upon the body politic, but it was only skin-deep, and disappeared as rapidly as it had come. At a somewhat later date the disturbance took a different form. A demand was made that the hours of labor should be reduced from ten to eight hours a day. To state this demand is to pronounce its fate. Existing conditions are not changed by twenty-per-cent leaps and bounds, and especially in times like these, when business is not even moderately profitable. Such a request simply meant that many employers of labor would not be able to keep their men at work at all. History proves, nevertheless, that the hours of labor are being gradually reduced. The percentage of men working from ten to eleven hours in this country in 1830 was 29.7. These ten-hour workers increased in 1880 to 59.6 per cent of the whole; while the classes who in 1830 worked excessive hours — from twelve to thirteen — constituted 32.5 per cent. In 1880 they were only 14.6 per cent; while the number of men compelled to work between thirteen and fourteen hours, which was in 1830 13.5 per cent, had fallen in 1880 to 2.3 per cent. Those working twelve hours are generally employed in double shifts, night and day. I do not believe that we have reached the limit of this reduction, but I do believe that any permanent reduction will be secured only by the half-hour at a time. If labor be guided by wise counsel, it will ask for reductions of half-hours, and then wait until a reduction to this extent is firmly established, and surrounding circumstances have adjusted themselves to that.

In considering the reasonableness of the demand for fewer hours of labor, we must not lose sight of the fact that the American works more hours, on an average, than his fellow in Great Britain. Twenty-three trades in Massachusetts are reported as working sixty hours and seventeen minutes a week, on the average, while the same crafts in Great Britain work only fifty-three hours and fifty minutes, showing that the American works an hour a day longer than his English brother. In British textile factories, the number of working hours in a week ranges from fifty-four to fifty-six. In mines, foundries, and machine-shops, fifty-four hours make a week's work, which is equivalent to nine hours a day, six days a week; but the men, in all cases, work enough overtime each day to insure them a half-holiday on Saturday. In some districts, notably in Glasgow, the men prefer to work two weeks, and make every other Saturday a whole holiday. This gives them an opportunity to leave on early morning trains, on excursions, and to spend Saturday and Sunday with friends. The Allegheny Valley Railroad Company, under the management of my friend Mr. McCargo, introduced the half-Saturday holiday in the shops some time ago, with the happiest results. Mr. McCargo found, by years of experience, that working-men lose about half a day a week. Since the half-holiday was established no more time has been lost than before. The men work five and one half days a week regularly. While they are not paid, of course, for the half-holiday, they could not be induced to give it up. This example should be followed, not only by all the railroads of the country, but by every employer of labor, and should be supported by every man who seeks to improve the condition of the wage-receiving classes.

I venture to suggest to the representatives of labor, however, that before they demand any reduction upon ten hours per day, they should concentrate their efforts upon making ten hours the universal practice, and secure this. At present, every ton of pig-iron made in the world, except at two establishments, is made by men working in double shifts of twelve hours each, having neither Sunday nor holiday the year round. Every two weeks the day men change to the night shift by working twenty-four hours consecutively. Gas-works, paper-mills, flour-mills, and many other industries, are run by twelve-hour shifts, and breweries exact fifteen hours a day, on an average, from their men. I hold that it is not possible for men working ten hours a day to enlist public sentiment on their side in a demand for the shortening of their task, as long as many of their fellows are compelled to work twelve or more hours a day.

The eight-hour movement is not, however, without substantial foundation. Works that run day and night should be operated with three sets of men, each working eight hours. The steel-rail mills in this country are generally so run. The additional cost of the three sets of men has been divided between the workmen and the employers, the latter apparently having to meet an advance of wages to the extent of 16-⅔ per cent, but against this is to be placed the increased product which can be obtained. This is not inconsiderable, especially during the hot months, for it has been found that men working twelve hours a day continuously cannot produce as much per hour as men working eight hours a day; so that, if there be any profit at all in the business, the employer derives some advantage from the greater productive capacity of his works and capital, while the general expenses of the establishment remain practically as they were before. Since electric lighting has been perfected, many establishments which previously could not be run at night can be run with success. I therefore look for a large increase in the number of establishments working men only eight hours, but employing the machinery that now runs only ten hours the entire twenty-four. Each shift, of course, takes turn of each of the three parts into which the twenty-four hours are divided, and thus the lives of the men are rendered less monotonous and many hours for recreation and self-improvement are obtained.

The literature called forth by the recent excitement is preponderatingly favorable to coöperation, or profit-sharing, as the only true remedy for all disputes between labor and capital. My April article has been criticized because it relegated that to the future. But the advocates of this plan should weigh well the fact that the majority of enterprises are not profitable; that most men who embark in business fail — indeed, it is stated that only five in every hundred succeed, and that, with the exception of a few wealthy and partially retired manufacturers, and a very few wealthy corporations, men engaged in business affairs are in the midst of an anxious and increasing struggle to keep their heads above water. How to pay maturing obligations, how to obtain cash for the payment of their men, how to procure orders or how to sell product, and, in not a few instances, how to induce their creditors to be forbearing, are the problems which tax the minds of business men during the dark hours of night, when their employees are asleep. I attach less and less value to the teaching of those doctrinaires who sit in their cozy studies and spin theories concerning the relations between capital and labor, and set before us divers high ideals. The banquet to which they invite the working-man when they propose industrial coöperation is not yet quite prepared, and would prove to most of those who accepted the invitation a Barmecide feast. Taken as a whole, the condition of labor to-day would not be benefited, but positively injured, by coöperation.

Let me point out, however, to the advocates of profit-sharing that ample opportunity already exists for working-men to become part-owners in almost any department of industrialism, without changing present relations. The great railway corporations, in all cases, as well as the great manufacturing companies generally, are stock concerns, with shares of fifty or a hundred dollars each, which are bought and sold daily in the market. Not an employee of any of these but can buy any number of shares, and thus participate in the dividends and in the management. That capital is a unit is a popular error. On the contrary, it is made up of hundreds and thousands of small component parts, owned, for the most part, by people of limited means. The Pennsylvania Railway proper, for instance, which embraces only the 350 miles of line between Pittsburg and Philadelphia, is to-day owned by 19,340 shareholders, in lots of from one fifty-dollar share upward. The New York Central Railway, of 450 miles, between New York and Buffalo, belongs not to one, or two, or several capitalists, but to 10,418 shareholders, of whom about one third are women and executors of estates. The entire railway system of America will show a similar wide distribution of ownership among the people. There are but three railway corporations in which the great capitalists hold a considerable interest; and the interest in two of these is held by various members of a family, and in no case does it amount to the control of the whole. In one of these very cases, the New York Central, as we have seen, there are more than ten thousand owners.

Steel-rail mills, with only one exception, show a like state of affairs. One of them belongs to 215 shareholders; of whom 7 are employees, 32 are estates, and 57 are women. Another of these concerns is owned by 302 stockholders; of whom 101 are women, 29 are estates, representing an unknown number of individuals, and 20 are employees of the company. A large proportion of the remaining owners are small holders of comparatively limited means, who have, from time to time, invested their savings where they had confidence both as to certainty of income and safety of principal. The Merrimac Manufacturing Company (cotton), of Lowell, is owned by 2500 shareholders, of whom forty-two per cent are holders of one share, twenty-one per cent of two, and ten per cent of three shares. Twenty-seven per cent are holders of over three shares; and not less than thirty-eight per cent. of the whole stock is held by trustees, guardians, and executors of charitable, religious, educational, and financial institutions.

I have obtained from other concerns similar statements, which need not be published. They prove without exception that from one fourth to one third of the number of shareholders in corporations are women and executors of estates. The number of shareholders I have given are those of record, each holding a separate certificate. But it is obvious, in the case of executors, that this one certificate may represent a dozen owners. Many certificates issued in the name of a firm represent several persons, while shares held by a corporation may represent hundreds; but if we assume that every certificate of stock issued by the Pennsylvania Railroad Company represents only two owners, which is absurdly under the truth, it follows that, should every employee of that great company quarrel with it, the contest would be not against a few, but against a much larger body than they themselves constitute. It is within the mark to say that every striking employee would oppose his personal interest against that of three or four other members of the community. The total number of men employed by the Pennsylvania Railroad Company is 18,911 — not as many as there are shareholders of record. And what is true of the Pennsylvania Railway Company is true of the railway system as a whole, and, in a greater or less degree, of mining and manufacturing corporations generally. When one, therefore, denounces great corporations for unfair treatment of their men, he is not denouncing the act of some monster capitalist, but that of hundreds and thousands of small holders, scarcely one of whom would be a party to unfair or illiberal treatment of the working-man; the majority of them, indeed, would be found on his side; and, as we have seen, many of the owners themselves would be working-men. Labor has only to bring its just grievances to the attention of owners to secure fair and liberal treatment.

The "great capitalist" is almost a myth, and exists, in any considerable number or degree, only in the heated imagination of the uninformed. Aggregate capital in railway corporations consists of many more individuals than it employs.

Following the labor disturbances, there came the mad work of a handful of foreign anarchists in Chicago and Milwaukee,[4] who thought they saw in the excitement a fitting opportunity to execute their revolutionary plans. Although labor is not justly chargeable with their doings, nevertheless the cause of labor was temporarily discredited in public opinion by these outbreaks. The promptitude with which one labor organization after another not only disclaimed all sympathy with riot and disorder, but volunteered to enroll itself into armed force for the maintenance of order, should not be overlooked by the student of labor problems desirous of looking justly at the question from the laborer's point of view. It is another convincing proof, if further proof were necessary, that whenever the peace of this country is seriously threatened, the masses of men, not only in the professions and in the educated classes, but down to and through the very lowest ranks of industrious workers, are determined to maintain it. A survey of the field, now that peace is restored, gives the results as follows:

First. The "dead line" has been definitely fixed between

[4] Though Carnegie may have been unruffled, he was not necessarily able to make fine distinctions. The eight-hour movement of May, 1886, aroused labor enthusiasm in Chicago and Milwaukee and became entangled with an existing labor dispute. In Milwaukee Paul Grottkau, who had once been in Chicago and associated with some of its apostles of violence, edited the *Arbeiter Zeitung*, played a role in the Central Labor Union, and had great influence with foreign-born workers, for he had once been expelled from Germany under its anti-socialist laws. But Grottkau now advocated conventional labor union tactics; he was more socialist than anarchist. The eight-hour drive in Milwaukee, involving "some lawlessness and riotous proceedings" and considerable excitement, had led to brushes with police and the militia. The latter on May 5th, breaking up an attack on the North Chicago Rolling Mills, fired on the crowd. Subsequently Grottkau and thirty-six others were arrested. Many were convicted and punished with fines or short jail terms. Grottkau went free on a technicality.

the forces of disorder and anarchy and those of order. Bomb-throwing means swift death to the thrower. Rioters assembling in numbers and marching to pillage will be remorselessly shot down; not by the order of a government above the people, not by overwhelming standing armies, not by troops brought from a distance, but by the masses of peaceable and orderly citizens of all classes in their own community, from the capitalist down to and including the steady working-man, whose combined influence constitutes that irresistible force, under democratic institutions, known as public sentiment. That sentiment has not only supported the officials who shot down disturbers of the peace, but has extolled them in proportion to the promptitude of their action.

Second. Another proof of the indestructibility of human society, and of its determination and power to protect itself from every danger as it arises and to keep marching forward to higher states of development, has been given in Judge Mallory's words: "Every person who counsels, hires, procures, or incites others to the commission of any unlawful or criminal act, is equally guilty with those who actually perpetrate the act, though such person may not have been present at the time of the commission of the offense." [5] The difference between liberty and license of speech is now clearly defined — a great gain.

Third. It has likewise been clearly shown that public sentiment sympathizes with the efforts of labor to obtain from capital a fuller recognition of its position and claims than has hitherto been accorded. And in this expression, "a fuller recognition," I include not only pecuniary compensation, but what I conceive to be even more important to-day — a greater

[5] Judge James A. Mallory of Milwaukee had been prominent during the eighties in a fusion movement or Citizens' ticket to unite Democrats and Republicans against a labor party, the program of which advocated enlarged municipal services. In 1886 fusion defeated the labor effort by a narrow majority. Mallory also presided over the grand jury hearing that handed up indictments for "inciting to riot" in the Milwaukee eight-hour day excitement. Carnegie quotes from his charge to the jury. Mallory did not preside over the trials because "affidavits of prejudice" were filed against him.

consideration of the working-man as a man and a brother. I trust the time has gone by when corporations can hope to work men fifteen or sixteen hours a day. And the time approaches, I hope, when it will be impossible, in this country, to work men twelve hours a day continuously.

Fourth. While public sentiment has rightly and unmistakably condemned violence, even in the form for which there is the most excuse, I would have the public give due consideration to the terrible temptation to which the working-man on a strike is sometimes subjected. To expect that one dependent upon his daily wage for the necessaries of life will stand by peaceably and see a new man employed in his stead, is to expect much. This poor man may have a wife and children dependent upon his labor. Whether medicine for a sick child, or even nourishing food for a delicate wife, is procurable, depends upon his steady employment. In all but a very few departments of labor it is unnecessary, and, I think, improper, to subject men to such an ordeal. In the case of railways and a few other employments it is, of course, essential for the public wants that no interruption occur, and in such case substitutes must be employed; but the employer of labor will find it much more to his interest, wherever possible, to allow his works to remain idle and await the result of a dispute, than to employ the class of men that can be induced to take the place of other men who have stopped work. Neither the best men as men, nor the best men as workers, are thus to be obtained. There is an unwritten law among the best workmen: "Thou shalt not take thy neighbor's job." No wise employer will lightly lose his old employees. Length of service counts for much in many ways. Calling upon strange men should be the last resort.

Fifth. The results of the recent disturbances have given indubitable proof that trades-unions must, in their very nature, become more conservative than the mass of the men they represent. If they fail to be conservative, they go to pieces through their own extravagance. I know of three instances in which threatened strikes were recently averted by the decision of the Master Workman of the Knights of Labor, supported by the best workmen, against the wishes of the less intelligent members of that organization. Representative institutions eventually bring to the front the ablest and most prudent men, and will be found as beneficial in the industrial as they have proved themselves to be in the political world. Leaders of the stamp of Mr. Powderly, Mr. Arthur, of the Brotherhood of Locomotive Engineers, and Messrs. Wihle and Martin, of the Amalgamated Iron and Steel Association, will gain and retain power; while such as the radical and impulsive Mr. Irons,[6] if at first clothed with power, will soon lose it.

Thus, as the result of the recent revolt, we see advantages gained by both capital and labor. Capital is more secure because of what has been demonstrated, and labor will hereafter be more respectfully treated and its claims more carefully considered, in deference to an awakened public opinion in favor of the laborer. Labor won while it was reasonable in its demands and kept the peace; it lost when it asked what public sentiment pronounced unreasonable, and especially when it broke the peace.

The disturbance is over and peace again reigns; but let no one be unduly alarmed at frequent disputes between capital and labor. Kept within legal limits, they are encouraging symptoms, for they betoken the desire of the working-man

[6] Powderly became Grand Master Workman of the Knights of Labor in 1879 and served until 1893. Under his leadership the Knights grew to be the country's largest labor organization in 1886 and then declined into a local, agrarian organization. Powderly induced the Knights to discard their religious and secret features. Like most Knights, he was the foe of strikes. P. M. Arthur (1831–1903), originally an immigrant from Scotland and after 1874 Grand Chief of the Brotherhood of Locomotive Engineers, incurred a discharge of epithets and abuse from organized labor's opponents for his part in the railroad strikes of 1877; later employers and capitalists came to regard both the union and its leader as "conservative," an opinion concurred in by radicals in the labor movement. William Martin, during the eighties Secretary of the Amalgamated Association of Iron and Steel Workers, had been born in Scotland. For Wihle (really Weihe) see Essay V, note 5; on Irons, note 3 above.

to better his condition; and upon this desire hang all hopes of advancement of the masses. It is the stagnant pool of Contentment, not the running stream of Ambition, that breeds disease in the body social and political. The working-men of this country can no more be induced to sanction riot and disorder than can any other class of the community. Isolated cases of violence under strong provocation may break out upon the surface, but the body underneath is sound to the core, and resolute for the maintenance of order.

For the first time within my knowledge, the leading organs of public opinion in England have shown a more correct appreciation of the forces at work in the Republic than some of our own despondent writers. The London "Daily News" said truly that "the territorial democracy of America can be trusted to deal with such outbreaks"; and the "Daily Telegraph" spoke as follows:

> There is no need for any fear to be entertained lest the lawbreakers of Chicago should get the better of the police, and, if it be necessary to invoke their aid, of the citizens of that astonishing young city. Frankly speaking, such rioters would have a better chance of intimidating Birmingham than of overawing Chicago, St. Louis, or New York. In dealing with the insurgents of this class the record of the great Republic is singularly clear.

Not only the democracy, but the industrious working-men of which the democracy is so largely composed, have amply fulfilled the flattering predictions of our English friends, and may safely be trusted in the future to stand firmly for the maintenance of peace.

· VII ·

Distant Possessions: The Parting of the Ways [1]

TWICE only have the American people been called upon to decide a question of such vital import as that now before them.

Is the Republic, the apostle of Triumphant Democracy, of the rule of the people, to abandon her political creed and endeavor to establish in other lands the rule of the foreigner over the people, Triumphant Despotism?

Is the Republic to remain one homogeneous whole, one united people, or to become a scattered and disjointed aggregate of widely separated and alien races?

Is she to continue the task of developing her vast continent until it holds a population as great as that of Europe, all Americans, or to abandon that destiny to annex, and to attempt to govern, other far distant parts of the world as outlying possessions, which can never be integral parts of the Republic?

Is she to exchange internal growth and advancement for the development of external possessions which can never be really hers in any fuller sense than India is British or Cochin China French? Such is the portentous question of the day. Two equally important questions the American people have decided wisely, and their flag now waves over the greater portion of the English-speaking race; their country is the richest of all countries, first in manufactures, in mining, and in commerce (home and foreign), first this year also in ex-

[1] From the *North American Review*, CLXVII (August 1898), 239–248.

ports. But, better than this, the average condition of its people in education and in living is the best. The luxuries of the masses in other lands are the necessaries of life in ours. The school-house and the church are nowhere so widely distributed. Progress in the arts and sciences is surprising. In international affairs her influence grows so fast, and foreshadows so much, that one of the foremost statesmen has recently warned Europe that it must combine against her if it is to hold its own in the industrial world. The Republic remains one solid whole, its estate inclosed in a ring fence, united, impregnable, triumphant, clearly destined to become the foremost power of the world, if she continue to follow the true path. Such are the fruits of wise judgment in deciding the two great issues of the past, Independence and Union.

In considering the issue now before us, the agitator, the demagogue, has no part. Not feeling, not passion, but deliberate judgment alone, should have place. The question should be calmly weighed; it is not a matter of party, nor of class; for the fundamental interest of every citizen is a common interest, that which is best for the poorest being best for the richest. Let us, therefore, reason together, and be well assured, before we change our position, that we are making no plunge into an abyss. Happily, we have the experience of others to guide us, the most instructive being that of our own race in Great Britain.

There are two kinds of national possessions, one colonies, the other dependencies. In the former we establish and reproduce our own race. Thus Britain has peopled Canada and Australia with English-speaking people, who have naturally adopted our ideas of self-government. That the world has benefited thereby goes without saying; that Britain has done a great work as the mother of nations is becoming more and more appreciated the more the student learns of world-wide affairs. No nation that ever existed has done so much for the progress of the world as the little islands in the North Sea known as Britain.

With dependencies it is otherwise. The most grievous burden which Britain has upon her shoulders is that of India, for there it is impossible for our race to grow. The child of English-speaking parents must be removed and reared in Britain. The British Indian official must have long respites in his native land. India means death to our race. The characteristic feature of a dependency is that the acquiring power cannot reproduce its own race there.

Inasmuch as the territories outside our own continent which our country may be tempted to annex cannot be colonies, but only dependencies, we need not dwell particularly upon the advantages or disadvantages of the former, although the writer is in thorough accord with Disraeli, who said even of colonies: "Our colonies are millstones round the neck of Britain; they lean upon us while they are weak, and leave us when they become strong." This is just what our Republic did with Britain.

There was something to be said for colonies from the point of view of pecuniary gain in the olden days, when they were treated as the legitimate spoil of the conquerer. It is Spain's fatal mistake that she has never realized that it is impossible to follow this policy in our day. Britain is the only country which has realized this truth. British colonies have complete self-government; they even tax the products of their own motherland. That Britain possesses her colonies is a mere figure of speech; that her colonies possess her is nearer the truth. "Our Colonial Empire" seems a big phrase, but, as far as material benefits are concerned, the balance is the other way. Thus, even loyal Canada trades more with us than with Britain. She buys her Union Jacks in New York. Trade does not follow the flag in our day; it scents the lowest price current. There is no patriotism in exchanges.

Some of the organs of manufacturing interests, we observe, favor foreign possessions as necessary or helpful markets for our products. But the exports of the United States this year are greater than those of any other nation in the world.

Even Britain's exports are less, yet Britain possesses, it is said, a hundred colonies and dependencies scattered all over the world. The fact that the United States has none does not prevent her products and manufactures from invading Japan, China, Australia, New Zealand, Canada, and all parts of the world in competition with those of Britain. Possession of colonies or dependencies is not necessary for trade reasons. What her colonies are valued for, and justly so, by Britain, is the happiness and pride which the mother feels in her children. The instinct of motherhood is gratified, and no one living places a higher estimate upon the sentiment than I do. Britain is the kindest of mothers, and well deserves the devotion of her children.

If we could establish colonies of Americans, and grow Americans in any part of the world now unpopulated and unclaimed by any of the great powers, and thus follow the example of Britain, heart and mind might tell us that we should have to think twice, yea, thrice, before deciding adversely. Even then our decision should be adverse; but there is at present no such question before us. What we have to face is the question whether we should embark upon the difficult and dangerous policy of undertaking the government of alien races in lands where it is impossible for our own race to be produced.

As long as we remain free from distant possessions we are impregnable against serious attack; yet, it is true, we have to consider what obligations may fall upon us of an international character requiring us to send our forces to points beyond our own territory. Up to this time we have disclaimed all intention to interfere with affairs beyond our own continent, and only claimed the right to watch over American interests according to the Monroe Doctrine, which is now firmly established. This carries with it serious responsibilities, no doubt, which we cannot escape. European nations must consult us upon territorial questions pertaining to our continent, but this makes no tremendous demand upon our military or naval forces. We are at home, as it were, near our base, and sure of the support of the power in whose behalf and on whose request we may act. If it be found essential to possess a coaling-station at Porto Rico for future possible, though not probable, contingencies, there is no insuperable objection. Neither would the control of the West Indies be alarming if pressed upon us by Britain, since the islands are small and the populations must remain insignificant and without national aspirations. Besides, they are upon our own shores, American in every sense. Their defense by us would be easy. No protest need be entered against such legitimate and peaceful expansion in our own hemisphere, should events work in that direction. I am no "Little" American, afraid of growth, either in population or territory, provided always that the new territory be American, and that it will produce Americans, and not foreign races bound in time to be false to the Republic in order to be true to themselves.

As I write, the cable announces the annexation of Hawaii,[2] which is more serious; but the argument for this has been the necessity for holding the only coaling-station in the Pacific so situated as to be essential to any power desirous of successfully attacking our Pacific coast. Until the Nicaragua Canal [3] is made, it is impossible to deny the cogency of this contention. We need not consider it a measure of offense or aggression, but as strictly defensive. The population of the islands is so small that national aspirations are not to be encountered, which is a great matter. Nor is it obtained by conquest. It is ours by a vote of its people, which robs its acquisition of many dangers. Let us hope that our far-outlying possessions may end with Hawaii.

To reduce it to the concrete, the question is: Shall we

[2] Hawaii was officially annexed by the United States by Joint Resolution of Congress in 1898 and was administered as a Territory until it achieved statehood.

[3] Prior to the building of the Panama Canal a passage at Nicaragua was projected (as early as 1850), and various concessions were granted, but the United States preferred the present site.

attempt to establish ourselves as a power in the far East and possess the Philippines for glory? The glory we already have, in Dewey's victory overcoming the power of Spain in a manner which adds one more to the many laurels of the American navy, which, from its infancy till now, has divided the laurels with Britain upon the sea. The Philippines have about seven and a half millions of people, composed of races bitterly hostile to one another, alien races, ignorant of our language and institutions. Americans cannot be grown there. The islands have been exploited for the benefit of Spain, against whom they have twice rebelled, like the Cubans. But even Spain has received little pecuniary benefit from them. The estimated revenue of the Philippines in 1894–95 was £2,715,980, the expenditure being £2,656,026, leaving a net result of about $300,000. The United States could obtain even this trifling sum from the inhabitants only by oppressing them as Spain has done. But, if we take the Philippines, we shall be forced to govern them as generously as Britain governs her dependencies, which means that they will yield us nothing, and probably be a source of annual expense. Certainly they will be a grievous drain upon revenue if we consider the enormous army and navy which we shall be forced to maintain upon their account.

There are many objections to our undertaking the government of dependencies; one I venture to submit as being peculiar to ourselves. We should be placed in a wrong position. Consider Great Britain in India to-day. She has established schools and taught the people our language. In the Philippines, we may assume that we should do the same, and with similar results. To travel through India as an American is a point of great advantage if one wishes to know the people of India and their aspirations. They unfold to Americans their inmost thoughts, which they very naturally withhold from their masters, the British. When in India, I talked with many who had received an English education in the British schools, and found that they had read and pondered most upon Cromwell and Hampden, Wallace and Bruce and Tell, upon Washington and Franklin. The Briton is sowing the seed of rebellion with one hand in his schools, — for education makes rebels, — while with the other he is oppressing patriots who desire the independence of their country. The national patriotism upon which a Briton plumes himself he must repress in India. It is only a matter of time when India, the so-called gem of the British crown, is to glitter red again. British control of India is rendered possible to-day only by the division of races, or rather of religions, there. The Hindus and Mohammedans still mistrust each other more than they do the British, but caste is rapidly passing away, and religious prejudices are softening. Whenever this distrust disappears, Britain is liable to be expelled, at a loss of life and treasure which cannot be computed. The aspirations of a people for independent existence are seldom repressed, nor, according to American ideas hitherto, should they be. If it be a noble aspiration for the Indian or the Cuban, as it was for the citizen of the United States himself, and for the various South American republics once under Spain, to have a country to live and, if necessary, to die for, why is not the revolt noble which the man of the Philippines has been making against Spain? Is it possible that the Republic is to be placed in the position of the suppressor of the Philippine struggle for independence? Surely, that is impossible. With what face shall we hang in the school-houses of the Philippines our own Declaration of Independence, and yet deny independence to them? What response will the heart of the Philippine Islander make as he reads of Lincoln's Emancipation Proclamation? Are we to practise independence and preach subordination, to teach rebellion in our books, yet to stamp it out with our swords, to sow the seed of revolt and expect the harvest of loyalty? President McKinley's call for volunteers to fight for Cuban independence against the cruel dominion of Spain meets with prompt response, but who would answer the call of the President of an "imperial" republic for free citizens to fight the Washington [4] and slaughter the patriots of some distant dependency which struggles for independence?

It has hitherto been the glorious mission of the Republic to establish upon secure foundations Triumphant Democracy, and the world now understands government of the people, for the people, and by the people. Tires the Republic so soon of its mission, that it must, perforce, discard it to undertake the impossible task of establishing Triumphant Despotism, the rule of the foreigner over the people? and must the millions of the Philippines who have been asserting their God-given right to govern themselves be the first victims of Americans, whose proudest boast is that they conquered independence for themselves?

Let another phase of the question be carefully weighed. Europe is to-day an armed camp, not chiefly because the home territories of its various nations are threatened, but because of fear of aggressive action upon the part of other nations touching outlying "possessions." France resents British control of Egypt, and is fearful of its West African possessions; Russia seeks Chinese territory, with a view to expansion to the Pacific; Germany also seeks distant possessions; Britain, who has acquired so many dependencies, is so fearful of an attack upon them that this year she is spending nearly eighty millions of dollars upon additional warships, and Russia, Germany, and France follow suit. Japan is a new element of anxiety; and by the end of the year it is computed she will have sixty-seven formidable ships of war. The naval powers of Europe, and Japan also, are apparently determined to be prepared for a terrific struggle for possessions in the far East, close to the Philippines — and why not for these islands themselves? Into this vortex the Republic is cordially invited to enter by those powers who expect her policy to be of benefit to them, but her action

[4] Anti-imperialists were fond of comparing Aguinaldo, the Philippine rebel, with George Washington.

is jealously watched by those who fear that her power might be used against them.

It has never been considered the part of wisdom to thrust one's hand into the hornet's nest, and it does seem as if the United States must lose all claim to ordinary prudence and good sense if she enter this arena and become involved in the intrigues and threats of war which make Europe an armed camp.

It is the parting of the ways. We have a continent to populate and develop; there are only twenty-three persons to the square mile in the United States. England has three hundred and seventy, Belgium five hundred and seventy-one, Germany two hundred and fifty. A tithe of the cost of maintaining our sway over the Philippines would improve our internal waterways; build the Nicaragua Canal; construct a waterway to the ocean from the Great Lakes, an inland canal along the Atlantic seaboard, and a canal across Florida, saving eight hundred miles' distance between New York and New Orleans; connect Lake Michigan with the Mississippi; deepen all the harbors upon the lakes; build a canal from Lake Erie to the Allegheny River; slack-water through movable dams the entire length of the Ohio River to Cairo; thoroughly improve the Lower and Upper Mississippi, and all our seaboard harbors. All these enterprises would be as nothing in cost in comparison with the sums required for the experiment of possessing the Philippine Islands, seven thousand miles from our shores. If the object be to render our Republic powerful among nations, can there be any doubt as to which policy is the better? To be more powerful at home is the surest way to be more powerful abroad. To-day the Republic stands the friend of all nations, the ally of none; she has no ambitious designs upon the territory of any power upon another continent; she crosses none of their ambitious designs, evokes no jealousy of the bitter sort, inspires no fears; she is not one of them, scrambling for possessions; she stands apart, pursuing her own great mission, and teaching all nations by example. Let her become a power annexing foreign territory, and all is changed in a moment.

If we are able to compete with other nations for foreign possessions, we must have a navy like theirs. It should be superior to any other navy, or we play a second part. It is not enough to have a navy equal to that of Russia or of France, for Russia and France may combine against us just as they may against Britain. We at once enter the field as a rival of Britain, the chief possessor of foreign possessions, and who can guarantee that we shall not even have to measure our power against her?

What it means to enter the list of military and naval powers having foreign possessions may be gathered from the following considerations. First, look at our future navy. If it is only to equal that of France it means fifty-one battle-ships; if of Russia, forty battle-ships. If we cannot play the game without being at least the equal of any of our rivals, then eighty battle-ships is the number Britain possesses. We now have only four, with five building. Cruisers, armed and unarmed, swell the number threefold, Britain having two hundred and seventy-three ships of the line built or ordered, with three hundred and eight torpedo-boats in addition; France having one hundred and thirty-four ships of the line and two hundred and sixty-nine torpedo-boats. All these nations are adding ships rapidly. Every armor- and gun-making plant in the world is busy night and day. Ships are indispensable, but recent experience shows that soldiers are equally so. While the immense armies of Europe need not be duplicated, yet we shall certainly be too weak unless our army is at least twenty times what it has been — say five hundred thousand men. Even then we shall be powerless as against any one of three of our rivals — Germany, France, and Russia.

This drain upon the resources of these countries has become a necessity from their respective positions, largely as graspers for foreign possessions. The United States to-day, happily, has no such necessity, her neighbors being power-less against her, since her possessions are concentrated and her power is one solid mass.

To-day two great powers in the world are compact, de-veloping themselves in peace throughout vast conterminous territories. When war threatens they have no outlying posses-sions which can never be really "possessed," but which they are called upon to defend. They fight upon the exposed edge only of their own soil in case of attack, and are not only invulnerable, but they could not be more than inconven-ienced by the world in arms against them. These powers are Russia and the United States. The attempt of Britain to check Russia, if the wild counsels of Mr. Chamberlain [5] were followed, could end in nothing but failure. With the irresistible force of the glacier, Russia moves upon the plains below. Well for Russia, and well for the world, is her ad-vance over pagan China, better even for Britain from the standpoint of business, for every Russian to-day trades as much with Britain as do nine Chinamen. Britain, France, Germany, Belgium, Spain, are all vulnerable, having de-parted from the sagacious policy of keeping possessions and power concentrated. Should the United States depart from this policy, she also must be so weakened in consequence as never to be able to play the commanding part in the world, disjointed, that she can play whenever she desires if she remain compact.

Whether the United States maintain its present unique position of safety, or forfeit it through acquiring foreign possessions, is to be decided by its action in regard to the Philippines; for, fortunately, the independence of Cuba is assured; for this the Republic has proclaimed to the world that she has drawn the sword.[6] But why should the less

---

[5] Joseph Chamberlain (1836–1914), the British statesman who, at first a Liberal, became a Conservative in 1895 and a spokesman for "the new imperialism" in Lord Salisbury's government.

[6] The Teller Resolution before the outbreak of the Spanish-American War disclaimed for the United States any intention "to exercise sovereignty, jurisdiction, or control" over Cuba.

than two millions of Cuba receive national existence and the seven and a half millions of the Philippines be denied it? The United States, thus far in their history, have no page reciting self-sacrifice made for others; all their gains have been for themselves. This void is now to be grandly filled. The page which recites the resolve of the Republic to rid her neighbor, Cuba, from the foreign possessor will grow brighter with the passing centuries, which may dim many pages now deemed illustrious. Should the coming American be able to point to Cuba and the Philippines rescued from foreign domination and enjoying independence won for them by this country and given to them without money and without price, he will find no citizen of any other land able to claim for his country services so disinterested and so noble.

We repeat, there is no power in the world that could do more than inconvenience the United States by attacking its fringe, which is all that the world combined could do, so long as our country is not compelled to send its forces beyond its own compact shores to defend worthless possessions. If our country were blockaded by the united powers of the world for years, she would emerge from the embargo richer and stronger, and with her own resources more completely developed. We have little to fear from external attack. No thorough blockade of our enormous seaboard is possible; but even if it were, the few indispensable articles not produced by ourselves (if there were any such) would reach us by way of Mexico or Canada at slightly increased cost.

From every point of view we are forced to the conclusion that the past policy of the Republic is her true policy for the future; for safety, for peace, for happiness, for progress, for wealth, for power — for all that makes a nation blessed.

Not till the war-drum is silent, and the day of calm peace returns, can the issue be soberly considered.

Twice have the American people met crucial issues wisely, and in the third they are not to fail.

· VIII ·

Americanism Versus Imperialism [1]

I

FOR several grave reasons I regard possessions in the far East as fraught with nothing but disaster to the Republic. Only one of these, however, can now be considered — the dangers of war and of the almost constant rumors and

[1] From the *North American Review*, CLXVIII (January and March, 1899), 1–13; 362–372. The Spanish-American War broke out in April 1898 largely because American public opinion had become so excited as to demand Spain grant Cuba independence. A small group of Americans, including Theodore Roosevelt, Henry Cabot Lodge (1850–1924), and A. T. Mahan, also hoped to utilize the conflict to acquire for the United States other Spanish territories, notably the Philippine Islands. Other "Great Powers," for example Germany, Japan and Great Britain, were naturally divided in their sympathies. The first two, while recognizing they could not turn back the *fait accompli* of American conquest — if such occurred — were themselves expansionist minded; Great Britain regarded American expansion more benignly. After the United States won a military decision, American Commissioners were dispatched to Paris to negotiate a peace with Spain without any definite instructions on Pacific acquisitions from President Mc-Kinley or W. R. Day (1849–1923), Secretary of State. The Commissioners debated among themselves what to do. So did the nation's press, politicians and other leaders of opinion. In October 1898 the President decided the United States must take the whole Philippine archipelago. The Senate ratified a treaty to that effect by a narrow two-thirds vote in February 1899. The Filipinos, whose opinion was not solicited, mounted an insurrection against their new masters. Throughout these events Great Britain's foreign policy saw in the United States a counterweight to her own rivals in the imperialist scramble in the Far East. Though English statesmen uttered avuncular approval for American expansion, no concrete understandings or engagements between representatives of the two nations resulted. Of course one of the most effective ways to smear an American policy politically was to arraign it as pro-British.

These events were the background of Carnegie's timely essay. His ideas had some support in the Cabinet, and one member tried to get him to change McKinley's annexationist course, but in an interview Carnegie found the President "obdurate."

threats of war to which all nations interested in the far East are subject. There is seldom a week which does not bring alarming reports of threatened hostilities, or of new alliances, or of changes of alliances, between the powers arming for the coming struggle. It is chiefly this far Eastern question which keeps every ship-yard, gun-yard, and armor-yard in the world busy night and day, Sunday and Saturday, forging engines of destruction. It is in that region the thunderbolt is expected; it is there the storm is to burst.

It is only four years since Japan defeated China and had ceded to it a portion of Chinese territory, the fruits of victory. Then appeared upon the scene a combination of France, Russia, and Germany, which drove Japan out of China. Russia took part of the spoils for herself, and Germany later took territory near by. Japan got nothing. Britain, the most powerful of all, stood by neutral. Had she decided to defend Japan, the greatest war ever known would have been the probable result; the thunderbolt would have fallen. Were the question to be decided to-day, it is now considered probable that Britain would support Japan.

Germany obtained a concession in China, and Britain promptly appeared, demanding that Germany should maintain the "open door" in all her Chinese territory; the same demand was made on Russia. Both perforce consented. The far East is a mine of dynamite, always liable to explode.

The relative strength of the powers contending for empire in the far East is as follows: Great Britain has 80 first-class ships of war, 581 war-ships in all; France has 50 first-class war-ships, and a total of 403; Russia has 40 first-class war-ships, 286 in all; Germany has 28 first-class war-ships, a total of 216. Japan will soon rank with Germany, and be stronger there because close to the scene of action.

The United States proposes to enter into the zone of danger with 18 first-class and a total of 81 ships. These would hardly count as half that number, however, owing to her greater distance from the battle-ground. Russia is 8000 miles, the other Europeans about 9000 miles from it. The United States is from 15,000 to 17,000 miles distant via the Cape and via the Straits; the route via Europe is about 12,000 miles, but that would be impracticable during war-time, as the American ships going via Europe would pass right into the trap of their European enemies.

The armies of the European nations are as follows: Germany's army on a peace footing numbers 562,352 men, on a war footing, 3,000,000 (and a large addition ordered); France's army on a peace footing, 615,413, on a war footing, 2,500,000; Russia's, on a peace footing, 750,944, on a war footing, 2,512,143. All Frenchmen and Germans over twenty, and all Russians over twenty-one years of age are subject to military service. They are, in fact, first soldiers, then citizens.

It is obvious that the United States cannot contest any question or oppose any demand of any one of its rivals which secures the neutrality of the other powers, as France, Germany, and Russia did that of Britain. She cannot stand alone. What the *Saturday Review* [2] says here is true:

> Let us be frank and say outright that we expect mutual gain in material interests from this rapprochement. The American commissioners at Paris are making their bargains, whether they realize it or not, under the protecting naval strength of England, and we shall expect a material *quid pro quo* for this assistance. We expect the United States to deal generously with Canada in the matter of tariffs, and we expect to be remembered when the United States comes into possession of the Philippine Islands, and above all we expect her assistance on the day, which is quickly approaching, when the future of China comes up for settlement, for the young Imperialist has entered upon a path where it will require a strong friend, and a lasting friendship between the two nations can be secured not by frothy sentimentality on public platforms, but by reciprocal advantages in solid material interests.

Bishop Potter has recently stated that we must become the "cat's-paw of Britain" if we venture into the arena, and

---

[2] This is the British publication of course.

that is true. By Britain's neutrality, and by that alone, were we permitted to take the Philippines at all from Spain. But for that, France, Germany, and Russia never would have stood aloof, and the price demanded President McKinley has had to pay — the "open door," which secures the trade of our possessions for Britain. Nothing more significant has occurred than the statement of Senator Davis,[3] chairman of the Senate Committee upon Foreign Relations, whose ability, influence, and position are alike commanding. He says:

I favor a treaty of alliance including the United States, Great Britain, and Japan, for the protection of all their interests north of the equator. The rest of the world would have a wholesome fear, synonymous with respect, for us.

We may assume after this that it is true that, just as we were allowed by Britain to take the Philippines from Spain, so our position in the East depends upon her continued support or alliance — rather a humiliating position, I should say, for the Republic. But let us see about alliances. Can we depend upon an alliance? National combinations change with alarming rapidity in Europe. France and Britain, allied, fought the Crimean War. They took Sebastopol as we took Manila. Their flags waved together there, but they did not consider that that fact gave them the right to demand territory. To-day Russia and France are in firm alliance against Britain and other nations. Germany fought Austria; to-day they are in the Triple Alliance together. Italy allied with France fought the battle of Solferino; to-day Italy is a member of the Triple Alliance against France. Europe is a kaleidoscope, where alliances change, dissolve, recombine, and take other forms with passing events. During the past week the bitter enmity which recently existed between Germany and Britain, owing to German interference in the Transvaal, is changed, and it is announced that "they see together upon

[3] Henry Gassaway Davis (1823–1916), Senator from West Virginia, served as delegate to the first two International American Congresses.

many points and expect to coöperate more and more in the future." This morning the question is, Shall France and Germany combine for some common ends? This would have been considered remarkable a short time ago, but statesmen will remember that Germany and France did combine with Russia to drive Japan out of China. There is no alliance, not even the most apparently incongruous, that cannot be made, and that will not be made, to meet the immediate interests or ambitions of nations. Senator Davis seems to rest satisfied with an alliance for his country with Britain and Japan. If he had an alliance to-day, it might not be worth the paper it was written upon to-morrow.

I say, therefore, that no American statesman should place his country in any position which it could not defend relying only upon its own strong right arm. Its arm at present is not much to depend upon; its eighty-one ships of war are too trifling to be taken into account; and as for its army — what are its fifty-six thousand regulars? Its volunteers are being disbanded. Both its navy and its army are good for one thing only — for easy capture or destruction by either one of the stronger powers. It is the protection of Britain, and that alone, upon which we have to rely in the far East — a slender thread indeed. Upon the shifting sands of alliances we are to have our only foundation.

The writer is not of those who believe that the Republic cannot make itself strong enough to walk alone, and to hold her own, and to be an imperial power of herself, and not the weak protégé of a real imperial power. But in order to make herself an imperial power she must do as imperial powers do — she must create a navy equal to the navy of any other power. She must have hundreds of thousands of regular troops to coöperate with the navy.

If she devoted herself exclusively and unceasingly to creating a navy equal to that of Britain, for instance, which is what she will need if she is not to be at the mercy of stronger powers, that will be the work of more than twenty years, building twenty war-ships per year; hitherto our navy has added only six per year. In order to get the men to man these ships, she must take the means to educate them. That she can do this there is no question; that the American either on sea or land is at least equal to the man of any other nation cannot be gainsaid. More than this, I know the American workman, especially the mechanic, to be the most skilful, most versatile, in the world — and victories at sea depend as much upon the mechanic below as upon the gunner on deck, and American gunners have no equals. It was no surprise to me that the American war-ships sunk those of Spain without loss. I spent last winter abroad in the society of distinguished men of European nations who congregate at Cannes. The opinion was universally held by them that for a time the Spanish navy would be master over us, although it was admitted the superior resources of the United States must eventually insure victory. I said then that, whenever any war-ships in the world met those of the American navy, the other war-ships would go to the bottom — for two reasons: first, our ships were the latest and their equipment was the best, and, second, I knew the kind of men who were behind the guns. If ever the Republic falls from her industrial ideals and descends to the level of the war ideals of Europe, she will be supreme; I have no doubt of that. The man whom this stimulating climate produces is the wiriest, quickest, most versatile of all men, and the power of organization exists in the American in greater perfection than in any other. But what I submit is that at present the Republic is an industrial hive, without an adequate navy and without soldiers; that she therefore must have a protector; and that if she is to figure in the East, she cannot be in any sense an imperial power at all. Imperialism implies naval and military force behind. Moral force, education, civilization, are not the backbone of Imperialism; these are the moral forces which make for the higher civilization, for Americanism. The foundation for Imperialism is brutal physical strength, fighting men with material forces, war-ships and artillery.

The author of "A Look Ahead," which first appeared in the *North American Review* [4] is not likely to be suspected of hostility to the coming together of the English-speaking race. It has been my dream, and it is one of the movements that lie closest to my heart. For many years a united flag has floated from my summer home in my native land, the Stars and Stripes and the Union Jack sewn together — the first flag of that kind ever seen. That flag will continue to fly there and the winds to blow the two from side to side in loving embrace. But I do not favor a formal alliance, such as that desired by Senator Davis. On the contrary, I rely upon the "alliance of hearts," which happily exists to-day. Alliances of fighting power form and dissolve with the questions which arise from time to time. The patriotism of race lies deeper and is not disturbed by waves upon the surface. The present era of good feeling between the old and the new lands means that the home of Shakspere and Burns will never be invaded without other than native-born Britons being found in its defense. It means that the giant child, the Republic, is not to be set upon by a combination of other races and pushed to its destruction without a growl coming from the old lion which will shake the earth. But it should not mean that either the old land or the new binds itself to support the other in all its designs, either at home or abroad, but that the Republic shall remain the friend of all nations and the ally of none; that, being free today of all foreign entanglements, she shall not undertake to support Britain, who has these to deal with. Take Russia, for instance. Only last year leading statesmen were pushing Britain into a crusade against that country. They proposed to prevent its legitimate expansion toward the Pacific — legitimate because it is over coterminous territory, which Russia can absorb and Russian-

---

[4] Carnegie's own article, in June 1893 (CLVI, 685–710), reprinted in the 1893 edition of *Triumphant Democracy*.

ize, keeping her empire solid. She knows better than to have outlying possessions open to attack. Russia has always been the friend of the United States. When Lord Palmerston, Prime Minister of Great Britain, proposed to recognize the South, Russia sent her fleet to New York. Russia sold us Alaska. We have no opposing interests to those of Russia; the two nations are the only two great nations in the world solid, compact, impregnable, because each has developed only coterminous territory, upon which its own race could grow. Even in the matter of trade with Russia, our exports are increasing with wonderful rapidity. Shiploads of American locomotives, American steel bridges, and American electrical machinery for her leave our shores. Everything in which our country is either supreme or becoming supreme goes to Russia. Suppose Britain and Russia clash in the Far East and we have an alliance with Britain, we are at war against one of our best friends.

The sister Republic of France and our own, from her very beginning, have been close friends. The services France rendered at the Revolution may be, but never should be, forgotten by the American. That some interests in France sympathized with Spain was only natural. The financial world in France held the Spanish debt. The religion of France is the religion of Spain. The enemies of the French Republic sided with the monarchy. But this can be said without fear of contradiction, that those who govern France stood the friends of our Republic, and that our enemies in France were also the enemies of the French government. An alliance with Britain and Japan would make us a possible enemy of France. I would not make an alliance which involved that. I would make no alliance with any power under any circumstances that can be imagined; I would have the Republic remain the friend of all powers. That has been her policy from the beginning, and so it should remain.

When "the world shall have a wholesome fear, synonymous with respect, for us," as Senator Davis desires, it will not be a good day for the Republic. Adherence to Washington's desire seems better to me — that we should be the "friends of all nations" — a wholesome friendship instead of a "wholesome fear."

Reference has been made to possible difference arising between the protector and its ward, but I do not wish to be understood as entertaining the belief that actual war is probable between them. Far from this, my opinion is that actual war will never exist again between the two branches of the English-speaking race. Should one have a grievance, the other would offer arbitration, and no government of either could exist which refused that offer. The most powerful government ever known in Britain was that of Lord Salisbury, when President Cleveland rightfully demanded arbitration in the Venezuelan case.[5] As is well known, Mr. Gladstone's government had agreed to arbitration. Lord Salisbury, upon coming into power, repudiated that agreement. Lord Salisbury denied President Cleveland's request, and what was the result? Some uninformed persons in the United States believe that he was compelled to withdraw his refusal and accede to President Cleveland's request by the attitude of the United States. That was only partially true. The forces in Britain supporting Lord Salisbury compelled him to reverse his decision. This is an open secret. Those nearest and next to him in power who sided with President Cleveland could be named; but the published cables are sufficient. The heir and the next heir to the throne cabled that they hoped and *believed* the question would be peacefully settled. That behind this cable was the Queen herself, always the friend of the Republic, need not be doubted.

[5] The boundary dispute between British Guiana and Venezuela, of long standing, came to a crisis in April 1895 with the arrest of two British officials. Cleveland, persuaded by the Venezuelan minister to invoke the Monroe Doctrine, sent a message to Congress virtually stating that British efforts to enforce claims on Venezuela without arbitration would be considered a cause of war. The question was eventually arbitrated in 1899. See also Essay XI, note 2.

The idea of actual war between Great Britain and the Republic can be dismissed as something which need not be taken into account; but what is to be feared is this: the neutrality of Britain — even to-day desired by other powers — in case her ward gave her offense, or was, as she supposed, ungrateful, and did not make full return for the protection accorded to the weakling, as we have said. It did not require the active hostility of Great Britain to thwart Japan and push her out of her possessions, but simply her decision not to interfere on Japan's behalf. Had Japan had satisfactory advantages to offer to Britain, she might have had Britain's support. It is the satisfactory bargain that alliances are founded upon in Europe; every European nation has its price, and every one of them has something which the other covets. France could give Britain a free hand in Egypt. Germany could concur in Britain's acquisition of Delagoa Bay [6] and end her troubles in the Transvaal. This is something Britain dearly covets. Russia could give Britain a desired frontier in India. These nations have all co-related interests and desires, and no man can predict what alliances will be broken and what made — it is all a matter of self-interest. The United States has not this position. She has little desirable to offer in exchange for alliance, and in all probability she would be sacrificed for the aims of her strong rivals — at least she might be, being herself powerless.

When a statesman has in his keeping the position and interests of his country, it is not with things as they are to be in the future, but with things as they are in the present, that

[6] In 1875 Marshal MacMahon, President of France, acting as arbitrator in a dispute between Great Britain and Portugal over the ownership of Delagoa Bay, awarded this port to Portugal, which began active colonization, extending westward and conflicting with British claims inland. The dispute lasted from 1880 to 1890, when Lord Salisbury delivered an ultimatum, as a consequence of which in 1891 Portugal conceded to Great Britain the right of preëmption to her possessions south of the Zambesi River. The Transvaal Republic wanted a seaport, but in 1895 Great Britain annexed the territory between Zululand and Mozambique, thus cutting the Boer Republic off from any port. German interests in Africa looked with disfavor on further British colonial expansion.

it is his serious duty to deal. The dream, in which no one perhaps indulges more than the writer, of the union of the English-speaking race, even that entrancing dream must be recognized as only a dream. The "Parliament of Man, the Federation of the World," [7] we know is to come. The evolutionist has never any doubt about the realization of the highest ideals from the operation of that tendency within us, not ourselves, which makes for righteousness. But he is no statesman — he is only a dreamer — who allows his hopes to stand against facts, and he who proposes that the United States, as she stands to-day, shall enter into the coming struggle in the far East, depending upon any alliance that can be made with any or all of the powers, seems unsuited to shape the policy or deal with the destinies of the Republic.

Just consider her position, solid, compact, impregnable. If all the naval forces were to combine to attack her, what would be her reply? She would fill her ports with mines; she would draw her ships of war behind them, ready to rush out as favorable opportunities might offer to attack. But she would do more than this in extremity: she would close her ports, — a few loaded scows would do the business, — and all the powers in the world would be impotent to injure her seriously. The fringe only would be troubled; the great empire within would scarcely feel the attack.

The injury she would inflict upon the principal powers by closing her ports would be much more serious than could be inflicted upon her, because non-exportation of food-stuffs and cotton would mean famine and distress to Britain and injure her to a greater degree than loss in battle. Even in France and in Germany the results of non-exportation would be more serious than the effects of ordinary war. It would only be a matter of a short time until the powers recognized how futile was their attempt to injure seriously this self-

---

[7] "Till the war drum throbbed no longer and the battle flags were furled In the Parliament of Man, the Federation of the world."
Locksley Hall, lines 127–128.

contained Republic, whose estate here lies secure within a ring fence.

The national wealth would not grow as fast during the blockade, but that is all. Our foreign trade would suffer, but that is a trifle, not more than four per cent of our domestic commerce. No expert estimates the annual domestic exchanges of the people at less than fifty thousand millions of dollars; those of exports and imports have never yet reached quite two thousand millions. The annual increase of domestic exchanges is estimated to be just about equal to the total of all our foreign trade, imports and exports combined. Labor would be displaced, but the new demand upon it caused by the new state of affairs would employ it all. We should emerge from the embargo without serious injury. So much for the impregnability of the Republic. To-day fortune rains upon her. For the first time in her history, she has become the greatest exporting nation in the world, even the exports of Britain being less than hers. Her manufactures are invading all lands; commercial expansion proceeds by leaps and bounds. New York has become the financial center of the world. It is London no more, but New York, which is to-day the financial center. This, however, is not yet to be claimed as permanent, but it promises to become so ere long, unless the Republic becomes involved in European wars through Imperialism. Labor is in demand at the highest wages paid in the world; the industrial supremacy of the world lies at our feet. Two questions are submitted to the decision of the American people: first, Shall we remain as we are, solid, compact, impregnable, republican, American? or, second, Shall we creep under the protection, and become, as Bishop Potter says, the "cat's-paw" of Britain, in order that we may grasp the phantom of Imperialism?

If the latter be the choice, then it is submitted that we must first begin quietly to prepare ourselves for the new work which Imperialism imposes.

We need a large regular army of trained soldiers. There is no use trying to encounter regular armies with volunteers — we have found that out. Not that volunteers would not be superior to the class of men we shall get to enlist simply for pay in the regular army, if they would enlist there and be trained, but because they are not trained. Thirty-eight thousand more men are to be called for the regular army; but it is easy "to call spirits from the vasty deep" [8] — they may not come. The present force of the army is sixty-two thousand men by law; we have only fifty-six thousand, as the President tells us in his message. Why do we not first fill up the gap, instead of asking for legislation to enlist more? Because labor is well employed and men are scarce in some States to-day; because men who now enlist know for what they are wanted, and that kind of work is not what American soldiers have been asked to perform hitherto. They have never had to leave their own country, much less to shoot down men whose only crime against the Republic was that they, too, like ourselves, desired their country's independence and believed in the Declaration of Independence — in Americanism. The President may not get the soldiers he desires, and whom he must have if he is not to make shipwreck of his Imperialism. There is very grave reason to doubt whether the army can be raised even to one hundred thousand men without a great advance in pay, perhaps not without conscription. But surely before we appear in the arena in the far East we must have a large regular army.

The second indispensable requirement is a navy corresponding, at least in some degree, to the navies of the other powers interested in the East. We can get this in twenty years, perhaps, if we push matters, but this means building twenty ships a year. The securing of men trained to man them will be as difficult a task as the building of the ships. When we have armed ourselves thus, but not till then,

[8] *Henry IV*, Act iii, scene 1, line 54.

shall we be in a position to take and hold territory in the far East "by the sole power of our unlorded will," as we should hold it, or not hold it at all. To rush in now, without army or navy, trusting to the treacherous shifting foundation of anybody's "protection," or "neutrality," or "alliance," is to court defeat, and such humiliation as has rarely fallen to the lot of any nation, even the poorest and most madly or most foolishly governed. It is not good sense.

This ends the subject upon which I undertook to write, but there remains the practical question, What shall we do with the Philippines? These are not ours, unless the Senate approves the treaty; but, assuming that it will, that question arises.

The question can best be answered by asking another: What have we promised to do with Cuba? The cases are as nearly parallel as similar cases usually are. We drove Spain out of both Cuba and the Philippines. Our ships lie in the harbors of both. Our flag waves over both. To Cuba the President in his message renews the pledge given by Congress — she is to be aided to form a "free and independent government at the earliest possible moment."

The magic words "free and independent" will be accepted by the people of Cuba, and our soldiers hailed as deliverers. So well assured of this is our government that only one half the number of troops intended for Cuba are now to be sent there.

Even if we were tempted to play false to our pledge, as the enemies of the Republic in Europe predict we shall, the aspirations of a people for independence are seldom quenched. There are a great number of Americans, and these of the best, who would soon revolt at our soldiers being used against the Cubans fighting for what they had been promised. The latest advices I have from Cuba are from a good source. This necessity is not likely to arise. Cuba will soon form a government, and, mark my prediction, she will ask for annexation. The proprietors of Cuba who will control the new government, and many Americans who are becoming interested with them in estates there, will see to this. "Free sugar" means fortune to all. Will the United States admit Cuba? Doubtful. But Cuba need not trouble us very much. There is no Imperialism here — no danger of foreign wars.

Now, why is the policy adopted for the island of Cuba not the right policy for the Philippine Islands? General Schofield [9] states that thirty thousand troops will be required there, as we may have to "lick them." What work this for Americans! General Miles [10] thinks twenty-five thousand will do. If we promised them what we have promised Cuba, half the number would suffice, as with Cuba, — probably less, — and we should be spared the uncongenial task of shooting down people who are guiltless of offense against us.

If we insist "the slaves are ours because we bought them," and fail to tell them we come not as slave-drivers, but as friends to assist them to independence, we may have to "lick them," no doubt. It will say much for the Filipinos if they do rebel against "being bought and sold like cattle." It would be difficult to give a better proof of their fitness for self-government.

Cuba is under the shield of the Monroe Doctrine; no foreign interference is possible there. Place the Philippines under similar conditions until they have a stable government, when eight millions of people can be trusted to protect themselves. The truth is that none of the powers would risk the hostility of eight millions of people who had tasted the hope of independence. "Free and independent" are magical words, never forgotten, and rarely unrealized.

[9] John McAllister Schofield (1831–1906), Superintendent of the United States Military Academy (1876–1881), commanding general of the army (1895), and noted, among other things, for his part in the acquisition of Pearl Harbor by the United States.

[10] Nelson Appleton Miles (1839–1925), succeeded to Schofield's position in 1895. He was active in the Spanish-American War and afterwards.

Only one objection can be made to this policy: they are not fit to govern themselves. First, this has not been proved. This was said of every one of the sixteen Spanish republics as they broke away from Spain; it was said even of Mexico within this generation; it was the belief of the British about ourselves. There is, in the writer's opinion, little force in the objection. In the far East I have visited the village communities in India, to find even there a system of self-government dating back for two thousand years. In no country, not even the most backward, are government and "orders and degrees" of men not to be found. The head men of tribes and others of lesser authority are often selected by the members. In the wild lands of the Afridis — a tribe in India which has just baffled seventy thousand soldiers, native and British, the largest army ever assembled there — there is a system of self-government, and a rigid one. Human societies cannot exist without establishing, as a rule, peace and order in greater or less perfection.

The Filipinos are by no means in the lowest scale — far from it; nor are they much lower than the Cubans. If left to themselves they will make mistakes, but what nation does not? Riot and bloodshed may break out — in which nation are these absent? Certainly not in our own. But the inevitable result will be a government better suited to the people than any that our soldiers and their officers could ever give.

Thus only can the Republic stand true to its pledge that the sword was drawn only in the cause of humanity and not for territorial aggrandizement, and true to the fundamental principles upon which it rests: that "government derives its just powers from the consent of the governed"; that the flag, wherever it floats, shall proclaim "the equality of the citizen," "one man's privilege every man's right"; that "all men are created equal," not that under its sway a part only shall be citizens with rights and a part subjects without rights — freemen and serfs, not all freemen. Such is the issue between Americanism and Imperialism.

II

In the January number of the *Review* I dealt with the danger of foreign wars and entanglements as one of several grave reasons against departing from the past policy of the Republic, which has kept it solid and compact upon its own continent, to undertake the subjection and government of subject races in the tropics. I now propose to consider one of the reasons given for such departure — the only one remaining which retains much vitality, for the two other reasons once so prominent have already faded away and now are scarcely ever urged. These were "commercial expansion" in peace and "increased power" in war. The President killed the first when compelled by Great Britain to give the "open door" as the price for her support; for to give the "open door" to the nearer foreigner meant the "closed door" to the products of the soil and mines of his own country. There never was and never can be any trade worth quarreling about in the Philippines; but what little there is or can be he has given away. When the country saw Dewey's fleet provisioned from Australia, instead of from our own agricultural land, the claim of possible expansion of American commerce there fell to the ground.

The second claim, that the Republic as a war power would be strengthened, held the field even for a shorter period than that of commercial expansion, for it was obvious that distant possessions would only give to our enemies, during war, vulnerable points of attack which had hitherto been wanting. As one solid mass, without outlying possessions, the Republic is practically unassailable. Should she keep the Philippines, any one of the great naval powers has her at its mercy. Hence Admiral Sampson [11] warned us but a few days ago that "our risks of and dangers from war had already increased a hundred per cent and that we needed to double our navy." The

---

[11] William Thompson Sampson (1840–1902), squadron commander in the Spanish-American war.

President has just asked that our army also be doubled.

Thus the claims of "commercial expansion" in peace and of "increased power" in war have bled to death of themselves.

There remains to-day, as the one vital element of Imperialism, the contention that Providence has opened for the American people a new and larger destiny, which imposes heavy burdens indeed upon them, but from which they cannot shrink without evading holy duty; that it has become their sacred task to undertake the civilization of a backward people committed to their charge. A foundling has been left at their door, which it is their duty to adopt, educate, and govern. In a word, it is "Humanity," "Duty," "Destiny," which call upon us again for sacrifice. These potent cries, which brought us to the drawing of the sword for oppressed Cuba, are now calling us to a more difficult task, and hence to a greater "duty."

It is encouraging to those who hold to Americanism that the chief strength of the imperialistic movement calling upon us to depart from our republican ideals, rests upon no ignoble foundation to-day. It is not the desire of gain, as our European critics assert, nor the desire of military glory, which gives vitality to the strange outburst for expansion and the proposed holding of alien races in subjection for their good. The average American, especially in the West, really believes that his country can govern these tropical people, and benefit them by so doing; he considers it a duty not to evade a task which, as he sees it, Providence has clearly imposed upon his country. The writer knows that the cynics, both at home and abroad, but especially the latter, will smile at this statement; but the extent of the ignorance of the American people in general, except in the South, about subject races and tropical conditions, cannot be realized by Europeans. This ignorance is truly as great as their belief implies. Their lack of knowledge is at fault, but the greater this lack the clearer is it that they can be credited with absolute sincerity, and with those very dangerous things when possessed without knowledge, "good intentions." The people of the South, who have knowledge of the problems of race, are with rare unanimity opposed to further accretions, and see it to be a "holy duty" to keep our Republic from further dangers arising from racial differences.

Our national history has not been such as to give our people experience in dealing with this new and essentially foreign question, but the American democracy has displayed in all national crises a highly creditable sensitiveness to the moral features of every issue presented. The deciding voice has been that of those who stood for what made toward its abolition until the issue was placed upon high moral grounds. In the issue of secession, patriotism played the first part, but the enthusiasm of the nation was greatly quickened the moment it became a question of the emancipation of the slaves. Even in the recent issue, when the debasement of the standard of value was proposed, those who stood for the maintenance of the high standard found their strongest weapon when they placed before the people the moral side of the question, and argued that debts contracted in gold should be paid in gold; that the savings of the people deposited in banks in gold should be so repaid; and that the soldiers' pensions should be paid in money equal to any. The justice of the matter, what was right, what was fair, — in other words, the moral side of the question, — was potent in determining the decision.

We hear much of the decline of the pulpit in our day, and upon theological questions and dogmas its influence cannot be what it once was. Yet, as far as our country is concerned, I should say that the power of the pulpit upon all moral questions has gained as much as it has lost upon theological issues. It is not less powerful to-day in this domain of the Republic than in Scotland, and far more so than in any other English-speaking country. In such questions its voice has been potent when decisively pronounced upon one side or the other, as it generally has been; but in regard to Imperialism it has been divided. Bishop Potter, Dr. van Dyke, Dr. Cuyler, Dr. Parkhurst, Dr. Eaton, and others equally prominent stand firmly against it. On the other hand, Bishop Doane, Dr. Lyman Abbott, and others have taken the opposite view, but solely from the standpoint of the good of the subject races, not in the slightest degree for our own advantage.[12] This view, and this alone, is what gives Imperialism most of its remaining vitality.

Here is the essence of the whole matter given by Professor Alden [13] of the University of Pennsylvania:

Apropos of the missionary argument for expansion, the clergyman under whose ministry I sat last Sunday offered the following petition on behalf of the Filipinos:

"We pray thee that those who prefer to remain in darkness, and are even willing to fight in order to do so, may, whether willingly or unwillingly, be brought into the light."

Instantly there came to my mind the naïve remark of the pious

---

[12] Carnegie here calls the roll of divines, most of whom were conspicuous in the Anti-Imperialist League, a spontaneous uprising of intellectuals against "imperialism." At least three were "first citizens" of New York City. Henry C. Potter (1835–1908), Episcopalian bishop of New York, a clerical and social liberal and leader in the fight against municipal corruption; Henry Van Dyke (1852–1933), Princeton graduate and pastor of the Brick Presbyterian Church, a fabulous preacher and teacher, a literary man and self-styled "adventurous conservative"; and Charles Henry Parkhurst (1842–1933), pastor of the Madison Square Presbyterian Church, whose blistering sermon (1892) on the alliance between politicos and vice forced him to collect the evidence and brought on the Lexow Investigation (1894) which led to the defeat of Tammany Hall. Theodore Ledyard Cuyler (1822–1909), Princeton graduate, was pastor in the Lafayette Avenue Presbyterian Church, Brooklyn, and a conservative in theology. Homer Eaton (1834–1913) after 1889 was Secretary of the Methodist Book Concern in New York and Treasurer of the denomination's Board of Foreign Missions. The deviant divines were W. C. Doane (1832–1913), first bishop of the Protestant-Episcopal Diocese of Albany, a high churchman with gifts as an administrator; and Lyman Abbott (1835–1922), Congregationalist pastor of the Plymouth Church (Henry W. Beecher's Church) in Brooklyn during the nineties, editor of the *Outlook* — the new name (1893) of the *Christian Union* — and a reconciler of evolution and historic Christianity. Abbott later became a zealous apostle of Theodore Roosevelt.

[13] Raymond M. Alden (1873–1924), later professor at the University of Illinois and at Stanford.

author of the "Chanson de Roland," in describing one of the victories
of Charlemagne over the Mussulmans:

> En la citet nen at remes paien
> Ne seit ocis, o devient crestiens.

That is to say: "There was not a pagan left in the city who was not
either killed or made a Christian." So may it be in Manila, when a
similar dilemma is prepared for its inhabitants.

Bishop Doane is the most prominent representative of the
religious world who upholds the missionary view, and he
would probably hesitate to push it to its logical conclusion,
as his less known ministerial adherent does. The Bishop gives
the argument of "Duty" in the following:

> Bishop Doane says that precedent seems to indicate that both by the
> inherent national right of sovereignty and under the existing Con-
> stitution we can provide for the government of the people whom we
> have rescued, but that if this supposition shall be found untrue, "then
> we must remember that, in the emergency, national life and duty are
> more important than the letter of a document, and that the Constitu-
> tion, not being, as some people seem to think it, a close and final
> revelation of God, can be amended. . . . No difficulties and no anxie-
> ties can alter the facts or change the situation or put back the advanc-
> ing movement of God's will, which tends to the final substitution of
> the civilization, the liberty, and the religion of English-speaking people
> for the lost domination of the Latin races and the Latin religion.
> God has called the people in America to be his instruments in a
> movement perhaps even greater in its consequences than the Reforma-
> tion in England or the liberation of Italy or the unification of Ger-
> many, and in the spirit of dependence on Him, with the quiet courage
> of patient faith, we must rise to the duty of the hour."

It is with the view Bishop Doane presents that we anti-
Imperialists have to deal, not with spouting party politicians
waving the flag, and descending to clap-trap phrases to
"split the ears of the groundlings." In the Bishop's words we
see some reason for the charge sometimes made against
ecclesiastics, viz., that, their attention being chiefly fixed
upon the other world, they seldom shine as advisers upon
affairs pertaining to this. The Bishop's remedy for overcoming constitutional obstacles, for instance, is easily sug-

gested; but such an amendment to the Constitution is impossible, since upon this question all the Southern States are attached to its present provisions, and against "rescuing" and governing subject races by force. Having in their own land some experience of race problems of which the North and West are ignorant, they stand for the old Americanism. Then, again, the Bishop reveals to us "God's will," which, he informs us, "tends to the final substitution of the civilization, the liberty, and the religion of English-speaking people for the lost domination of the Latin races and the Latin [Catholic] religion." It may be open even for a layman who cannot pretend to know the designs of the Creator to observe that, in the case of the tropics, the Unknown Power seems to have placed an insurmountable barrier against the English-speaking race. Professor Worcester,[14] who knows most about the Philippines, tells us that our race cannot settle there and make permanent homes; neither can it in other parts of the tropics, nor has it ever done so. It has tried to do so in India, but failed. If a British child be born there, it must be sent home. In the Philippines it is even worse. Can Bishop Doane point to any considerable or successful settlement of our race in the tropics? He cannot do so, and this fact would seem to imply that perhaps the Bishop may have misinterpreted God's will. It would seem that, perhaps, in his own way he intends the people he has placed in the tropics to develop a

[14] Dean C. Worcester (1866–1924), born in Thetford, Vermont, and educated there and at the University of Michigan, was a naturalist on the Michigan faculty and participator in scientific expeditions to the Philippine Islands in the eighties. In 1898 he published a book, *The Philippine Islands and Their People,* which came to the attention of President McKinley; not surprisingly, he appointed Worcester in January 1899 a member of the Philippine Commission, one of the three civilians. The duties of this group were to determine how American "authority" should be extended humanely over the islands. Worcester believed the United States must retain the islands and govern them for a considerable period. He remained on the Commission until 1913 and served as Secretary of the Interior in the Philippine Insular Government from 1901 to 1913. Worcester's opinion, here quoted by Carnegie, is in the former's volume, p. 67. It reads, "It is doubtful, in my judgment, if many successive generations of European or American children could be reared there."

civilization for themselves, and is keeping his loving, fatherly eye upon his children there just as tenderly as upon the Bishop. In my travels, I have found the universal laws everywhere working to higher and higher standards of national life. All the world steadily improves. Only impatient men, destitute of genuine faith in the divine government throughout all the world, doubt that all goes well. The Bishop's eminent colleague, Bishop Potter, sees "God's will," our "holy duty," so differently from Bishop Doane. When bishops in the same church disagree, it is difficult to decide.

Perhaps we are not justified in quoting Dr. Abbott as still an Imperialist, since his latest article in the *Outlook* is entitled "An Official Disclaimer of Imperialism." After quoting the Cuban Resolution passed by Congress, he asks:

Why should not Congress at the present juncture pass a similar resolution respecting the Philippines? . . . When pacification is secured, our mission is at an end. . . . The above resolution respecting Cuba was simply an affirmation of the principles of this government wrought into its Constitution, vital to its life, affirmed and reaffirmed at many periods of its history. It denies that we wish either to hold people in subjection or to possess their territory as our own. Under no circumstances do the American people desire to hold under military government against their will a discontented and resisting people.[15]

These sentiments justify the title. They are indeed a disclaimer of Imperialism, but it seems that, like Bishop Potter, Dr. Abbott has not been favored with the revelation of God's will made to Bishop Doane, for, according to him, "whenever the subject races are pacified our mission ends"; while it is only after pacification that the Bishop's "Holy Mission" can begin to enforce "God's will" by the crusade against the Catholic (Latin) form of religion, for the introduction of "the religion of English-speaking people," of which we have in our land more than two hundred and fifty different forms, all used and loved by those who speak the English tongue.

[15] In the *Outlook*, LXI, 207 f.

Even our valued Catholic friends are often "English-speaking people."

Nevertheless, we must recognize that, diametrically opposed as Bishop Doane and his school, and Dr. Abbott and his school are in their conclusions, they both have as their aim what they believe to be the good of the poor backward races, and neither pecuniary gain nor military glory for their own country. None of these earnest, good men have anything in common with the ranting political school. They see only serious and unsought "duty" where the others find "gain" or "glory," if not for the nation, at least for themselves as politicians.

Imperialism can become a "holy duty" only if we can by forcible interference confer blessings upon the subject races; otherwise it remains what the President once said it was, "criminal aggression." Let us see, therefore, whether good or evil flows from such interference. This is easily ascertained, for there are many dependencies of European powers throughout the world, and many races held in subjection. Has the influence of the superior race upon the inferior ever proved beneficial to either? I know of no case in which it has been or is, and I have visited many of the dependencies. Where is there anything to show that it has been? On the contrary, the mass of authority declares that the influence of a superior race upon an inferior in the tropics is not elevating, but demoralizing. It is not difficult to understand why. Take the Philippines, for instance. The prevailing religion is our own Christian religion, Catholic, of course, but Christian, as in France and Belgium. In the interior there are Mohammedans, next in importance. Mr. Bray, the resident English consul, gives in the *Independent* a picture of happy life in Manila, which reminded me of what I had found in the East.[16]

---

[16] Howard W. Bray, British consul at Singapore and a behind-the-scenes negotiator between the Americans and the Filipinos, published "The Character and Rights of the Filipinos," in the *Independent*, L (1898), 1312–1316.

One of the great satisfactions in traveling around the world is in learning that God has made all peoples happy in their own homes. We find no people in any part of the world desirous of exchanging their lot with any other. My own experience has impressed this truth very strongly upon me. Upon our journey to the North Cape, we stopped in the Arctic Circle to visit a camp of Laplanders in the interior. A guide is provided, with instructions to keep in the rear of the hindmost of the party going and returning, to guard against any being left behind. Returning from the camp, I walked with this guide, who spoke English and had traveled the world round in his earlier years as a sailor, and was proud to speak of his knowing New York, Boston, New Orleans, and other ports of ours. Reaching the edge of the fiord, and looking down upon it, we saw a hamlet upon the opposite side, and one two-story house under construction, with a grass-plot surrounding it, a house so much larger than any of the adjacent huts that it betokened great wealth. Our guide explained that a man had made a great fortune. He was their multi-millionaire, and his fortune was reported to reach no less a figure than thirty thousand kroner (seven thousand five hundred dollars), and he had returned to his native place of Tromsö to build this "palace" and spend his days there. Strange preference for a night six months long! But it was home. I asked the guide which place in all the world he would select if ever he made such a fortune — with a lingering hope that he would name some place in our own favored land. How could he help it? But his face beamed with pleasure at the idea of ever being rich, and he said finally: "Ah, there is no place like Tromsö!"

Traveling in southern India, one day I was taken into the country to see tapioca roots gathered and ground for use. The adults working in the grove, men and women, had each a rag around the loins, but the boys and girls, with their black, glossy skins, were free of all encumbrance. Our guide explained to these people that we were from a country so

far away, and so different from theirs, that the waters were
sometimes made solid by the extreme cold and we could walk
upon them; that sometimes it was so intensely cold that the
rain was frozen into particles, and lay on the earth so deep
that people could not walk through it, and that three and
four layers of heavy clothes had to be worn. This happy
people, as our guide told us, wondered why we stayed there,
why we did not come and enjoy life in their favored clime.

It is just so with the Philippines to-day, as one can see
from Mr. Bray's account of them. It is astonishing how much
all human beings the world round are alike in their essentials.
These peoples love their homes and their country, their
wives and children, as we do, and they have their pleasures.
If, in our humanitarian efforts and longing to benefit them,
under the call of duty or destiny, we should bring a hundred
to New York, give them fine residences on Fifth Avenue, a
fortune conditioned upon their remaining, and try to "civi-
lize" them, as we should say, they would all run away if not
watched, and risk their lives in an attempt to get back to
their own civilization, which God has thought best to provide for them in the Philippines. They have just the same
feelings as we have, not excluding love of country, for which,
like ourselves, as we see, they are willing to die. Oh, the pity
of it! the pity of it! that Filipino mothers with American
mothers equally mourn their lost sons — one fallen, defender
of his country; the other the invader. Yet the invader was
ordered by those who see it their "duty" to invade the land
of the Filipinos for their civilization. Duty, stern goddess,
what strange things men sometimes do in thy name!

Another reason which, we submit, renders it beyond our
power to benefit these people is that, with the exception of
a few men seeking their own gain, the only Americans whom
the Filipinos can ever know must be our soldiers, for American women and children cannot make their homes there.
No holy influence flowing from American homes, no Christian
women, no sweet children; nothing there but men and

soldiers, the former only a few adventurers who, failing to succeed at home, thought they could make money there. Now, every writer upon the subject tells that the presence of soldiers in any town in the tropics is disastrous to both native and foreigner; that the contact of the superior race with the inferior demoralizes both, for reasons well understood. Forty-six per cent of the British army in India is at all times diseased. What imperialistic clergyman or intelligent man but knows the soldiers in foreign camps, so far from being missionaries for good, require missionaries themselves more than the natives? It would all be so different if Americans could settle and establish their homes in the Philippines, and amalgamate with the people, making a colony. It is in colonies, not in dependencies, that Britain has done good work. Soldiers will not benefit the inferior race in the Philippines. Men there for gain will not. Missionaries there are already in abundance. Beyond a few of a different sect of Christianity, we have nothing more we can send, and these will find welcome there if we cease warfare upon the people, while to-day they would be regarded as enemies. It is not civilization, not improvement, therefore, that Imperialism can give to the Philippines, should we hold permanent possession. It is serious injury both to the Filipinos and to our soldiers, and to the American citizens who go there. It is a bad day for either soldier or business man when, in a foreign land, he is bereft of the elevating influences which center in the home.

The religious school of Imperialists intends doing for the Filipinos what is best for them, no doubt; but when we crush in any people its longing for independence, we take away with one hand a more powerful means of civilization than all which it is possible for us to bestow with the other. There is implanted in the breast of every human community the sacred germ of self-government, as the most potent means of Providence for raising them in the scale of being. Any ruler, be he President or Czar, who attempts to suppress the growth of this sacred spark is guilty of the greatest of public crimes. There is no people or tribe, however low in the scale, that does not have self-government in a greater or less degree. The Haitians and the San Domingans do not require our interference. Why is it not seen to be our duty to force our ideas upon these, our neighbors? The Filipinos are not inferior to these people. On the contrary, we have Admiral Dewey and General Merritt [17] both stating that the Filipinos are more capable of self-government than the Cubans. It may be taken as a truism that a people which is willing to fight and to die for the independence of their country is at least worthy of a trial of the self-government it seeks. The Filipinos have done this. Even if they had not, it is better for the development of a people that they should attempt to govern themselves, this being the only school in which they can ever learn to do so. No matter through what years of failure they have to struggle, the end is certain, the successful development of the faculty of government. Through this stern but salutary school our own race traveled for centuries in Britain, with varying fortunes, but the end was the evolution of constitutional government. The cost is great, but the result is beyond price. No superior race ever gave it to an inferior without settling among and amalgamating with that race. In the Philippines, and in the tropics generally, this is impossible. The intruding race cannot be grown there, and where we cannot grow our own race we cannot give civilization to the other. We can only retard, not hasten, their development.

India has been subject to British rule for nearly two hundred years, and yet not one piece of artillery can yet be intrusted to native troops. The people have still to be held down as in the beginning. It is so in every dependency in which the superior power assumes the right to govern the inferior, without being able to settle there and amalgamate

[17] Wesley Merritt (1834–1910), commander of the first Philippine Expedition in the Spanish-American War.

with it. We challenge the Imperialist to give one instance to the contrary in all Britain's possessions.

The impulse which carried many clergymen and other good people away at first was creditable to their hearts and emotions. But Dr. Abbott's remarkable article just quoted may be taken as evidence that the reason is now demanding audience, and not what we should like to do, but what conditions render it possible for us to do, or wisely undertake, is now to be soberly considered.

The press also, like the pulpit, has done its part to stir the impulse to meet the demands of the "New Destiny"; but one of the most prominent organs of all in this work, and the leading government organ in the West, the "Times-Herald" of Chicago, — to judge from a recent editorial, — is also finding its hot passion chilled at the throne of reason, as it confronts and examines the conditions of the situation. It says:

> The conscience of the American people will not tolerate the slaughter of Filipinos in a war of conquest. We do not seek their land; we do not wish to replace the yoke of Spain with one bearing the more merciful and just label of the United States. Let the President announce that we have no intention to annex Asiatic territory, and that the pledge of Congress as to Cuban independence will be the pledge of the American nation to the Philippines.

If the President had said this in his message to the Filipinos there could not to-day rise before him the specter of nearly five thousand human beings "mowed down like grass," as the cable describes, and sixty of our own fellow-citizens sacrificed and several hundreds wounded.[18] This is the effect of his failure to say to the one people what he said to the other. His responsibility is great.

I write upon the eve of the birthday of the greatest public man of the century, perhaps of all the centuries, if his strange history be considered — Abraham Lincoln. Washington, Franklin, and Jefferson may have become "back num-

[18] On September 15, 1898, the Filipinos declared their independence. On February 4, 1899, fighting broke out between them and American troops.

bers," as we have been often told, for, as men of the past century, they could not know our destiny; but here is the man of our own time, whom many of us were privileged to know. Are his teachings to be discarded for those of any now living who were his contemporaries? Listen to him: "No man is good enough to govern another without that man's consent. I say this is the leading principle, the sheet-anchor of American republicanism." [19] It is not fashionable for the hour to urge that the "consent of the governed" is all-important; but it will be fashionable again one of these days.

It seems as if Lincoln were inspired to say the needful word for this hour of strange subversion of all we have hitherto held dear in our political life. Our "duty" to bear the "White Man's Burden" [20] is to-day's refrain, but Lincoln tells us: "When the white man governs himself, that is self-government; but when he governs himself and also governs another man, that is more than self-government; that is despotism." Lincoln knew nothing of the new "Duty" and new "Destiny," or whether it is "Duty which makes Destiny" or "Destiny which makes Duty"; but he knew the old doctrines of Republicanism well.

One other lesson from the great American: "Our reliance is in the love of liberty which God has planted in us. Our defense is in the spirit which prizes *liberty as the heritage of all men in all lands everywhere. Those who deny freedom to others deserve it not for themselves*, and under a just God cannot long retain it." [21]

Are these broad liberty-loving and noble liberty-giving principles of Americanism, as proclaimed by President Lincoln, to be discarded for the narrow liberty-denying, race-subjecting Imperialism of President McKinley when the next appeal is made to the American people? We have never for

[19] From Lincoln's speech at Peoria, October 16, 1854.
[20] Title of the much-quoted Kipling poem.
[21] This is somewhat inaccurately quoted from Lincoln's speech at Edwardsville, Illinois, September 11, 1858.

one moment doubted the answer; for they have never yet failed to decide great issues wisely nor to uphold American ideals.

Never had this nation greater cause to extol Abraham Lincoln than upon this the ninetieth anniversary of his birth, and never till to-day had it cause to lament that a successor in the Presidential chair should attempt to subvert his teachings.

· IX ·

Democracy in England [1]

THE most interesting political problem which the world presents to-day is undoubtedly that now pressing for solution in England. For the first time in their history, the majority of her people have power. Henceforth England is democratic. Cajoled, overruled, thwarted for generations by the aristocratic classes, who have doled out to them from time to time only such small measures of reform as were necessary to prevent revolution, the people have never been fully heard. A climax was reached, however, last session, when an act was forced upon the House of Lords which at once transferred power from the privileged few to the masses. It is this fact which renders the situation there so interesting to the political student.

To understand the position, it is needful to look for a few moments at the scope of the great act just referred to. The electoral system of England was quite fair when established centuries ago. The centers of population then lay in the south of England, and this district very properly sent to Parliament a majority of representatives. Those were the days when pretty little Bideford in Devonshire was required

[1] From the *North American Review*, CXLII (January 1886), 74–80. The advance toward parliamentary electoral reform is conventionally associated with the passage of three loosely-called reform bills; the first in 1832, the second in 1867, and the third in 1884–1885. Their general tendency was to extend the suffrage from a landed class, constituting a minority of the nation, to all males who possessed or occupied some property; and to redistribute seats in Parliament so that representation would have a more direct relation to population. When Gladstone was Prime Minister, the Act of 1884, adding about 2,000,000 voters to the rolls, in effect gave agricultural workers the franchise; that of 1885 pretty generally established single member constituencies approximately equal in population.

to send sixteen sail against the Armada, while Liverpool's quota was but two. But as population shifted to the middle and north of the island, the great cities like Birmingham, Leeds, Manchester, and Glasgow, each sending but two representatives, were offset by the two members from some decaying village in the south. Seventy thousand electors, say in Birmingham or Glasgow, had no more weight than a few hundred in Woodstock or Eye. To aggravate this injustice, the aristocratic landholders kept firm hold of the counties by restricting the right of voting to such as paid a rental sufficiently high to exclude all but the farmers, and traders who were wholly dependent upon them.

All this has been changed. The bill of last year gave the suffrage to residents throughout the country districts. Even the hitherto despised farm-laborers are now voters. The total electorate is increased about forty per cent. The squires and parsons who have for generations designated the county representatives, now find themselves powerless against the populace. The influence of this revolution is already seen in the character of the representatives whom they have just returned. The old-fashioned country squire has been discarded, and a rising barrister, rich merchant, or large employer of labor, has taken his place. Most significant was the remark of one of the Liberal managers to me, that he had on his list thirteen titled gentlemen ready to serve the state in Parliament, for whom no satisfactory constituencies could be found, their titles being regarded as elements of weakness before the new voters.

Even more important than the vast addition of voters to the electorate is the redistribution of seats which the measure enacts. One hundred and sixty-seven have been taken from the smaller constituencies and given to the great cities. All constituencies less than ten thousand in number have been abolished. What England is and has been, under the rule of a privileged class chiefly intent upon preserving their privileges, and restricted at every turn by feudal traditions, is well known. What she is to become under the rule of a democracy, in which no barriers exist between the popular will and its prompt execution, is now the question.

To this but one reply can be given. The people of England will proceed to assimilate their political institutions to those of all other English-speaking communities. The institutions will be rapidly colonialized and Americanized. This process began some years ago, and has continued without cessation. And just in proportion as the people have been able to influence their rulers has the movement been accelerated. The record of recent legislation shows only a copying of our institutions.

The first and by far the most important step ever taken in this direction was the adoption some years ago of a system of public education. Every child in the land now receives an education equal to that which we bestow. Small fees are still collected from parents, but the local school boards have authority to pay these fees should parents be unable to do so. Attendance is compulsory. The first generation of those who have benefited by this system are now appearing upon the stage of action with the inevitable result: they are radical. Education is everywhere a sure destroyer of privilege. The boy who can read the Declaration of Independence may be trusted to feel its force sooner or later. The doctrine of political equality, once known, enters the heart of man a welcome guest. Following us again, as we have seen, the Electoral Act is a great step toward our plan of equal districts and universal suffrage. Legislation upon law, a department in which Britain has long been considered supreme, has recently been in the direction of combining law and equity, after our practice. The patent laws of England have just been modeled after our own, although there is yet much to be done to bring them to our standard. In regard to married women's property, the year before last witnessed the discarding of feudal ideas and the adoption of our American law upon the subject. In a short time we are to see marriage with a deceased wife's sister allowed in England, as it is in other English-speaking lands. If we except legislation upon Irish land, which Mr. Gladstone and every member of the government pronounced exceptional and only justifiable upon the plea of necessity, it would be difficult to point out any change made in the laws of Britain during the past twenty years which is not in the direction of the colonial and republican practice. If we regard prospective legislation, we again find the parent land is politically under the influence of her children; her part for some years is to follow them.

England's position is indeed unique among nations. Time was when not only all English-speaking communities, but the thinkers of all nations, looked to her for lessons in political development. The mother of nations was the mother of parliaments. Trial by jury, *habeas corpus*, freedom of the press, constitutional government itself — all these are her work; but they are of the past, and are accepted as the law of gravitation is, there being no further dispute about them. The world requires the solution of new problems, fitting a more advanced condition; and toward this the fondest admirers of the dear old land must blush to own her contribution has been but scanty. A new English-speaking community, about to found a state, might indeed still look to England, but it would be to learn, not what to adopt, but what to avoid. Instead of standing forth a model, she has become a warning. No state would think of adopting throne, hereditary chamber, primogeniture and entail, union of church and state, or any other of the remains of feudal institutions with which England is afflicted. Her more enterprising children seem to stand reminding her that

> *To have done* is nothing
> But to stand, like rusty mail,
> In monumental mockery.[2]

[2] Quoted inaccurately from *Troilus and Cressida*, Act III, scene 3, lines 151 ff.

It is not to be supposed, unless Britain's star has set, and Britons are Britons no more, that the people — now educated, and becoming more and more apprised of the truth that they have been indulging in a Rip Van Winkle sleep — will rest content, deprived of the position they once held as the foremost nation of the world, the pioneer in political progress. I am quite sure that Britons are still Britons, a mighty race, whose part in the world, great as it has been, is not yet played to a finish. England has risen from her slumber.

The appeal to the people which has just taken place has unfortunately resulted in an equivocal response. For several reasons the towns which voted first have deserted the Liberals for the Tories. First, the Irish vote, from dictates of policy, was thrown against their natural allies, the Liberals. Second, the premature explosion of the issue of church disestablishment on the eve of the election frightened many Liberal churchmen into opposition. The Englishman regards every new question as a bogy, and has to be led up quietly to the object, and accustomed to it before he can be driven on. A third reason, no doubt more potent than a surface view would indicate, was a deep aversion to the Liberal policy in Egypt and in the Sudan,[3] which resulted in a loss of thousands of lives, and added twenty millions sterling to the budget. A fourth cause is found in the theory of "Fair Trade" as opposed to "Free Trade." Great distress prevails in the manufacturing districts, and many operatives were carried away in the hope that there might be some virtue in the fair trade idea. Thus the Liberals fought at enormous disadvantage in the towns, and lost a great many seats which are safe for them under normal conditions.

Turning to the country districts, the reverse is found. All that the most advanced Radical hoped for has been accomplished, and more. The enfranchised voters have turned upon

[3] The defeat of the Liberals and the decline of Gladstone's influence resulted in part from the disaster to General Charles Gordon at Khartoum, where, failing to evacuate the Sudan as expected by the home government, and unrelieved until too late, he was besieged by the Mahdists and killed.

their former oppressors, the parson and the squire, and their class, and have driven them from the field. The new Parliament will differ from other Parliaments in nothing so much as this: that the members from the country are Radical instead of being Tory magnates as hitherto. The gains in the counties have equalized the losses in the towns, and all to the advantage of the Radical wing of the Liberal party. Left to struggle with the Tories alone, Mr. Gladstone and his followers would have had a triumphant majority, and been able to carry the Liberal program complete. But here comes in the most important factor of all. As Richelieu says to the king, of Cromwell, "A great man has arisen in England" — Parnell. His triumph is complete. He holds both parties at his mercy. The scales of power are in his hand. In presence of this great fact speculation concerning the Radical program is vain. The question of Ireland overshadows all. Nothing else will be heard of. Not even the reform of the rules of procedure of the House, which is a crying necessity, can be accomplished except by arrangement with the "uncrowned King of Ireland." The natural course would be an alliance between Mr. Gladstone and Mr. Parnell, when probably a few of the Whigs — Goschen and Hartington — would go sulking to their tents. Rosebery and Harcourt, and even Granville, if he does not finally retire, which is probable, may be depended upon, however, to remain with the advanced wing, which is headed by Chamberlain, Morley, Dilke, and Trevelyan. Even with this alliance it is probable that an appeal would have to be made to the country next year upon the one vital question of Home Rule for Ireland; and as the Liberals would then have the Irish vote, the result cannot be doubtful.[4]

[4] Since Carnegie is here dealing with events both complicated and critical, it is not surprising that his analysis and forecasts went awry. The parliamentary election of December 1885 had an outcome exceptional in English history. The Liberal Party under Gladstone won a plurality of seats but the combined total of Conservatives and of the followers of Charles Stewart Parnell (1846–1891) equaled it. Parnell was at the crest of his

But neither Mr. Gladstone nor the Marquis of Salisbury, not even Parnell, nor any other man, can tell what combination the kaleidoscope of British politics is to form during the next sixty days. It is useless, therefore, for me to speculate further upon it. This much, however, is certain: The democracy are in power, and their measures will be carried, if not this session, then in some early Parliament. And included in these will be Home Rule for Ireland, with rights similar to those enjoyed by the States of the American Union — a further imitation of her giant child by the motherland. When this great question is settled, but not till then, the Radical program of further democratic reforms will be in order.

The most important consideration of all is the future attitude of Great Britain toward other nations. Is the British democracy to be pacific or belligerent? Is Britain to continue to embroil herself in wars in all parts of the world? Is she to maintain her costly and useless interferences in the quarrels of Europe? I think not. I believe that the British democracy is to be pacific, and that the American doctrine of non-intervention will commend itself to it. Britain will be more and

influence. A Protestant, Irish landowner, Parnell hated England. He had consolidated, as far as any man could, the various sects and programs of Irish discontent; his Land League drew sympathy and financial support from America. Though he did not publicly condemn the violent acts of Irish terrorists, Parnell primarily sought to wring concessions from the English Parliament by making himself a nuisance through procedural delays and by dramatizing his cause. Even before the election of 1885 Gladstone had decided upon a measure for Irish home rule; afterwards it seemed a practical necessity. By sponsoring it he split from his party the old Whigs and many of the Radicals. Chamberlain and Sir George Otto Trevelyan (1838–1928) resigned from the Cabinet; Rosebery and Morley stayed in; Sir Charles Wentworth Dilke (1843–1911) voted for the bill. The Commons defeated home rule by thirty votes; ninety-three Liberals voted against it. Gladstone resigned and Salisbury returned to office. The other statesmen mentioned are Viscount George Joachim Goschen (1831–1907), member of the Gladstone Cabinet (1868) and, with Spencer Compton Cavendish, Marquis of Hartington (1838–1908), an active Liberal Unionist on the Irish question; George Leveson-Gower Granville (1815–1891), colonial secretary in the Gladstone ministry of 1868, and foreign secretary (1870–1874, and 1880–1885), a firm supporter of Gladstone on home rule; Sir William Granville Harcourt (1827–1904), Liberal.

more inclined to follow the example of America in regard to foreign affairs, as she has done in home affairs. "Friendship with all, entangling alliances with none," is to become the common platform of the democracy on both sides of the Atlantic. I believe, further, that it will not be long ere both parties in Britain will pledge themselves, as both parties here have done, to offer arbitration for the settlement of international disputes before drawing the sword. In short, Herbert Spencer's great law will be further vindicated: "As power is held arbitrarily by king or chief the military type is developed, and wars of dynasties and aggression ensue. As power passes to the people the industrial type is developed, and peace ensues."

In all this we see the unceasing movement of the various divisions of the English-speaking race throughout the world to assimilate their political institutions, each division taking that which the others have proved to be best. English law is already universal; the decisions of the Supreme Court of Washington are quoted wherever our language is spoken. Religion, too, may be said, in a broad sense, to be universal. Our speech is also the tongue of a hundred million Anglo-Saxons; our literature is also the same, and political institutions are rapidly becoming assimilated. The world is soon to see this community of language, religion, and political forms merge into the great Anglo-Saxon democracy. The child now lives who will see every English-speaking community living under institutions founded upon the extremest view of the rights of man, as formulated in our Declaration of Independence, without a vestige of privilege from birth, without king or aristocracy, without united church and state, without great standing armies, unhampered by primogeniture and entail, with equal electoral privileges and equal districts. In short, with only such slight variations of laws as are necessary to adjust them to differing conditions and climates, the various divisions of the English race will live in peaceful brotherhood, each governing itself as a free and independent nation, but held to the others with bonds stronger than those of conquest, feudal dependency, or colonial relationship, and ready to help one another in need. This is the ideal federation of the English-speaking people of the world. It is also the only one possible or desirable.

The great parent land, it is true, lags behind at present. It is characteristic of her to be slow; but it is no less characteristic of her that what she once sets her hand to do, that she accomplishes. Twenty years' reign of the people will place her abreast of the most advanced of her children, and twenty years more may restore to her the political leadership of the **world.**

· X ·

Home Rule in America [1]

M_R. President, Ladies, and Gentlemen: I have first to thank the officers of the Junior Liberal Association for giving me the great privilege of standing before a vast audience of my fellow-countrymen here in the second city of the Empire, in that city which has done more than any other city to draw closer the two branches of the great English-speaking race, my native and my adopted land. The great ships which you are sending forth every year to ply to and fro across the Atlantic are shuttles weaving a glorious web between the two nations. Already we have spelled out in the glorious pattern international arbitration, and there is yet to come, as we draw closer and closer together, eternal friendship and good will.

The recent appointment of a commission to settle the fisheries dispute proves once more that never henceforth is a drop of blood of one branch of the race to be shed by the other branch. And, in speaking of that Fisheries Commission, permit me to say that I, for one, and I believe all Liberals and all British people, were rejoiced that a man like Mr. Chamberlain should have found a position in which he can do more good to his country than in any which he could find at home. It is a great work, this upon which he has embarked. I know that the *Pall Mall* represents him as a Jonah thrown overboard to the fishes, but I trust that he too, like Jonah,

[1] Address before the Glasgow Junior Liberal Association, St. Andrew's Hall, Glasgow, September 13, 1887. Published in the *Scottish Leader*, September 1887.

will return from the excursion wholly uninjured, with increased reputation, and able to boast that he has done something which no other traveler has ever done.[2]

When I accepted the invitation to deliver a political address before this audience, I stated that it would be unbe-
coming in me to enter into the quarrels — the temporary and
passing quarrels — which, unfortunately, have existed in the
Liberal party, but which, I am happy to say, between the
date of my acceptance and the date of my appearance, have
largely vanished into thin air. The recent elections did not
show much of a schism in the Liberal party, and therefore
I approach the subject of Home Rule in America to-night,
feeling that I in nowise become a party to the dissatisfac-
tions and to the jealousies which have existed among you.
For I tell you this: be he Liberal Gladstonian, be he Liberal
Unionist, be he Conservative, or be he Tory, — I believe I
have described all the variations, — in the soul of every
honest and fair and patriotic citizen of this great land there
lies like a weight the conviction that, whatever may come,
the present condition of affairs in Ireland must cease. You
must no longer disgrace the English name, and make us
blush in America for the land of our fathers — the land that

[2] Over the details of the fisheries question in the waters to the northeast
of the United States there had been quarrels since the treaty closing the
Revolution. Aside from the justice or injustice of the issues in dispute, it was
difficult to secure an adjustment between Great Britain and the United
States because the former "stood as broker between the United States and
Canada, and had great difficulty in managing their Canadian clients." As
for the United States, Maine and Massachusetts were usually furthering
circumstances that would make the importation of fish from Canada impossible, either by embargoes or tariffs. At this particular time "Blaine &
Company" — Republicans — were trying to stir up anti-British feeling to
win "the Irish heart (the Irish vote)." In spite of these handicaps, President
Cleveland and his Secretary of State, T. F. Bayard (1828–1898), and the
Salisbury ministry resolved upon an effort at conciliation. In the fall of 1887
a Fisheries Commission met in Washington; Joseph Chamberlain was the
leader of the British delegation. In February 1888 Cleveland submitted the
Bayard-Chamberlain Treaty to the Senate. Partisanship on the eve of the
presidential election of 1888 contributed to its rejection by the Senate. In
any case Chamberlain made the acquaintance of the American lady who
became his wife.

has been the pioneer of liberty. The mother of nations must no longer stand before the world confessing that at her own doors, in a part of her own empire, she is unable to found just laws which commend themselves to the public sentiment of the governed. Home Rule is certain, and therefore I enter upon no disputed question when I venture to lay before you the phase of Home Rule which we have in America, hoping that when your bill is prepared, you may find some hints there which may be of use to you in solving this great and pressing question.

Now, gentlemen, it will be necessary for me to say a few words upon the American Constitution. What is it? I will tell you upon what it is founded. It is founded upon your own Constitution, and it is largely the work of a Scotsman. I appeal to any scholar here, to any man who has read the proceedings antecedent to the adoption of the Constitution. I ask you to read the "Federalist," and you will find that the draft of the American Constitution submitted by Alexander Hamilton was adopted, with very few amendments, and is to-day that Constitution. I do not think that will cause it to be less favorably considered before a Glasgow audience. Well, the eulogies of that Constitution have been so great and so many, recently, that I will not trouble you with quotations; but in the works of Matthew Arnold, Froude, Freeman, Dicey, and last, but not least, Mackenzie, a Scotsman who has written a wonderful history of America, — a Dundee man, I believe, — and Sir Henry Mayne,[3] you can read

[3] Examples of eulogies to the Constitution are provided by Matthew Arnold, "A Word More about America," *Nineteenth Century*, XCVI (February, 1885), 219–236; E. A. Freeman, *Some Impressions of the United States* (1883), pp. 111–119, 134–137; A. V. Dicey, "Parliamentary Sovereignty and Federation," *Lectures Introductory to the Study of the Law of the Constitution* (1885), pp. 126–165; Sir Henry S. Maine, *Popular Government, Four Essays* (1886), pp. 196–254. This burst of interest in American institutions followed the British Reform Acts of 1881–2, in effect establishing universal manhood suffrage. British observers were interested in seeing how democracy worked. These were also days when a belief in the superiority of Anglo-Saxon culture touched academic circles on both sides of the Atlantic; English scholars consequently detected commendable similarities or even

pages of eulogy which, as an American, my modesty will not permit me to repeat. I will, however, venture to quote from the leaders of your two parties, that you may see how they corroborate the views expressed by these writers.

My lord Salisbury has said: "The Americans have a Supreme Court which gives a stability to their institutions, for which we look here in vain; the Americans have a Senate wonderful in its power and efficiency; would that we could have such a second chamber here!" I will tell Lord Salisbury how he can have it. There is no patent for its exclusive use — and there is only one way of getting anything good in a nation. The United States Senate springs from the people. There is not the poison of hereditary privilege in its veins, and that is what makes it so powerful and wonderful in its strength and efficiency; and if my friend Lord Rosebery, when he brings in his bill to reform the House of Lords, which he has promised, can only persuade Lord Salisbury to agree to exclude the hereditary poison, why, then you can get a Senate chamber equal to the American in strength and efficiency. You cannot get it any other way, and unless this is conceded, Lord Rosebery will find that his only safety lies in taking the advice Hamlet gave to the players: "Reform it altogether." Well, now, a greater man than Lord Salisbury — do not cheer; I am not going to give the name, but when I mentioned the name in Edinburgh, all the audience jumped to their feet and cheered, and I enjoyed it very much. As I said, a greater authority than Lord Salisbury, and one who has done a great deal more in improving constitutions, has pronounced the American Constitution the most wonderful work ever struck off at one time by the brain and purpose of man. I do not know whether Mr. Gladstone, being a Scotsman, may not be a little partial to the work of a Scotsman like Alexander Hamilton, but these are his

superiorities in American institutions. Finally, as American higher education attained status, the interchange of academic personnel across the Atlantic quickened; observations on the spot dispelled old misconceptions about the United States and revealed unsuspected merits in American institutions.

words. The day after to-morrow there will assemble in the city of Philadelphia representatives from all parts of the United States, with the judges of the Supreme Court and the President at their head, to celebrate the centenary of the adoption of the Constitution.[4] The Constitution, a hundred years ago, was adopted by a population of three millions which fringed the Atlantic coast. To-day it holds peaceful sway over the majority of the English-speaking race — more English-speaking people than all Great Britain and all her colonies, even were the latter doubled in population; and although this branch of the British people has extended from the Atlantic to the Pacific, and southward from the coast of Maine to the Gulf of Mexico, they have not outrun the benefits or the protection of that Constitution.

Let me now describe that Constitution to you. The government of the United States, under the Constitution, is divided into three departments — the legislative, the executive, and the judicial. The Legislature consists of two houses — a House of Representatives, elected for two years by a direct vote of the people; and a Senate, composed of two senators from each of the thirty-eight States, elected for six years by the State Legislature, but so elected that every two years one third of the entire body retires to the people to seek reëlection and have the chance of being displaced by worthier servants. These representatives receive as a compensation for their services one thousand pounds each, per annum. They sit from ten o'clock in the morning till four o'clock in the afternoon, and having paid for the services of these gentlemen, the nation exacts regular attendance. It exacts their abilities and attention when these are fresh, and it would not tolerate for a moment one hundred and sixty-eight barristers, as in your present Parliament, who do all their work in the daytime and come to you to muddle your

---

[4] In mid-September 1887 a three-day civic celebration was held in Philadelphia to commemorate the centenary of the completion of the work of the Constitutional Convention.

business at night. I have sat a great deal in your House of Commons. It is largely a debating club for the display of vanity, and it is no longer a sober, thoughtful legislative chamber. It never will be, as long as its members consider that they give you a gentlemanly class that condescends to serve you in Parliament. Your legislators are always your masters here, but in America they are our paid servants.

You know that celebrated story of a gentleman who lost a great deal of money by a false play at whist on the part of his partner. He scolded him, and the matter was referred to the leading expert of the whist club. The question was this: Could a man make such a stupid play as that which was described? And the decision of the referee was that he thought he might — after dinner. That is one point not embraced in Home Rule — but I mention it incidentally.

Well, then, the power of the two houses of Parliament is very much akin to your own in one respect. As far as the House of Representatives is concerned, they have the power of the purse, but the Senate of the United States is of equal power with the House. No act becomes an act without its approval. No treaty can be signed by the President, no appointment made of a petty postmaster, no appointment of an ambassador or minister or agent, without the consent and vote and approval of the most august legislative assembly in this world — the American Senate. There is where we hold our chief ruler. The President must carry with him that body of senators. We have our executive in the President. We make our king every four years, and we pay him a tremendous salary. I suppose all you people would grudge it for a crowned head. We pay him ten thousand pounds per annum, and we have nothing to do with his brothers and his sisters and his cousins and his aunts. And at the end of four years, if we do not like him, we put him down and elect another one. My fellow-countrymen, I would like you to cast your eye over the list of American Presidents and compare them for the last hundred years with certain individuals that you have been cursed with on your throne. Compare them, man for man, and see where you will land. This President nominates his Cabinet; but, mark you, not a man is a member of his Cabinet until the Senate says, "Approved." He may dismiss them, but when he nominates others, every new man must go through that ordeal before be becomes a member of the Cabinet.

The President is not only the first civil magistrate: he is the first military magistrate. We bring the civil power right where we want the civil power to be — at the head; and we put the military power where the military power ought always to be — at the foot. The President of the United States is the commander-in-chief of the army and of the navy, and of the military forces of the States when he chooses to call them into service. This is no shadowy power. When General Grant was at the top of his fame, it was rumored that he was about to conclude a convention with General Lee which touched upon the policy to be pursued; and I saw the telegram which President Lincoln wrote with his own hand: "TO MAJOR-GENERAL GRANT, near Richmond, Virginia: You will hold no conventions with General Lee except for the capitulation of his army. You will not confer, nor discuss, nor conclude any question of any political import whatever. The President holds these questions in his own hands, and he will not submit them to any military conference whatever." That is the kind of power we give our President, and we hold him responsible for the exercise of that power, and at the end of four years he gives us an account of his stewardship. At his call to-day seven millions of men capable of bearing arms, accustomed to bear arms, and only too ready to bear arms in defense of the Union, would stand forth. But two years from now that President would be one of the seven millions shouldering his musket in his ranks.

Now, then, our Cabinet does not appear in our House of Congress. They make written communications. They answer all questions which either House requires, but they do not deliberate with the House, because the American people are most jealous of any interference between the legislative and the executive. Now, to regulate all the rights of these people, the Supreme Court, the object of Lord Salisbury's admiration, has been created. It consists of nine judges. They receive two thousand pounds a year each for their services, and the Chief Justice of the United States receives one hundred pounds more than his fellows. He passed through your country the year before last, the head of the American government in one sense, because the court is above the President, as it interprets the acts of Congress, and is the arbiter of the community. He passed along unnoticed. The aristocracy and the court paid no attention to the Chief Judge of the United States. That is very much to be wondered at, because Buffalo Bill had not then arrived. But when your Chief Justice visited America, he was received as became a man in his position. The President of the United States received him, the cities received him, and he was everywhere entertained in a manner which, I trust, some future day, the Chief Justice of the United States may experience when he visits this country when the democrats are in power.

This Supreme Court has a veto on all laws passed by the House, the Senate, and the President. It does not make a particle of difference if the House of Representatives pass a law, and if the Senate pass it, and if the President approve it, any man can make an issue and appeal to the Supreme Court, "Is that law constitutional?" If it is decided to be unconstitutional it is waste paper. But great as are the powers which our Supreme Court possesses, remember the Supreme Court can start no issue. It can only decide issues which are brought before it, so that it is only when the law would work injustice or create popular discontent that the Supreme Court is appealed to at all. Now, then, having briefly described to you the three departments of the American government, allow me to say that the Supreme Judges remain for life, subject to removal by the President and the Cabinet for misbehavior or inability to serve.

Now, then, we come to the great question, How is it possible that not only one nation but thirty-eight nations — thirty-eight States covering a continent almost as big as Europe — how are their legislative and political matters managed? In no way is that possible but by Home Rule. Let me show you how deep down the principle of Home Rule goes and how far it extends, how wide-spread it is under this American system. The land of America is divided by government surveyors — and you will understand that I speak now not of the small Atlantic States which were divided before the Constitution was adopted, but of the great West and Northwest in which the majority of the American people dwell. It was divided into six mile-squares. These are called townships, and a few settlers make up a township. By and by they feel the want of roads, they feel the want of everything, and they decide to have a meeting. Now, here is a record of a meeting of a similar character to that which has created thousands and thousands and thousands of councils. You will see it is most interesting. Just listen to where Home Rule begins; see its beginnings — its roots. It always reminds me of that beautiful poem of Ballantine's about the brook when

It dropped from a gray rock
Upon a mossy stone.[5]

Yes, away up there — that is where the Home Rule stream starts. Here is what you find. Here is the township of Burlington, in Calhoun County, Michigan. "Organized in 1837, and held its first township meeting April 3 of that year, electing Justus Goodwin, supervisor; O. C. Freeman, town clerk; Justus Goodwin, Gibesia Sanders, and Moses S. Gleason, justices of the peace; Leon Haughtailing, constable and collector." That is the German element, you see, coming into

[5] James Ballantine (1808–1877), Scottish poet.

America. "Established six road districts; voted one hundred
dollars to build a bridge across the St. Joseph River and
fifty dollars for bridging Nottawa Creek; voted fifty dollars
for common schools." Ah, gentlemen, that is a vote! Fifty
dollars! The first meeting of a few stragglers in the Western
wilderness, and the first thing they do is to vote fifty dollars
for common schools to educate all their children free of
price. Now you are getting at the roots of democracy, gentlemen. But that meeting did another thing. It voted five
dollars for wolf-scalps. That throws a great light upon the
situation when the wolves were so numerous that they gave
a pound premium for every scalp that was brought in. Well,
now, that is a beautiful picture of Home Rule. There was no
superior officer there. They made themselves and created
themselves into a political community. It was universal suffrage — there was no privilege. I do not find anything about
who Leon Haughtailing was, or where or when he was born,
or who was his grandfather; he was elected, not because he
was the richest man, but because his fellow-citizens thought
him the best man at their command. That is the first meeting
of the little township of six miles. By and by other settlers
come into the neighborhood and form other squares; and
they hold similar meetings, and they vote for common
schools. In the course of time fifteen or twenty communities have been created, and they combine. They find that
they have not good enough school accommodation for each
township, and that they cannot have a court-house and all
the provisions for government upon so small an area; and
they say, Let fifteen or twenty of us townships combine and
send representatives elected by universal suffrage in proportion to our population. A convention is created for the
county, and they go forward and elect county officers in
the manner in which they elected their township officers,
and they elect their judges. And I have sufficient faith in the
democracy to say, Give me the judge elected by the people.
No community in America that has ever tried the experi-

ment has regretted it. I tell you the democracy is most interested in the purity of its judges. It is the poor man, the working-man, who is interested in his judges. And as all humanity has its bias, I tell you frankly that your gentlemen have the prejudices of the gentleman class, and your newly made baronets have the prejudices of the aristocracy worse than any old baronets, and your newly made lords are a disgrace to Mr. Gladstone. Well, the county goes forward — the second and larger circle of Home Rule. Observe, now, there is not what we might call a foreign element. There is no outside element, but all an outgrowth from the democracy itself. There is no divine right about it. It is a healthy, grand, glorious growth of the body politic itself. Very well, then; the county gets a little too small for their growing life. They want railroads, churches, halls. They want everything that a civilized people wants. They want everything that is good, and they get everything that is good, so far as human nature can get perfection. Twenty or thirty of these counties conclude that they will make a State, and they elect officers by a convention as in the case of townships and counties, and they meet and establish a capital, about the center of the proposed State generally. They elect a governor and a House of Representatives, and the State Legislature is composed of two houses, one called the House of Representatives, and the other called the State Senate. The word "Congress" is never used except when the national meeting at Washington is meant. The word "Congress" is sacred to the great central power, as I trust that in the great Home Rule Bill the word "Parliament" will be sacred to that great body which will meet at Westminster and attend to international affairs. Well, now, gentlemen, the State is born in that way. Every State has its own governor; it has its own militia, its own courts, and its own judges, and it manages its own taxation. It does everything that a State can do, everything that pertains to the State itself. That is a very, very broad platform of Home Rule; but the broader you make the Home Rule principle, always provided that it is subordinate to the national or federal principle, the better for the rulers, and the better for the people themselves.

Well, then, the several States, as you are aware, banded together and formed the nation. There were thirteen of them originally. The States being, as you know, before the general government, the people of America gave the general government certain delegated powers, and a comprehensive clause of the Constitution says that all powers not expressly delegated are retained by the States themselves. That is the principle of Home Rule in America. The national government is the sun of our system, and round the government the States revolve, each one on its own axis, some at one angle, some at another, all State communities governing their own affairs in the way that seems best to them. And therefore it is impossible you can ever have a State revolution in America, any more than it is possible for a man to turn and rend himself. The State Constitution is part and parcel of its people. It is their own work; they made it, and if they do not like it they can mend it.

Now, then, will you permit me, having sketched the American Constitution to you, to apply its provisions to the case of Home Rule at home? And in doing so you will all clearly understand that I do not represent anybody but myself. I bind nobody. The Liberal party — Gladstonian — is not responsible for what I describe as the operations of the American Constitution; and the Unionist is not responsible; and no Tory or Conservative may be alarmed upon the head of his responsibility for anything which I say. Now, then, if we were to deal with the Home Rule question, — taking this great Constitution for our guide, — I will mention in rotation four points, and just tell you how we would settle them — and we *would* settle them. When the democracy of America puts its foot down it stays there. The first condition is the supremacy of the national Parliament. I do not like the word "imperial." You may have an empire soon enough. You have very nearly an Empress now, and when you get an Emperor you can use "imperial," but I prefer "national." Well, it goes without saying that when two men ride a horse one must ride behind. There must be no mistake about the powers in the general government. I will not say whether the recent bill introduced was faulty or not in its expression of that power. Unionists may contend that it was, and they have the highest possible authority for thinking the words were unfortunately vague. But of this I have not the slightest doubt, that it never entered into the brain of any man that any assembly given to Ireland or Scotland would not have to bow before the national assembly — the Parliament. The American Constitution provides this: "This Constitution, and the acts under it passed by the national government, as interpreted by the Supreme Court, are the supreme laws of the land, anything in the State laws or State constitutions to the contrary notwithstanding." And if I were called on to settle the Home Rule question, that is the language I would put into the new bill. Mind you, that power being there, it has never to be exercised. It has only been exercised once in a hundred years upon an important issue, and that issue was one which no human constitution, nor all the human powers on earth, could have averted. The man or nation that tries to bind together in harmonious development freedom and human slavery has attempted the impossible, and when the great democratic forces came face to face, in the development of that country, with the slave power, which disputed its rights, one or the other had to fall; and you know which one fell. You might as well try to bind democracy and privilege. The two are antagonistic forces; and I believe the "Scotsman" newspaper of the 16th of August, in an editorial on the Northwich election, used the most significant words I have heard since I took up my residence among you. "Democracy means" — I quote the "Scotsman" — "Democracy means, and rightly means, that privilege shall cease."

Well, now, after what had been said about the supremacy
of the national government, I ask any Unionist here to consider in his mind to-night whether he has the shadow of a
fear that that will not be provided for in the new bill. Has
not Mr. Gladstone said, "All parliaments, all assemblies, with
statutory powers, are necessarily subordinate to their creator,
and I have no objection to name the delegated powers."
Now, then, when he names the delegated powers, he will
follow the American Constitution.

The other point on which great stress is laid, and laid
rightly, in my opinion and in the opinion of the American
Constitution, is the question of the continued representation of Ireland in the national assembly. Well, gentlemen, a
great deal has been said in this controversy about American
opinion. I have asked hundreds of Americans — and you
have got some intelligent Americans, no doubt, in Glasgow;
ask their opinion yourselves. There is not an American living
that will not answer this question as every one has answered
to me: "Would you agree that the State of Virginia should
have a Legislature of its own, and be absolved from the
duty of sending representatives to the national Congress at
Washington to deliberate equally with all other representatives, and hence be bound equally with the others for all
its acts?" And the reply is, "Never." And with the new bill
I would say to any Unionists, — because I am most anxious
to restore the harmony of the Liberal party, — "Gentlemen,
you have a hard enough fight before you; you have many
measures, the adoption of which lies deep at your heart; you
need every vote and every influence at your command for
this campaign." Very well, I ask any Unionist to-night to
consider whether he has the slightest doubt but that the
representatives of Ireland and Scotland will continue to be
sent to the imperial Parliament at Westminster. I do not
see how he can have a doubt. I had my doubts when the
bill was cabled across the Atlantic. I could see that point
clearly myself, and I took prompt measures to point out to

friends here what I thought was the weak point in that
bill. But, gentlemen, I thought I could do most good within
the party. I have known what Mr. Gladstone has already
done. There is no man living can carry reforms as he can,
and if his life be spared, he *will*, I am satisfied, — I will not
say I am satisfied; I *know*, because he has said it, that he
will, — deal with this question without touching the question
of Irish representation.

We come to the third point — Ulster. Now I am going
to apply the American Constitution to Ulster, and I tell you
it is not without force in Ulster or in any part of Ireland.
They will not seek anything beyond what the Americans
give their States. If they do, every son of an Irishman in
America — and there are a million of such — and every American will denounce the demand as something which upon no
consideration they themselves would ask, and which every
well-wisher of Great Britain prays she never will give. As
to Ulster, speaking as an American Home Ruler, that is too
trifling a subject to talk about among statesmen. The
province of Ulster is very nearly Nationalist, and divided by
the aggregate of the poll, it is Nationalist to-day. I reject
with contempt and indignation the attempt, in this nineteenth century, to stir up sectarian jealousy. You know, and
I know, what Scotland has done for civil and religious
liberty. If there be any body of Protestant Irishmen who
wish to keep themselves apart and nurse those bitter hatreds,
those feuds that give rise to disturbance of the peace — if
they want to do that, I am against them; and if there be any
body of Catholics that wish to nurture such feuds, and keep
themselves apart from their Protestant fellow-citizens, I am
against them also. There is no difficulty about Ulster. Whenever you give Ireland Home Rule you will stir up a patriotic
flame. And they will all be Irishmen first, and Ulster men
and Tipperary men afterward, and the presence of Catholics
and Protestants meeting in an assembly laboring for the
national good will soften all asperities and make them under-

stand each other better than they have hitherto done. The question of Ulster will settle itself. Left to a plebiscite of the Ulster people, you will hardly find a man that will not say, "Let us go with our country"; and I would not respect the man that did not say so, were he a hundred times a Protestant of the Protestants. That is not the Protestant religion. It is founded on private judgment and free thought, and the Irish Protestants have much to learn yet as to the fundamental principles of the faith of which they would boldly stand forth as the main adherents.

I now come to the fourth point. You will notice I am following the four contentions of the Unionists. Do not laugh at the Unionists. Let me tell you there were reasons for their contentions, much as I differ with them as to the mode which they took to enforce them. I think the Unionists within the councils of the Liberal party would have been much more powerful — I know the representatives of the Unionists in Parliament would have been more powerful — if they had labored within the lines of the party under the banner of the only possible chief; but the Unionists whom I have met and wrestled with have always told me, "Mr. Gladstone is all wrong." I will tell you a story in point. Henry Clay was the most popular man America had. Well, he voted against his constituents upon the slavery question, which was the only burning question of the time, and he offered himself for reëlection. There was not a ghost of a chance of his being returned to Washington, any more than there is of any Unionist being returned to the next Parliament. Well, Henry Clay saw that there was no use in conducting his canvass if he stood up to defend what he had done, so he went before the farmers of Kentucky and made one speech all over the State, "Now, boys," he said, "you have all got good, trusty rifles. Think of the game your rifle has brought down. Did your rifle ever miss fire? I have shot a good deal, and my rifle missed fire now and then. Did you on that account throw it away, or did you pick it up and try it again?" There

was no resisting such an appeal, and Clay was reëlected by
the greatest majority he ever received. Now, admitting all
that the most conscientious or contentious Unionist has to
say, I think if he has much of human nature in him, much of
gratitude for past services, much of admiration for the
noblest political career, he will pick up that old rifle — Gladstone. Just let the old man have another shot.[6] I will wager
ten to one he will bring down the game. I will tell you
another thing: I know your public men pretty well, but I do
not believe you have got a rifle in the whole army, in the
whole state, in the whole House of Parliament, that can
bring down the game like Mr. Gladstone. Now, then, I come
to the judicial question. We want to be thorough, the Tories
say. We are not thorough when we oppress the people and
thrust laws upon them which they do not want; we are only
thorough when we go to the root of popular dissatisfaction
and make our laws just. Now, the American States elect
their own judges, who determine all issues between the
citizens of the same State. A Pennsylvanian has the right to
be tried by the courts of Pennsylvania, and to have his case
decided by his fellow-citizen — the judge whose character
he knows and trusts. There is no appeal beyond the Supreme
Court of Pennsylvania in an issue pertaining to Pennsylvania;
but, under the national Constitution, any issue between men
of different States may be proceeded with in the courts of
the United States. The Supreme Court of the United States
sits at Washington, but it has judges in each district of the
country. Sometimes one State will have one federal judge,
sometimes two. Pennsylvania has two, one at Pittsburg and
the other at Philadelphia, three hundred and fifty miles apart.
That is matter of arrangement, and you can there have an
appeal to the United States Court. Apply that to Ireland.
In the first place, Irish judges already exist, and they will be

---

[6] Gladstone, at the age of eighty-three, won "another shot" in the election of 1892. He got Home Rule by the Commons, but the Lords defeated
it. In 1895 the Conservatives under Salisbury returned to power.

retained. It is not likely a good judge would be dismissed. Therefore I think the Irish executive would take over the Irish judges. It is a *prima facie* case that a judge is a good judge unless he can be proved bad. It will be for the Irish executive to reappoint or choose their own judges. What I want to point out to you is that if you pay regard to the lesson of Home Rule in America, you will allow the Irish Assembly to appoint Irish judges and to determine Irish affairs; and you will hold, of course, through the delegated powers, the right, in any issues of an international character, to appeal from these courts to the imperial power, such an appeal as every Scotchman has now to the judicial lords of the House of Lords. Now, that would settle the judicial question; but if you are going to give Ireland Home Rule, and withhold from her or from Scotland, when she gets Home Rule, as I trust she soon will, the control of the highest function, and the very essential of all government, — namely, the right to execute justice and administer the laws among her own citizens, — you are going to give them a mockery; you are going to play "Hamlet" with Hamlet left out, and you will have the Irish question upon you again and again in worse forms than it is now.

You must make the judicial power in Ireland respected in Ireland, and you cannot do that unless it derives its powers from the Irish government. I do not profess that the Liberal party has quite clearly sounded this note, but I trust the democracy will watch with clear eye the clause giving judiciary powers to Ireland. You cannot give Home Rule to Ireland if you take from the government the power to enforce its decrees; you may as well bind the government, Mazeppa-like,[7] on a wild horse, without whip, spur, or bridle, and expect peace and good government and loyalty in Ireland if you deny to the Irish executive the highest of all

[7] A reference to the famous story of the young Pole, tied naked to the back of a wild horse by the jealous husband of the lady with whom he had an intrigue. Among various literary treatments, that of Byron's *Mazeppa* is perhaps the best known.

political functions — the administration of law and the maintenance of peace and order. So says the American Constitution.

Now, I will touch upon one point — the land question. Every State of the American Union has a right to make a kirk or a mill of its land if it pleases. It is its own. If the soil of a nation is not the property of that nation, and if you are not going to allow Ireland to manage its own land, what are you going to allow it to manage? The land question is at the foundation of everything in the State, and you find that the Land Bill [8] is discarded — rightly so, and Mr. Gladstone has said that the sands have run for the landlords. That is too good to believe. I doubt even Mr. Gladstone's power to make a bill as it ought to be in regard to land, because in the Liberal councils you have lots of Irish landlords. Lord Hartington is a large Irish landlord with a rental of thirty thousand pounds a year. I know he is a sincere and honest man, but I know Burns says that

> When self the wavering balance shakes,
> It's rarely richt adjusted.[9]

No man should sit as a judge in its own cause, and in America no man who is directly interested in an act of Legislature can constitutionally vote upon it. I am afraid you will have to buy out the landlords before you can get done with them. The poor democracy, the toiling millions of Great Britain, will be mulcted in an enormous sum. Many members of

[8] One means of pacifying Irish discontent had been the Gladstonian effort to make more just the arrangements under which Irish tenants held land. These tenants often held their land "at will," subject to six months notice; their rent, a "rack rent," was fixed by competitive bidding, and if evicted from their holdings they received no compensation for improvements or repairs they had made. In 1870 Gladstone in an Irish Land Act compelled landlords to pay for improvements if tenants were evicted through no fault of their own. Parnell and the Irish Land League agitated for fixity of tenure, fair rent set by the courts, and free sale by tenants of their interests to other tenants. Gladstone's Land Act of 1881 granted these three F's. In 1885 Parliament passed an act for state assistance to land purchases by tenants; the aim was a peasant proprietary.

[9] Robert Burns, "Epistle to a Young Friend, May, 1786," stanza 3.

Parliament are interested in land, and there is that tone in society which seems to say that property in land is different from property in everything else, because for hundreds of years the land has been held up by infamous laws to maintain a class of people who, if left to the free competition of economic forces, would go down in the struggle for existence.

Well, what is the solution to the land question? It is a very easy one. Let it alone; let the Irish executive settle with the Irish landlords. The democracy has never been anything but generous in its acts, and it will be generous to the Irish landlords when upon their executive is placed the responsibility of settling with them — if it decides to buy the land at all. I am not in favor of the executive of Ireland touching the land of Ireland, or of the executive of Great Britain touching the land of Great Britain. Let me give a hint to the democracy. You are past the days of unearned increment, and upon the days of earned decrement, and any man foolish enough to counsel the people of Great Britain to take over the land to-day in a falling market may have his own interest at heart, but he cannot have yours. It is said that the people of Ireland will not do justice to the landlords. No, I hope not. In my wildest and most vindictive moments I have never yet gone so far as to wish that the Irish landlords had justice. No; let us remember that mercy should in that case season justice. But they will get generous treatment, and the democracy of Great Britain can be absolved from all trouble with the land of Ireland if they strengthen Mr. Gladstone's hands, and tell him in unmistakable tones that there are a great many things the democracy of this country will do, and a great many things they will suffer, but, as the Lord helps them, they will never be found on the side of Irish landlords as against Irish tenants, or pay one penny toward buying their land.

There may be some exceedingly patriotic men here who have been saying in their hearts, "We do not want to Americanize our institutions." Why not? The Americans have taken from you everything they could lay their hands upon. They have taken your Constitution and bettered it; they have

taken your literature, your laws; they have taken your
language, and if you would take from America everything
that America has to give you, or everything that America
ever will have to give you, there would remain a huge,
incalculable balance yet left in favor of the parent land. Why
should you not take things from your child if you know they
are for your good? But your own colony of Canada has
practically the same Constitution, as far as Home Rule is
concerned. If there be any man who forgets that America is
your own child, let him look to Canada — she is practically
the same. Do you think that the English-speaking race
throughout the world, with the same language, the same
traditions, — because all Americans claim your traditions, —
with the same literature, with the same religion — do you
think that it is in the power of man to prevent all English-
speaking people ultimately from having the same political
institutions? I will not venture to say what the political institutions of the English race may be in the future. It may be
that the "Scotsman" is right, and that democracy means that
privilege shall die, and it may be that all English-speaking
people will range themselves together upon a platform which
develops the extremest rights of man, and the political
equality of the citizen. That is possible. It may be possible,
on the other hand, you may say, that the majority of the
English-speaking race will turn its back upon this advanced
political development, and, seeking out some prince, will go
back and make him a perpetual king, and make his children
kings hereafter, whether they be fools or idiots or not, and
spend hundreds of thousands of their hard-won earnings
every year to support the entire brood in vulgar riot and
ostentation; and it may be that we will create another
aristocracy, and that I shall so far forget myself and my
lineage, as the direct descendant of weavers and shoemakers
— glorious Radicals some of them have been, who have gone
to jail just for attending such a meeting as was interrupted
in Ireland the other day! — it may be that I will forget that
and parade before you as a baronet. Then you will say, "We

don't know how we will treat Mr. Carnegie coming to visit us; he is not a nobleman, and he has ceased to be a gentleman." But whatever be the system of political institutions adopted in the future, — you may have it either way, — one point I venture to stand by, and that is that the English-speaking race throughout the world is to have the same institutions. If you can adopt some of the provisions of the American Constitution for this emergency, you will have hastened by so much the day when your institutions shall be the same as the institutions of the English-speaking race. How long will it take after that assimilation is perfected before we have a federal council that will forever render it impossible that the blood of the English-speaking man can be shed by English-speaking man? Where lies your greatest hope that your own race, the dominant power of the world, shall coalesce and form a union against which nothing on earth shall stand? In the assimilation of your institutions. There lies the point. And where is the hope of that great day which the poet sings of —

> When the drum shall beat no longer, when the battle-flags are furled,
> In the Parliament of Man, the Federation of the World? [10]

It lies in the great beneficent principle of Home Rule — Home Rule for each of the divisions, with a central authority over all to keep them in order; and in that congregation of English-speaking people, in that future Parliament — I know not how many divisions, I know not what their size or number, I know not their positions, but I know the position of one power is fixed, immovable, perpetual, and secure — that of this glorious little island. There may be many children clustering around her in that Parliament of Man; there can only be one mother. I say cursed be the arm and withered the tongue of any man, wherever found, who would strive to keep apart, by word or by deed, those children from that mother.

[10] See Essay VIII, note 7.

· XI ·

Does America Hate England?[1]

This question has been much discussed of late in Britain: and the answer has generally been given in the affirmative; even the *Spectator*, a powerful and true friend of the Republic, has been reluctantly driven to that side.

But the correct answer to this inquiry depends upon what is meant by hatred; for this may be of two kinds — one deep, permanent, generally racial, which creates hereditary antipathy and renders the parties natural enemies; the other only temporary and skin-deep — indignation and resentment aroused by specific questions, which pass with their settlement, leaving no serious estrangement behind.

That several causes exist which must always create more or less irritation in the United States against Great Britain is obvious. The Canadian question must always do so. Imagine Scotland republican, owing allegiance to the United States, and constantly proclaiming its readiness to attack Britain at their bidding. The industrial question also has its effect. A score of articles "made in Germany" are causing irritation in England. What can a thousand articles "made in England" be expected to do in the United States? Industrial competitors, and the workmen employed by them, are very sensitive and easily irritated; and in our day, when every nation of the front rank aspires to manufacture and produce for its own wants, "Foreign Commerce" and "Free Trade" do not always make for peace and good will among

[1] From the *Contemporary Review*, LXXII (November 1897), 660-668.

nations, but the contrary. Nations are disposed to resent industrial invasion, Free-Trade Britain not less than Protective Germany.

But deeper than these causes of irritation there does lie at the core of the national heart of the Republic a strong and ineradicable stratum of genuine respect, admiration, and affection for the old home. The pride of race is always there at the bottom — latent, indeed, in quiet times, but decisively shown in supreme moments when stirred by great issues which affect the safety of the old home and involve the race. The strongest sentiment in man, the real motive which at the crisis determines his action in international affairs, is racial. Upon this tree grow the one language, one religion, one literature, and one law which bind men together and make them brothers in time of need as against men of other races. This racial sentiment goes deeper and reaches higher than questions of mere pecuniary import, or of material interests. The most recent proof that this pride of race exists in America in an intense degree was given, even at the very height of the Venezuelan dispute,[2] when it was suspected that a combina-

[2] The Venezuelan dispute, one of the major diplomatic fireworks of the nineties, went off because Venezuela and Great Britain could not agree upon the boundary between the former and British Guiana. Venezuela had for years proposed arbitration; in 1895 Cleveland and his Secretary of State, Richard Olney, insisted Britain arbitrate, since the application of her claims violated the Monroe Doctrine. Salisbury rejected the proposal and denied the American interpretation of the Monroe Doctrine. Cleveland proposed to Congress the appointment of a commission to investigate the merits of the disputants and added that after the investigation the United States would resist as aggression any "appropriation" of Venezuela's lands by Great Britain. Britain's freedom of action was limited by the outbreak of violence between British "outlanders" and the Boers in the Transvaal in South Africa. The German Emperor openly congratulated President Paul Kruger of the Boers for maintaining the independence of his country. Britain under Salisbury and Chamberlain, Secretary for Colonial Affairs, decided to liquidate the American quarrel and concentrate on South Africa. Consequently, England and Venezuela in February 1897 agreed to arbitration; on the tribunal of reference were two Justices of the American Supreme Court as well as British and neutral representatives. The award came in 1899.
    Carnegie's picture of the American reaction to the Boer War is inaccurate. There was a "wild cheer," but it was not out of character. American opinion is predisposed to support under-dog nations, especially when an

tion of European Powers was behind Germany's action in regard to the Transvaal, which had for its aim the humiliation and ruin of Britain, and was taking advantage of the family quarrel to begin the partition of the possessions of the only other member of our race. When the plucky little island took up the challenge and prepared without a moment's hesitation to meet the world in arms, the American continent, from Maine to California, might be said to have burst forth in one wild cheer — a cheer which meant more than prosaic people will believe, and more, perhaps, than uncontrollable outburst; nor can one tell how far this impulse, which he could not check, would lead him when once in full swing. Senator Wolcott [3] only expressed in the Senate what the outside millions felt; the average American just said to himself: "This is our own race; this is what *we* do; this is how *we* do it. Of course we have some difference of our own with her, and we do not intend to let even our motherland light the torch of war upon our continent; she must arbitrate all questions concerning territory here — but this is a little family matter between ourselves. It does not mean that German, Russian, and Frenchman, or any foreigners, may combine to attack our race to its destruction, without counting us in. No, sir-ee."

No combination of other races is likely to estimate at a tithe of its true value the strength of this sentiment throughout our race, or correctly to gauge how very much thicker

---

issue of independence is involved. Irish-Americans and German-Americans were anti-British; and so were the *New York World* and the *New York Times*, though not the Hearst papers. Bryan and the Democrats were pro-Boer. Official opinion, on the other hand, accorded with the Carnegie formula. John Hay (1838–1905), Secretary of State, wrote: "I hope, if it comes to blows, that England will make quick work of Uncle Paul"; and President McKinley stood off all demands for American intervention. "Uncle Paul" is of course Paul Kruger (1825–1904), president of the Transvaal.

Carnegie's real opinions on the issues were as tangled as the issues themselves. He deplored Cleveland's attitude on the Venezuelan affair. In a private letter, later than this essay, he wrote he was with the Boers heart and soul.

[3] Edward Oliver Wolcott (1848–1905), Senator from Colorado.

than water our race-blood will be found if it is ever brought to the test.

The message which President McKinley sent to Queen Victoria at her Jubilee was another evidence of race pride, and was no mere formal effusion. More men in the United Kingdom than in the United States would hesitate to compliment and praise her Majesty and sing "God Save the Queen" with enthusiasm. She is universally recognized there as the truest of the true friends of the Republic, for she stood a friend when a friend was needed.[4]

It is strange that such evidences of race unity at bottom, and of genuine, cordial friendship, should not outweigh some alleged lack of courtesy of expression in a message written by a President to his own Congress or by a Secretary of State to his own minister. Yet the *Spectator* concludes that Americans hate England, and this opinion it bases upon such trifles as these.[5]

Much stress has been laid in the discussion upon American school-books reciting the facts of American history; this is held to make every American boy and girl a hater of England. This is undoubtedly true; and the pity of it is that there is no possible escape, for American history begins with the revolt of the colonies and their struggle for the rights of

[4] Victoria and her subjects celebrated the Queen's "diamond jubilee" in 1897. She had reigned sixty years. The allusion to the friendship of the Queen is probably to her supposed preference for the North during the Civil War. Actually it was the Prince Consort, with his immense influence over the Queen, who slowed down ministerial belligerence against the Federal Union.

[5] In the Venezuela crisis Cleveland's special message to Congress on October 17, 1895, proposing to investigate the merits of claims to disputed territory and to support Venezuela's rightful claims, contained both cautious conditional clauses and cryptic utterances foreboding war. The latter made a great impression at the time. Richard Olney (1835–1917), Secretary of State, had previously dispatched a communication to the American Minister in London, directing him to find out if Britain would arbitrate the dispute and asserting, "Today the United States is practically sovereign on this continent." While the *Spectator* regarded with pleasurable anticipation the possibility that the Monroe Doctrine would make the Anglo-Saxon supreme in Latin America, it objected to the schoolmasterish and pompous tone of these American utterances.

Britons. The Republic has never had a dangerous foe except Britain, for the short campaign against Mexico made no lasting impression upon the nation. It is impossible to do otherwise than state the facts as they occurred; and even if there were added the further facts that some of the greatest and best of British statesmen opposed the attempt to tax the colonies even at that early day, and that now the kindness and consideration with which Britain reigns over her colonies gives an example to the whole world, these things would make no impression upon children. The young American must begin in our day as an intense hater of England; and this we must accept: generations will elapse before it can be greatly modified.

On the other hand, it is impossible for any American to acquire further and more detailed knowledge of the struggle for independence, of the later treatment of her colonies by Britain, and of British history and the part his race has played in the Old World, without becoming her admirer, and, should he have British blood in his veins, — which most Americans can boast, — without being very proud of his race. It is upon this foundation that we have to build our hopes of closer union between the old and the new lands. Englishmen and Hessians fighting Washington must give place in the minds of the young, as they grow older, to other pictures in which Britain and America are seen standing side by side, the two great pillars of civil and religious liberty throughout the world, and the sole members of our race. Later must come the knowledge of Shakspere, Milton, Burns, and Scott; then the political history of England, Cromwell, Sidney, Russell, Hampden, Chatham, Burke, and the many others, until the young American learns that from Britain he has derived, not only his language, but his laws, religion, and even his free institutions; and that the political institutions of the two countries are similar — one crowned, the other uncrowned, yet both republican, since in both there is government of the people, for the people, and by the people, which is the essence of republicanism. This is the chief point which influences the ardent young politician, and gives the old land at last a warm place in the heart of young America. From this time on, the race sentiment grows stronger and stronger in his heart as knowledge increases.

How different with the young Canadian and Australian, who learn with their first lessons that the rights of Britons have never been denied them, and find in Britain the most generous, most illustrious, and kindest of mothers, whom they reverence and love from the beginning. Such are the opposite results of tender and proper regard for colonies and dependencies, and of denial to them of the rights and liberties enjoyed at home.

Whether at this day seeds of future hatred or affection are being sown in the hearts of the millions to come in various parts of the world, should be the vital question for statesmen engaged in empire-building. What an expanding nation would here do "highly, that should she holily," for assuredly empire founded upon violent conquest, conspiracy, or oppression, or upon any foundation other than the sincere affection of the people embraced, can neither endure nor add to the power or glory of the conquerer, but prove a source of continual and increasing weakness and of shame.

While, in the opinion of the writer, there is no deep-seated, bitter national hatred in the United States against Britain, there is no question but there has been recently a wave of resentment and indignation at her conduct. This has sprung from two questions:

First, Ambassador Pauncefote and Secretary of State Blaine, years ago, agreed upon a settlement of the Bering Sea question,[6] and Lord Salisbury telegraphed his congratula-

---

[6] The migratory fur seals generally resorted for breeding purposes to islands over which the American government, after the purchase of Alaska, exercised jurisdiction. The American government sought to save the fur seals from extinction by domestic protective legislation. Since seals could still be taken on the high seas, these steps were inadequate. Pursuant to a treaty of 1892, negotiated by Pauncefote (1828–1902), British ambassador

tions, through Sir Julian Pauncefote, to Mr. Blaine. The two nations were jointly to police the seas and stop the barbarous destruction of the female seals. Canada appeared at Washington and demanded to see the President of the United States upon the subject. Audience was denied to the presumptuous colony; nevertheless, her action forced Lord Salisbury to disavow the treaty. No confidence here is violated, as President Harrison referred to the subject in a message to Congress. Britain was informed that if she presumed to make treaties in which Canada was interested without her consent, she would not have Canada very long. It will be remembered that Canada took precisely the same position in regard to international copyright. It is this long-desired treaty-making power which Canada has recently acquired for herself, at least as far as concerns fiscal policy, so that she need no longer even consult her suzerain. She can now appear at Washington and insist upon being received when new tariff measures are desired, having suddenly become a "free nation," according to her Prime Minister. There are surprises in store here for the indulgent mother.

The repudiation of the Bering Sea settlement aroused a deep feeling of resentment, not only among the uninformed, but among the educated class of Americans, who were and are Britain's best friends; and this has been greatly embittered by charges, commonly made in British publications, that the United States has failed to adhere to the findings of the Bering Sea tribunal. Nothing could be more baseless than such a charge. The tribunal decided that the United States were liable for certain vessels seized which carried the British flag, and payment was directed to be made, either of a stated sum by mutual agreement, or, failing this, of damages to be assessed by a commission. The United States Secretary

in Washington, and Blaine, the Bering Sea claims were referred to an international tribunal. It rejected the American claims to the exercise of a wide oceanic jurisdiction and enforced a payment to Canadian sealers for vessels illegally taken. In 1911 Russia, Japan, Britain, and the United States joined in a treaty protecting the seals in the North Pacific.

of State agreed to a fixed sum with Ambassador Pauncefote, "subject to an appropriation by Congress" — those are the very words of the agreement. When the bill was presented in Congress for an appropriation, the ex-chairman of the Committee on Foreign Relations, Mr. Hitt,[7] rose and stated that it had been discovered that the fishing-boats in question were really owned, to a great extent, by naturalized Americans. Evidence had been found that a blacksmith in San Francisco, a British subject, had been paid one hundred dollars to take title to these boats, so that the British flag could be prostituted to cover the killing of the female seals, which was unlawful under American law. Only about one fifth of the amount claimed was due to Canadians; the remainder of the claim belonged to naturalized Americans, who had broken American laws by engaging in this nefarious and unlawful traffic. Mr. Hitt asked that the right of the Government, under the award, to have these claims examined by a commission, be exercised. Congress agreed to this, and the Commission was promptly appointed and ratified by the Senate unanimously. It is now sitting, and the result, we venture to prophesy, will vindicate the contention of the United States Government — viz., that a fraud has been attempted. Yet many British papers at intervals have repeated the charge that the United States Government has been false to its obligations under the Bering Sea award. Charges of national dishonor — and such a charge involves this — always cause intense bitterness. Writers who make them falsely, as in this case, have much to answer for.

Much offense had been taken in Britain at Secretary Sherman's [8] recent message about the destruction of the seals. It is said that he has not observed the usual diplomatic reserve and courtesy. Granted; but had he not some excuse for plain speaking? It is stated that before Mr. Sherman's letter was written — to his own minister, be it remembered,

[7] Robert R. Hitt (1834–1906).
[8] John Sherman was Secretary of State, 1897–1898.

not to the British Government — Lord Salisbury had already refused a conference on the subject. After that letter Lord Salisbury thought better of it, and agreed to the conference, which is to meet immediately in Washington. How this matter is viewed in America is shown by the following cable from Washington in to-day's (September 20) newspapers:

> The officials of the State Department are not disposed to comment upon the correspondence which has been published relating to the fur-seal question between Great Britain and the United States. They say, however, that it shows that the object sought by the Government of the United States for the past three years has been attained by the agreement of Great Britain to participate in a conference to be held in October. They point out that the refusal of the British Government heretofore to consent to such a conference led to the transmission to Mr. Hay, United States ambassador in London, of Mr. Sherman's note of May 10, which was followed by Lord Salisbury's reply agreeing to hold a conference.

The whole Bering Sea business has been mismanaged by Britain — as is believed, contrary to her real wishes — simply because she could not govern her colony; the colony has governed her, as she will under Sir Wilfrid Laurier [9] and his successors hereafter, as time will show.

The second cause of the bitter hostility which has been aroused recently against Britain is her conduct upon the Venezuela question. Let us look at the facts in this case. For many years the United States Government urges upon Great Britain in the most courteous manner that the territorial dispute with Venezuela, her small republican neighbor, should be settled amicably by arbitration. The sixteen American republics having agreed to settle their disputes by arbitration,[10] it is hoped that Britain will not attempt to light

[9] Laurier (1841–1919) was the first French Canadian to become Premier.

[10] Blaine, long an advocate of inter-American co-operation, when he became Secretary of State in Harrison's administration pushed hard to establish an Inter-American Union. The first Inter-American conference assembled in Washington in 1889. The conference failed to establish a customs union, as Blaine had hoped it would, and fell short of tangible short-run accomplishments on other matters. Carnegie had been appointed as one of ten United States delegates to the conference and was partially

the torch of war upon the American continent. Mr. Gladstone's administration, through Earl Granville, foreign minister, agree to arbitrate. Lord Salisbury enters upon office, and
immediately withdraws from the agreement and refuses to
arbitrate. Repeated requests from the United States are made
without result. Finally, President Cleveland appears upon
the scene. Now, President Cleveland has one great wish —
namely, to bring about a treaty of arbitration between Great
Britain and the United States. It was my privilege to introduce the first Parliamentary committee that approached him
upon the subject. The interest he took in it was surprising,
and his intimate friends well know that the consummation
of the treaty of peace lies nearest his heart of all public questions. He is, beyond all things, a believer in the peaceful
arbitration of international disputes.

He asks Britain for a final reply. Will she, or will she not,
arbitrate this territorial dispute with Venezuela? Upon his
return to Washington, one evening, from a journey, he reads
the refusal of Lord Salisbury, and writes his message before
he retires for the night. It gives great offense in Britain, but
this is because the British people do not know that for
fifteen years the United States Government has been begging
Great Britain to arbitrate this question, and that Britain has
agreed to do so. The message is not addressed to the British
Government, but to the American Congress, and the President concludes by stating in effect that it will be the duty of
the United States Government to protect Venezuela should
Britain presume to enforce her own views of her territorial
rights.

There is no question but that the United States would have

---

instrumental in finding a way through the arbitration thicket which confused the conference debates. The conference failed to adopt arbitration as
a principle of "American international law" or to compel recourse to it.
It did make conquest in defiance of arbitration inadmissible. Nor did the
governments later ratify this feature of the conference's work. However, the
conference did succeed in establishing a permanent secretariat at Washington which developed into the Pan-American Union. Andrew Carnegie
later gave a building to house the Union's activities.

fought, or will to-day fight, any nation — even Britain — in defense of the principle of peaceful arbitration upon questions relating to the territorial rights of foreign Powers upon the American continent. Sixteen of the seventeen American republics have agreed to arbitrate their differences, and why should a European Power be permitted to make war on that continent thus dedicated to arbitration? Nations have their red rags. Every one knows that Great Britain would fight in defense of her right of asylum. Every one knows that she would defend her colonies to the extent of her power. There should be no mistake made by the British people upon this point, that the United States will not permit any European nation to attack an American State in consequence of a territorial dispute. These claims are to be settled by peaceful arbitration.

It is not alone the uninformed masses of the American people whose passions would be inflamed in support of war in defense of this principle, but the educated classes who will be found most determined in its defense; and it is upon these educated classes, for reasons stated, that Britain must depend for friends, because it is with education alone that there can come a just estimate of the past, and a knowledge of the position which the British people hold to-day in regard to colonial liberties and to international arbitration. It is deeply to be regretted that, although public sentiment in Britain forced Lord Salisbury to accept peaceful arbitration, as requested by the United States Government, nevertheless the majority of the American people cannot be successfully reached and impressed with that fact. The educated people, who follow foreign affairs, do know and appreciate that the best people in America had with them the best people in Great Britain in favor of settlement by arbitration, but to the masses it must unfortunately appear that Britain refused arbitration until forced to accept it by the United States. The truth, however, fortunately for our race, is that Lord Salisbury was forced by his own people to recede from his position. The questions which Britons might ask themselves, when seeking for some explanation of the hatred aroused in the United States recently against their country, seem to be these: Does not a nation deserve to be hated which refuses to fulfil its agreement to arbitrate a territorial dispute with a weak power? Is not irritation justified against a nation which, having agreed to a treaty settling seal fisheries, repudiates it at the dictation of a colony with which the other contracting party has nothing whatever to do?

These are the only two questions which have recently aroused the United States against Britain. In that of Venezuela, we have seen that the unfortunate hatred engendered was wholly unnecessary and caused solely by Lord Salisbury refusing to carry out the agreement of his predecessor. Arbitration asked for by the United States has now been agreed to, and the question will soon be out of the way, and, let us hope, soon forgotten, although the triumph of the principle of peaceful arbitration in this case should ever be remembered.

The other question, that of pelagic sealing, is now to be in conference again, as before asked for by the United States, but also refused by Lord Salisbury, — at first, — and in a fair way toward settlement; and let us hope it is soon also to be forgotten, always excepting that in this case also the principle of peaceful arbitration was invoked and peace preserved through the Bering Sea tribunal, even after the treaty agreed to was canceled upon Canada's demand.

With the removal of these two causes of hatred there remains not a serious cloud upon the horizon between the two branches of our race at present. The proposed general treaty of arbitration is again to be taken up under happier conditions. It is greatly to Lord Salisbury's credit that he proposed it; and in recognition of this service to the cause of peace and good will between the two nations, Americans are disposed to forgive and forget his unfortunate refusal to abide by the agreement of his country to arbitrate the

Venezuelan question. As for the denunciation of the Bering Sea treaty which had been agreed upon with Secretary Blaine, no one conversant with the circumstances holds him responsible. He could not have successfully withstood Canada, and there was nothing for him to do but to repudiate.

The treaty, which failed of ratification, obtained, let it always be remembered, within six votes of the necessary two-thirds majority of the Senate. A greater number than these six votes was thrown against it for reasons with which the treaty itself had nothing whatever to do. Into the personal and political history of the opposition to the treaty, which President McKinley declared it was our duty to pass, it would, however, be unprofitable to enter. It is impossible to obtain a two-thirds majority for any measure which becomes involved in the vortex of party politics and personal quarrels. A treaty of peace between the two branches of our race is certain to come. The pulpit, the press, the universities of the United States are its ardent supporters, President McKinley and his Cabinet being among the foremost. No other question before the nation enlists such general enlightened support from the best men of both parties. There is, therefore, no reason in the world why the two nations should not now again draw closer and closer together. On both sides of the Atlantic each should be careful hereafter to give to the other no just cause of offense, and it may be taken as true that, Briton and American being of the same race, what would be offensive to the one would be equally so to the other.

Both Briton and American can dwell with the greatest satisfaction upon this fact, which recent events have conclusively proven, that there is in each country so powerful an element favoring peace within the race that no Government, however strong, either in the old land or in the new, can decline peaceful arbitration, when offered by the other, as the Christian substitute for the brutal test of war. No small compensation this, even for the estrangement which has arisen over two questions, but which is now rapidly passing away, leaving fortunately unimpaired in the Republic that element which may be trusted to determine international action in a crisis — pride of race, a force lying too deep in the national heart to be revealed upon calm seas, but which, under the recent swing of the tempest, bared its great head high enough above the surge to be seen and noted of all men — a dangerous rock upon a fatal shore for other races in combination to strike against, if ever they attempt to sail that unsailed sea.

· XII ·

Imperial Federation [1]

THE time seems opportune for acting upon the suggestion
of the editor of this review, that I should elaborate an idea
expressed in a previous article touching the unity of the
English-speaking race, and the relations which the parts
thereof are to bear to each other; for the "Imperial Federation" and the "United Empire Trade League" are prominently
upon the stage, and the monthly magazines and daily press
freely discuss the subject. Each of the two societies named
has recently been granted an interview with the Prime Minister, and each has been advised by him in turn to take the
first forward step and furnish at least rough outlines of its

---

[1] From the *Nineteenth Century*, XXX (September 1891), 490–508. A
renewed interest in colonies and the nature of their relationship with the
mother country arose in the eighties. The movement has often been called
the "new imperialism"; in England it took the form of a difference of
opinion and sentiment between "Little Englanders" and the advocates of a
"Forward" movement. In 1884 the Imperial Federation League brought
together politicians, journalists, and intellectuals, like Sir John Robert Seeley
(1834–1895), James Bryce (1838–1922), and Froude, on a vague platform
advocating closer imperial ties. While the League had a concrete accom-
plishment in the calling of the First Colonial Conference in 1887 at the
time of Victoria's golden jubilee, it was always riven by schisms over matters
of free trade and preferential tariffs within the Empire. Either of these
suggested programs involved a modification of the English traditional
policy of free trade. The passage of the McKinley Tariff Act of 1890 by the
United States, with its high rates and proffer of reciprocity between the
United States and certain raw-material-producing nations, so alarmed more
extreme English imperialists that they formed in 1891 the United Empire
Trade League. Its founder and secretary announced: "The whole object of
empire is commerce and the extension of commercial relations." Neither
manifestoes nor zeal could budge politicians in places of responsibility, including Salisbury, or still quarrels within the Imperial Federation League.
It dissolved in 1894; the United Empire Trade League continued.

plans. It is a fact of much significance that so antagonistic are the views held by these two organizations that the second to be heard by Lord Salisbury thought necessary, previous to its interview, to request that he should not commit himself to the ideas of the first — evidence of an anxiety which seems to have been wholly unnecessary, as it is evident from Lord Salisbury's reply that neither of the societies, so far, has been able to lay before him anything requiring consideration. He has wisely called for a bill of particulars, having had enough of glittering generalities. This is a challenge which admits of no denial if these societies are to justify their continued existence. If they cannot formulate a plan, surely they will retire.

Before the permanent relations of the parts of the race to each other can be properly considered, however, we must pay some attention to the two phases of the "federation idea" represented by them.

The United Empire Trade League attends strictly to business; there is no sentiment about it — trade all over, and nothing but trade. We have, therefore, only to consider, as far as it is concerned, whether Britain and her colonies would make good bargains by banding together against the outside world, and giving to each other more favorable terms than to outsiders. Reduced to this, it becomes simply a matter of figures. The Zollverein idea is here, but the Kriegsverein absent.[2] Let us, therefore, first consider how Britain would fare under the proposed new departure. She exports about £250,000,000 of her products yearly. Of these, the English-speaking self-governing colonies take £31,000,000, or one eighth; India takes about the same amount; all the other British possessions £20,000,000; in all, about £82,000,-000, leaving fully double that amount taken by other countries. It is proposed to discriminate against the customers

---

[2] In the first part of the nineteenth century various German states under the leadership of Prussia formed the customs union known as the Zollverein. Kriegsverein, to employ the Carnegie vernacular, went beyond trade to joint action in time of war.

who consume £166,000,000 in favor of those who consume half that amount. With British imports it is just the same, for in 1889 imports and exports to colonies, etc., were only £187,000,000 out of a total of £554,000,000 — one third to the dependencies against two thirds to the foreigners. If there were a prospect of the former trade growing more rapidly than the other, it might be held that the future would justify the sacrifice, but there is nothing to encourage this view; on the contrary, colonial and Indian trade both tend to decline, while that with foreign nations increases. The reason is clear; the older nations have developed their resources, and trade with them is now practically upon its final basis; the colonies have only recently begun to supply their own wants, and are yet to extend their capacity greatly in this direction. It is scarcely to be expected that with double their present population their demands upon Britain will be much increased. Indeed, the present tendency to decline may continue for a time.

The important question is, What response would the nations of the world make to a declaration of industrial war against them? Had Britain and her colonies remained a compact free-trade Empire, like the forty-four States of the Republic, which furnish the world with the best proof of the blessings of free trade, other nations would have no right to object. It is quite a different matter, however, if, when their trade has been established and business built upon the other basis, change and disaster should now be visited upon them. A change in the policy of Britain toward other nations, I submit, must now be followed by a change of their policy toward Britain. Discrimination must produce discrimination. The Republic of the United States, for instance, is Britain's greatest customer, taking more of British products than all the English-speaking colonies combined, and more and more every year, while the trade with the colonies is, at best, stationary, notwithstanding their increase of population. It has slightly declined during the past five years. What the

Republic would do if she were discriminated against needs no guess, for she has recently lodged in the President power to go so far as to prohibit entirely the products of any country that does so.[3] Britain is called upon to justify her discrimination against American cattle, for instance, and nothing is surer than that the American people will have to be entirely satisfied that there is good cause for it, or the President will be forced by public sentiment to exercise this power, conservative, patient, and most peace-loving though he be. There would not be two parties upon this issue.

How about Germany? She takes from Britain every year products to the amount of about £18,000,000, twice that taken by the whole of British North America, and not far from that taken by the whole of Australasia (£22,000,000). She sends Britain about £3,000,000 per year of flour and cereals, of butter and eggs £1,500,000, of timber £1,500,000. What is to be the answer of the irrepressible Emperor if the products of his country are discriminated against in favor of the food products and timber of Canada and Australia? Italy, again, takes about as much of British products as the whole of British North America, £7,000,000, and she finds here each year a market to the extent of £3,000,000 for her hemp, fruits, etc. The Argentine Republic takes from £10,-000,000 to £11,000,000 per annum from Britain; the whole of British North America only £8,000,000. What is to be the return shot fired by her if her mutton, wool, and grain which

[3] Carnegie is manipulating a "paper dragon." The McKinley Tariff of 1890 threatened a prohibition of trade as a means of securing reciprocity; the device was directed against certain products and certain nations, for example Latin America, rather than against Great Britain. The trade in fresh beef to Great Britain took the form of exports of live animals and, after the application of refrigeration to transportation, of chilled or frozen meat. Both of these trades threatened beef producers in Great Britain, but their powerful interest was never able to induce the government to embargo or discriminate by tariff against the American product. Occasionally the British government, alarmed by Texas fever or the "lung plague," pleuropneumonia, clapped on quarantines or enforced them more strictly. A minor dust-up on this score occurred in 1891. In spite of such episodes the fresh beef trade to Great Britain expanded enormously from the seventies on.

she sends here are to be discriminated against? But why continue the list? It is the same story everywhere.

Britain has the foreign trade of all her colonies almost exclusively already, except that of Canada, of which she has nearly one half, the United States possessing rather more. All the other colonies deal with foreign nations only to the extent of from five to ten per cent for articles which Britain does not produce. The parent-land, therefore, has nothing to gain by any change in fiscal relations between herself and the colonies; her colonial trade, except perhaps to a small extent with Canada, could not be increased thereby. Why, then, should she jeopardize the control of the markets of the world to the extent of two thirds of her total exports, for nothing? The fabled dog which dropped the bird from his mouth had for excuse that its shadow in the stream seemed infinitely larger. The Imperial Trade League is not so excusable. It would sacrifice a real turkey in hand for nothing in the bush. This wondrous little island is dependent upon the world for two thirds of its food-supply; equally dependent upon the markets of the world for the sale of its products. There never was so great a people so artificially maintained. What the race has accomplished here under these conditions dwarfs the triumphs of all other races; it is marvelous, and if it were not before our eyes, it would be held impossible that a nation so placed could have yet led the world. One asks instinctively what such a breed of men will do when they control continents possessed of unbounded supplies of agricultural and mineral resources combined; but that she, being so placed, should be counseled by a body of able men to inaugurate an industrial war against the world seems something not to be accounted for by any process of reason. Russia, the Argentine or the Brazilian Republic, with its ports blockaded for ten years, would suffer only more or less inconvenience. The United States would emerge from such an embargo stronger and more independent of the world than before. Close the ports of this island for a year, and her people would suffer for food. Britain's house is a whole Crystal Palace — she of all nations should be the last to begin stone-throwing.

From something in the national character, but much more in the part she has had to play in the world, Britain has excited the envy, jealousy, and ill will of some of the most powerful nations; but I do not believe that my native land has an enemy so bitter as to wish her to plunge into an industrial war which would be so cruelly fatal to her, for even the worst foe must feel that the human race owes an incalculable debt to Britain. It would be a different matter if the imposition of protective duties were proposed bearing equally upon the products of all other countries, for this is a matter for each nation to settle for itself, and other nations could take no offense if Britain decided to reimpose such duties. This would be no declaration of industrial war against other nations, but only a matter of home policy. There is no vital objection to this being tried; although I am certain that free trade is Britain's only policy as I am a thorough disciple of John Stuart Mill — and, I am pleased to add, of his worthy successor, Professor Marshall [4] — in believing that the countries which have the necessary resources within themselves do well to encourage the starting of industries by protecting them for a time against the competition of those firmly rooted in other lands, always, however, with the view of ultimately obtaining a surer and cheaper source of supply within themselves. But the question for Britain is this: Given a nation with a thoroughly equipped manufacturing system producing more than its own people can consume, and which, on the other hand, is dependent for its food-supply upon other nations, what is its policy? The answer seems clear: Peace and free trade with all the world. Cobden and Bright [5] were right for Britain, and only wrong in assuming, in their enthusiasm, that what was wise

[4] Alfred Marshall (1842–1924), British economist.
[5] Richard Cobden (1804–1865); John Bright (1811–1889).

for an old country producing more articles than it could consume was necessarily wise for every country, including those which had diversified home industries yet to establish. Mill and Marshall are right for new countries, always provided such have within themselves the necessary resources and adequate market to eventually furnish the articles at less cost to the consumer than would have to be paid if dependent upon a foreign supply. Thus the United States has succeeded by protection in getting the millions of square feet of plate-glass she uses per annum at less cost than a similar article costs in Europe. She often has her steel rails at less than these could be imported for free of duty. She has failed, however, to produce cheaply her supply of sugar by protection. Hence she wisely abandons the attempt, and makes foreign sugar free. Now, because Britain has not the requisite territory to increase greatly her food-supply, any tax imposed upon food must be permanent. The doctrine of Mill does not, therefore, apply, for protection, to be wise, must always be in the nature of only a temporary shielding of new plants until they take root. It will surprise many if Britain ever imposes a permanent tax upon the food of her thirty-eight millions of people, with no possible hope of ever increasing the supply, and thereby reducing the cost, and thus ultimately rendering the tax unnecessary. A tax for a short period that fosters and increases production, and a tax for all time which cannot increase production, are different things.

But if, in the near future, Britain decides to try the old system of protection again, no irremediable injury need ensue, for results will soon prove that free trade is for her the very breath of her nostrils, and she may be able successfully to return to it because she will not have outraged the feelings and incurred the hostility of her former best customers. All will have been treated alike, and therefore none will have reason to complain; although it is always to be remembered that trade once diverted is most difficult to regain.

The loss owing to this will not be small. While, therefore, it is open to Britain to try "protection," and pay the cost of the experiment, and retrace her steps, he is a bold man who ventures to place an estimate upon the permanent loss to his country which is surely involved in entering upon the "Empire trade" crusade.

Turning from the British and the foreigners' points of view in regard to the proposed industrial crusade against the world, the reply of the colonies to an invitation to join it has yet to be considered.

Let us begin with Canada, the greatest of these. As already stated, she finds a market for more of her products in the neighboring Republic than in the parent-land. She also finds it to her advantage to purchase more from the former than from the latter. During the winter months she is indebted to the courtesy of the Republic for regular communication with the outside world; her steamships land at Portland in Maine, and her traffic, in bond, and her people travel through American territory to reach Quebec or Montreal. Her boasted east-and-west railway system would scarcely pay expenses — it certainly would yield no returns — except that the Republic generously permits it to connect with American railways and compete with them upon equal terms for the traffic to and from Chicago and the great West to Boston, New York, and the East, and to transport foreign goods in bond to Chicago and the West. The Canadian Pacific traverses the entire width of the State of Maine. All the ships of Canada receive rights in American ports which are denied to American fishing-vessels in Canadian ports. Any day the Republic thinks proper to resent the acts of her saucy little neighbor, which have recently been annoying, she can practically "bottle up" Canada without giving any cause of complaint from an international point of view. She has simply to withhold privileges now generously granted. It need not be feared that so strong and forbearing a nation will act tyrannously to one so completely in her power. The Republic has always been the kindest and most neighborly of neighbors to all her less powerful sisters; *but the power is there,* and this being so, I should like to ask our United Empire Trade League friends what answer Canada would be likely to make to their proposition to discriminate in favor of Britain as against the Republic. Canada may yet, in justice to herself, be compelled to do just the reverse. There is a large party in Canada in favor of such a step. An invitation from Britain to enter upon the policy of discrimination would require Canada to consider for her own interests in whose favor the discrimination should be. The idea suggested by the League may thus return to plague the inventor. Truly our friends of the Trade League have found and are brandishing a dangerous weapon.

With the Australasian colonies the case is different. These have no overshadowing giant alongside; but there is another element there which I submit is equally potent. New South Wales, the largest of the group, imports £23,000,000; exports just about the same. Her total trade with Great Britain, exports and imports, is only one third of this — something over £15,000,000. Victoria, the other great colony, imports and exports £37,500,000; Britain has of these between £12,-000,000 and £13,000,000 — just about one third, as in the case of New South Wales.

But Britain need not be jealous in regard to the remainder; for, as before stated, with the exception of from five to ten per cent of the total, which she cannot supply, she has it all. So far has Australasia advanced under the policy of encouraging home manufactures that the various colonies are able to supply the wants of one another to the extent of about two thirds of their total requirements — a most encouraging state of affairs, as promising the creation of a mighty nation of English-speaking people in the near future. Does any member of our "Fair Trade League" believe that a proposition would be entertained for a moment to lower duties upon articles from Britain, and hence to injure or destroy the manufactures of their sister colonies? Has any indication been seen of a desire upon the part of any of these colonies to abandon the high aim each has set before itself of becoming a great power with diversified industries, capable of supplying its own necessary wants? The members of the League should endeavor to place themselves in the position of Canada and of Australia, and judge in the case of Canada what its reply to their idea *must* be, and in the case of Australia what it *would* be. The officials of that society are, no doubt, preparing their answer to the challenge given by the Prime Minister, and it is to be hoped that it will deal with the points here suggested.

Turning now to the Imperial Federation League, we find no business whatever in its program; no considerations of trade; bargains are not thought of; sentiment reigns supreme. Still, it is not so grandly sentimental as it was. A painful falling away is noted. In its early days it pleased many to note that, in their praiseworthy desire for federation, the majority of the English-speaking race in the Republic was never forgotten; but we find no trace of this in the recent proceedings; even my friend Mr. Bolton seems to have abandoned the great idea which first roused his enthusiasm, and which still stirs mine. In his article in the July number of this review he regretfully says:

> If it may not be given to us to realize that grand idea, the confederation of *all* the nations which have sprung from the race nurtured in these isles, should we not at least use all our energies to promote the union and political consolidation of the Greater Britain which still owns one flag and acknowledges one sovereign? [6]

We have not yet heard from Lord Rosebery, the president, for reasons which call forth for him the deepest sympathy of all.[7] It is still possible we shall find, in the first address he

[6] S. B. Bolton, "Sir John Macdonald on Imperial Federation," *Nineteenth Century*, XXX (July 1891), 159–160.

[7] Rosebery was one of the charter members of the Imperial Federation League and a member of its executive body. Compelled to assume political responsibilities, he stood against extremists in the League. He thought it

delivers upon the subject, that his hopes of the union of the entire race may still be brighter than those expressed by officials who have spoken for the Federation in his absence. For the present, I take it, we must assume that, like the Trade League, it seeks no longer harmony and coöperation among the various parts of the race. It stands now as a body whose effort is to combine only the minority of the English-speaking race in a solid phalanx, leaving out the majority. While, in the case of the first society, it was necessary to go into particulars, in that of the latter it seems only necessary to examine its aim as recently presented.

It is deemed possible to create a solid empire, under one head, of parts of the English-speaking race, one the mother country, another in Canada, the third in Australia, each with different environments and totally different problems to solve; and one of the three parts under wholly different institutions from the other two, the latter being democracies without a trace of hereditary privilege, aristocracy, church and state, or entails of the soil, and the very air breathed there instilling ideas of political equality in the citizen. It is notable that this hope is chiefly confined to the parent-land, and to those born here who have played great parts till now in the colonies. Such men as Sir John A. Macdonald, Sir Henry Parkes, Sir Samuel Griffith, and others,[8] are not colonists but natives of Britain, and must ever reverence and love her. But the population of Australasia is already nearly three native to one British-born. In Canada, in 1881, more than four fifths were native-born, and every year the percentage of British-born grows less and less. Not one of five thousand native-born Canadians, nor of ten thousand born Australians, has ever seen or ever can see Britain, which to

---

should be "educational" and encourage colonial and imperial conferences, but he could not fit imperial preference into his program.

[8] Sir John A. Macdonald (1815–1891) was frequently after 1857 a Conservative prime minister of Canada; Sir Henry Parkes (1815–1896) after 1872 served often as prime minister of New South Wales; and Sir Samuel W. Griffith (1845–1920) was prime minister of Queensland.

the masses is only a name — no doubt a name which they can never mention without pride and gratitude, but still only a name, not a country; and a country every man worthy of the name of man will have and worship.

The native-born Australian is Australian first and last; the native-born Canadian the same. The public ear of my native land is sadly led astray about the feeling of her colonies, because she hears only the voices of her own people, native-born Britons, or a few rich visitors speaking in the name of the colonies. It is these who principally visit the old home, crossing the seas, drawn hither by longings, as pilgrims to their Mecca. The masses of the people in the colonies permit and even encourage upon the part of these native-born Britons the expression of the tenderest sentiments toward their native land; for they know that men are not worthy of the confidence and respect of the communities in which they dwell if they fail in affection for the land which gave them birth, and that the colonist who does not love his native land is not likely to prove much of an acquisition to his adopted one. But it will save much disappointment if the people at home can be made to understand and believe that the following truly represents the sentiments of ninety-nine out of every hundred native-born Canadians and Australians. I quote the words of the Premier of the important province of Quebec, Mr. Mercier,[9] who, being asked, whether he was opposed to federation, replied:

Yes, I am. I regard that policy as treason to Canada. Imperial federation means that Canada must join Britain in her wars throughout the world, and must weigh the interest of the whole Empire before looking to her own. A tie that would thus subject Canada completely to European dominion would be a most unnatural one, and there are not fifty men in the province of Quebec who are favorable to so unpatriotic a policy. The time has, in fact, come to consider in a very peaceful yet very serious way the right of European Powers to govern people living on the continent of America, whose interests and general tendencies, commercial or other, are in certain respects opposed to those of the people of Europe. Accordingly, instead of being disposed

[9] Honoré Mercier (1840–1894), premier and attorney-general (1887).

to strengthen the ties at present existing between Britain and Canada, we are, in fact, looking forward with some anxiety to the time when we shall ask for our independence. We shall request it with all due respect to Great Britain, and without any ill feeling toward her people, just as a young man of full age, on leaving his father's home, may sometimes do it with reluctance, but with the proud feeling that he, too, is called upon to take a free and independent share in life. What I say about the province of Quebec may, I believe, be said of the inhabitants of all the other provinces.

It surely cannot have failed to attract the attention of the members of the Imperial Federation League that even Sir John Macdonald, a native-born Briton, was forced, certainly much against his will, to announce that Canada was no longer to be dependent, but the ally, of Briton, and even going so far only enabled him to escape defeat by a greatly reduced majority.

In future, England would be the center, surrounded and *sustained by an alliance*, not only with Canada, but with Australia and all her other possessions; and there would thus be formed an immense confederation of freemen — the greatest confederacy of civilized and intelligent men that ever had an existence on the face of the globe.

Alliances are made between independent nations. Sir John must also have had in mind the Republic, for this is necessary to make the greatest confederacy of intelligent and civilized men. A confederacy of all others of our race would be much smaller than the United States alone.

Sir John asserted the independence of Canada to the fullest extent when he recently commanded Lord Salisbury to tear up a treaty which had been agreed upon by Sir Julian Pauncefote and Secretary Blaine, with Lord Salisbury's cordial approval, which the British Government had presumed to make without consulting Canada. The recent protest of Newfoundland is another case in point.[10] The public is informed that the difficulty has been compromised, but the

---

[10] On the Pauncefote-Blaine treaty see Essay XI, note 6. In 1890 and again in April 1891 Newfoundland sent deputations to London to protest against the principle and arrangement by which France and England arrived at a modus vivendi involving the fishing industry in the colony.

compromise has necessarily been all on one side. The form of arbitration with France is to be adhered to; but after this has been duly performed, Newfoundland's demands will be complied with. Any treaty rights France is found to possess are to be purchased. There was no other course open to Britain. She cannot govern her colonies; for they are full grown and almost of age and now dictate to her. They must be provided with homes of their own speedily if the filial tie is to be preserved.

The Imperial Federation has only to grapple with the initial difficulty to be overthrown, which is this: the native-born Australian wants at maturity a country of his own to live for, fight for, and, if necessary, to die for; the native-born Canadian wants the same. The native-born Briton has this, the American, German, Frenchman. Why not the people of Canada and Australia? The native-born colonist has not the slightest idea of permitting the parent-land, distant thousands of miles, or any land, to have anything to say in or to his own country. That any of their statesmen should favor the proposition that the representatives of his country should be sent across seas to be swamped in a Parliament in London, and the destinies of his country subjected to the votes of strangers, would probably be considered by the medical faculty of the colony as a *prima facie* proof of mental aberration; his incarceration in a lunatic asylum would be imminent. To endeavor to satisfy this commendable and patriotic devotion to the idea of country by offering them part of a land thousands of miles away, which they can never see, is futile. They might as well be asked to consider themselves citizens of the moon, and so to rest and be thankful. These ambitious, enterprising peoples with British blood in their veins are not crying for the moon. There is no rest for such movements; once started, national aspirations are not to be quenched. The sooner these are gratified, the better for all.

What lesson has the past to teach us upon this point?

Spain had great colonies upon the American continent: where are these now? Seventeen republics occupy Central and South America. Five of these have prepared plans for federating. Portugal had a magnificent empire, which is now with the Brazilian Republic. Britain had a colony. It has passed from its mother's apron-strings and set up for itself, and now the majority of all our races are gathered under its republican flag. What is there in the position of Britain's relation to Australia and Canada that justifies the belief that any different result is possible with them? I know of none; on the contrary, all that I know of the sentiment of the people in the colonies satisfies me that there exists this healthy growth toward national life. They would be unworthy of their sires if they did not possess it. It was not a question of taxes that produced the independence of the United States; this was the incident only which precipitated what was bound to come a few years sooner or later, independent of any possible home policy. Franklin and Adams had no idea of separating from the mother-land when they led in the refusal to be taxed from Westminster; but they soon found themselves compelled by a public sentiment, until then latent, to advance to independence. Australasia has begun the natural movement toward change in her relations to the old home. Her leaders — still native-born Britons chiefly — kindly propose that Britain may still be allowed to send an ornamental Governor-General. The tie will be slight, but it is now seen, especially in the most important of the colonies, New South Wales, that, as in the case of America, the British-born leaders may be pushed by the native-born Australians into a movement for complete independence. If it does not evolve now it must do so later, for the "Speaker" (July 18) truly says: "It is the fading class of the home-born which keeps alive the traditions and sentiment of the English connection. Every five minutes throughout Australasia an Imperialist dies; every four minutes a Republican is born."

The constant reader of the *Spectator* knows that journal to be equally well informed, and the *Times* has more than once recently shown that it is not ignorant of the true state of colonial affairs. But these able organs of public opinion seem to be almost alone.

It is of the utmost importance that the people of Britain should promptly realize her true relation to the colonies, which is just this: she is the motherland, and no nation has ever been blessed with a family so numerous, enterprising, and creditable. The only part open to her is to play the mother, and, as her children grow beyond the need of her fostering care, to endeavor to inculcate in them the ambition to go forth and manage for themselves. She should doubt the blood in any weakling content to remain under her protection when the age of manhood comes. True, few departures from the old home are unaccompanied by tears, but, after all, tears of affection, of joy, in the happiness of the child who starts in life for himself. There are only two modes that can be pursued: either the colonies will leave the parent nest with the parent's blessing, carrying in their hearts undying love and reverence for her to whom they owe all, or the parting will be made under conditions which must necessarily bring both parent and child lifelong bitterness and lifelong sorrow. The American boy is forever to be in youth the hater of the old home, for in his early years he is fed with stories of the Revolution — of the struggles and sufferings of Washington and his patriot army, of the desire of his native land for independence, and of the mistaken efforts of Britain to hold it in subjection.

This early impression of Britain as the oppressor of his country is not easily removed. It is a thousand pities that the majority of our race is to learn first that the parent-land was their country's only foe. Britain can choose whether Australia and Canada and her other colonies, as they grow to maturity, can set up for themselves with every feeling of filial devotion toward her, or whether every child born

in these lands is to be born to regard Britain as the American
child must. There is no other alternative, and I beseech our
friends of the Imperial Federation to pause ere they involve
their country and her children in the disappointment, humiliation, and antagonism which must come if a serious
effort be made to check the development and independent
existence of the colonies, for independence they must and
will seek by virtue of the blood that is in them, and obtain,
even by force if necessary. They were not true Britons else.

Lord Salisbury has recently said that if Home Rule were
granted to Ireland, other portions of the Empire might be
"wrenched from the power of the Queen." As he could not
mean that there was a danger of foreign nations attempting
to "wrench" any of the colonies, he must have meant that
the colonies would "wrench" themselves away. Nothing
should be left undone to prevent such "wrenches" from coming. To encourage the colonies to follow the example of
their mother-land and become nations themselves is the
only way to prevent such a "wrench" as took place between
the parent and the Republic. I should prevent all feeling of
"wrenching" upon one side or the other by having the parent-
land start her children in life in due course, as her Majesty
starts her children. With rare wisdom, she favors early mar-
riages. Britain, as a nation, should imitate the example of
her wise Queen, and start her colonies for themselves in
homes of their own as soon as they become restless under
the old roof-tree, with a God-speed, and a fond, proud
mother's blessing.

It may be said that the destiny indicated for the parent-
land is one unworthy of her past. I cannot share such a
thought. The world is still young. As each child of Britain
reaches proper growth and departs, another child will be
born to her. No limit can be set to this stage of the world's
development, no time fixed when the mother will not have
quite enough of a family to care for. Generations must pass
before the two hundred and eighty millions of India are

ready to federate into a great nation and govern themselves, while Africa was born to her only yesterday. Besides this, the United Kingdom, even of itself, and without colonies, would remain one of the principal nations. Her colonies weaken her powers in war, and confer no advantages upon her in peace. Her population about equals that of France, and will, I believe, eventually equal that of Germany, probably exceed it, leaving only Russia more populous in Europe. Her store of minerals surpasses all others except the United States; she has at her foot the markets of the world for the chief manufactured articles, for, whatever may be said of foreign competition, it cannot possibly amount to much in the future: her navy can control the seas. One of the purest fallacies is that trade follows the flag. Trade follows the lowest price current. If a dealer in any colony wished to buy Union Jacks, he would order them from Britain's worst foe if he could save a sixpence. Trade knows no flag. Britain's greatest customer is the American Republic; and, as we have seen, Germany and France, with a tithe of the population, consume as much as India of British products, and more than all the Australian and Canadian colonies combined. Canada trades more with the Republic than with Britain. The independence of the colonies will not lessen British trade with them, but increase it, because independence will stir their energies and make them much more enterprising. Hence wealth will be produced faster, and the market for fine articles from Britain be correspondingly increased. This is proved by the result of American independence.

With full appreciation of the patriotic sentiment which pervades the two leagues, I cannot refrain from asking their members to consider whether they are not working in the wrong direction, and aiding to thwart and not to promote the true mission of their country in the future. The position which Britain should aim to occupy is no less than the "headship of the race," as the parent of all. Now, even if the various parts of the race in the Empire could be federated under one sovereign — of which there is as little likelihood as that the Republic could be induced to enter — and thus the whole aim of the Federation League be accomplished, what then? Eleven millions of people will have been confederated with her — only this and nothing more — and Britain then would only be first in the smaller division of the race. It would not be such a prodigious gain for her, after all. We should have "Hamlet" with Hamlet left out. Few persons have a correct knowledge of the numbers and increase of the various parts of our race. During the past ten years the United States added to its numbers more than the total present number of English-speaking people in all other parts of the world, outside of the United Kingdom. Her increase was 12,500,000. The increase of the United Kingdom and all her English-speaking colonies was not one half as great — about 5,000,000. Britain added slightly more than 3,000,000; Canada only 500,000, a rate of increase not greater than that of Britain; New South Wales (last eight years) only 471,000; Victoria (last nine years) 710,984; all other colonies only trifling numbers. Thus, if we place the Republic in one scale, and all the other parts of the race in the other, the yearly increase in the first scale would more than double that in the second. Even if the United States increase is to be much less rapid than it has been hitherto, yet the child is born who will see more than 400,000,000 under her sway. No possible increase of the race can be looked for in all the world combined comparable to this. Green [11] truly says that its "future home is to be found along the banks of the Hudson and the Mississippi." Why should the parent-land, then, be counseled by the Imperial League to endeavor to form closer ties with her other children than with her eldest born, who must dwarf all the rest of the family together? What kind of federation is that which leaves the Republic out? There is no obstacle to forming any tie with the Republic that can possibly be formed with

[11] John Richard Green (1837–1883), British historian.

the commonwealth of Australia or the Dominion of Canada, for, just as soon as these are asked to forego their inborn desire for independence similar to that of the United States, their answer will settle the question, if, indeed, the League ever requires to go so far as to ask for Imperial Federation and be refused. It should not be necessary for it to place the parent-land in a position so humiliating, for that its idea is impracticable can be learned in every quarter without exposing itself to the inevitable and wholly unnecessary rebuff.

If the United Empire Trade League ever succeeds in getting the government to call a conference of the colonies, to meet in London, as it proposes, to consider its aim, the end of that idea also will have arrived, for few colonial governments could survive the support of a bill appointing delegates even to consider the question of discriminating against other nations in favor of Britain. But, as in the case of the Imperial Federation League, so the United Empire Trade League should be able to satisfy itself, before asking a conference only to be refused, that there is no possibility of obtaining the coöperation of any English-speaking community.

Mistaken, impracticable, and pernicious, however, though the aims of these two societies be, yet it is to their membership that we can best look for efforts in the right direction for such coöperation of the entire race as it is possible to effect; for their hearts are in the right place, and their heads can easily be brought to the favorable consideration of an idea which postulates for their country a much higher position, a much grander mission, than that which they have set themselves to secure — a position which will keep her in the rightful attitude of parent toward the entire race which has sprung from her.

I respectfully ask the patriotic, sympathetic, and enterprising men of these leagues to permit me to submit for their consideration a summary of the ideas which have forced themselves upon me from a study of the question, made with an earnest desire to secure, first, the unity of our race, and through that, for it, the mastery of the world, for the good of the world.

First. The great aim of the federationists should be to draw together the masses of all English-speaking countries, and to make them feel that they are really members of the same undivided race, and share its triumphs; that all English-speaking men are brothers who should rejoice in one another's prosperity and be proud of one another's achievements. The little faults or shortcomings of the other members should be overlooked, and all should dwell upon what is best in each, for, as members of the same race, what disgraces one necessarily reflects upon the entire family. Impossible Imperial Federation and Empire Trade League should give place to Race Alliance, and so embrace all in one common bond, the only test being

> If Shakspere's tongue be spoken there,
> And songs of Burns are in the air.

Pursuance of this policy during our generation will do much to lay the foundation for a true federation of the whole race, as far as it is possible to combine sovereign powers; and how far that is possible is for future generations, not for this, to learn. That it is possible to a degree, we of to-day already see. Once earnestly kept in view and labored for, and lower aims excluded, it is probable that things now deemed impossible dreams may prove easy of getting. Indeed, the "Parliament of Man" itself is only a question of time in the mind of the evolutionist who sees no bounds to the advance of man in the line of brotherhood. If we may not look into the future and tell what germ is to grow, we can at least do our duty in the present, and cultivate the soil and plant the germ which *ought* to grow among the members of the same race, leaving to posterity the duty of nurturing the precious seed, and, we trust, the fruition of our hopes.

Second. The parent-land should be urged to encourage her colonies, as an able mother encourages her sons, to go forth at maturity and play the part of men — loving and reverencing her, but independent. The idea of federation among colonies should also be encouraged; for no greater calamity could happen than that the various English-speaking communities should be divided into small nations, jealous of one another. The sad condition of Europe to-day, an armed camp, contrasted with that of the United States, which is ere long to contain an English-speaking population as great as the whole of Europe, without any necessity for a standing army, should be continually in mind and proclaimed. The Australian colonies do not require the lesson. These are wise and will federate, and, as one irresistible power, keep the peace and rule that quarter of the globe without armies, for they, like the Republic, can have no neighboring foe; but the union of England and Scotland should be held up to Canada and the United States. I should not like to think that I ever had said or ever should say a word that would tend to perpetuate upon the American continent two divisions of the race, or to feel that I had not exerted myself to produce union. The mother-land can do much by reminding Canada of her own union with Scotland, and the happy results which flow from it. The present unfortunate division of the race in America, so fraught with danger, is Britain's work; the duty upon her to correct the evil is imperative. Nor is she unequal to the task, for she has done things that other nations cannot parallel. The cession of the Ionian Islands to classic Greece, the recent cession of Helgoland to Germany, show her capable of generous, even sublime, action.[12] She can rise at times to great heights and

[12] In 1864 the Ionian Islands, the principal of which is Corfu, a British protectorate, were formally ceded to the Kingdom of Greece. The British seized Heligoland (Helgoland) in 1807 from the Danes but in 1890 ceded the island to Germany.

teach nations magnanimity. All she has done of this nature combined were but little in comparison with the uniting of the two children whom her policy separated a century ago. She should tell Canada that whenever it becomes, as it is becoming, a question of separate independent existence, or of union with the other division of the race, a mother's blessing would attend her union with the Republic. With the appalling condition of Europe before us, it would be criminal for a few millions of people to create a separate government instead of becoming part of a great mass of their own race which joins them, especially since the federal system gives each part the control of all its internal affairs, and has proved that the freest government of the parts produces the strongest government of the whole. The most eminent man in Canada to-day is certainly Goldwin Smith.[13] He remains an Englishman with allegiance unimpaired, yet he tells Britain that her position upon the American continent is the barrier to sympathetic union with her great child, the Republic. He is right.

Third. Much is done to prevent harmony in the race by the position that has until recently been held tenaciously by the parent-land in regard to the fiscal policy which every colony has found it best to pursue. Seeing that strictly agricultural communities can never amount to much under present conditions, it should be regarded as a natural and patriotic desire upon the part of Canadians and Australians to give their countries diversified industries, that the various aptitudes of the people may find scope. Britain need have no fear about her trade. Indeed, it is very doubtful if, with all her resources developed to the utmost, she can long continue to meet the demands for her products which must be made upon her, no matter what tariffs may be adopted. Where the iron and steel can be had to supply the coming wants of the

---

[13] British historian and publicist (1823–1910), author of *Canada and the Canadian Question* (1891). From 1868–1871 he was a professor at Cornell. He was an ardent spokesman for Anglo-Saxon union and supremacy.

world is already troubling Bell, Atkinson, Hewitt, and other high authorities.[14] A writer in the *Times* (July 12), Mr. Harvey, one of the most prominent citizens of Newfoundland and a loyal subject, states this point admirably, and asks that it "be granted by the majority of the people of England and Scotland that a man may doubt the infallibility of the doctrine of free trade under all circumstances, and not be considered a fool or worse." Britain is quite right in adopting free trade for herself, but every colonist visiting the old home should not be attacked and denounced, I might even say abused, because he ventures to think his new country requires a different system for a time.

Fourth. The process of assimilating the political institutions of all English-speaking countries should be continued, for it should never be forgotten by true federationists that different political conditions form a great barrier to close sympathetic union. No Parliament since that which passed the Reform Bill deserves greater thanks than the present one in this respect. It has done much to bring Britain's institutions in accord with the democratic standard of all the other English-speaking nations. County councils, and especially free education, are important steps toward the unification of our race. In like manner, the recent Copyright Act of the Republic removes a difference. Australasia has also done her part by placing the Republic under obligation, her greatly improved system having already been adopted with beneficial results in many of the States. She has also the simplest and best system of land laws in the world, for which we hope the Republic is soon — and the United Kingdom later — to discard its own. Thus each of the three parts,

[14] Of these authorities Sir Isaac Lowthian Bell (1816–1904) was an English metallurgist and businessman, organizer of the British Iron and Steel Institute, author of books on the industry. Abram S. Hewitt (1822–1903), son-in-law of Peter Cooper, an ironmaster, was a pioneer in the introduction into the United States of metal rolling and steelmaking and a successful Democratic politician. On Edward Atkinson see Editor's Introduction, above, p. x.

improving for herself, improves also for the benefit of the others. The race enjoying the same language, religion, literature, and law should also have the harmonizing blessings of common political institutions.

The ground once cleared of Empire Trade League efforts to array one part of the race against the other part, and equally of Imperial Federation aims which would shut out the vast majority of the race and limit the mother-land's connection to the smaller portion, and especially if the division of the race upon the North American continent were healed by union, upon the advice of the parent, the efforts of all could then be concentrated upon realizing what Mr. Bolton calls "that grand idea, the confederation of all the nations which have sprung from the race nurtured in these isles." The first-fruits of this movement would probably be seen in the appointment, by the various nations of our race, of international commissions, charged with creating a system of weights, measures, and coins, of port dues, patents, trade-marks, and other matters of similar character which are of common interest. If there be a question upon which all authorities are agreed, for instance, it is the desirability of introducing the decimal system of weights, measures, and coins; but an international commission seems the only agency capable of bringing it about.

The habit of producing uniform arrangements for the whole of the race having been created by such commissions, the step would be easy to a further development of the international idea. For under harmonious conditions Britain would soon be regarded by the English-speaking people throughout the world as the mother they all revere, and there must inevitably begin a gradual drawing together of the whole race. Even to-day, every federationist has the satisfaction of knowing that the idea of war between the two great branches is scouted on both sides of the Atlantic. Henceforth war between members of our race may be said to be already banished, for English-speaking men will never again be called upon to destroy one another. During the recent differences — not with Britain, for Britain and the Republic agreed, but with disapproving Canada, which was naturally more irritating to the Republic — not a whisper was ever heard upon either side of any possible appeal to force as a mode of settlement. Both parties in America and each successive government are pledged to offer peaceful arbitration for the adjustment of all international difficulties — a position which it is to be hoped will soon be reached by Britain, at least in regard to all the differences with members of the same race.

Is it too much to hope that after this stage has been reached and occupied successfully for a period, another step forward will be taken, and that, having jointly banished war between themselves, a general council should be created by the English-speaking nations, to which may at first be referred only questions of dispute between them? This would only be making a permanent body to settle differences, instead of selecting arbiters as required — not at all a serious advance, and yet it should be the germ from which great fruits would grow.

The Supreme Court of the United States is extolled by the statesmen of all parties in Britain, and has received the compliment of being copied in the plan for the Australian commonwealth. Building upon it, may we not expect that a still higher Supreme Court is one day to come, which shall judge between the nations of the entire English-speaking race, as the Supreme Court at Washington already judges between States which contain the majority of the race?

At first the decisions of the council would probably be made subject to ratification by all the principals, but the powers and duties of such a council, once established, may be safely trusted to increase; to its final influence over the race, and through the race over the world, no limit can be set; in the dim future it might even come that the pride of the citizen in the race as a whole would exceed that which he had in any part thereof — as the citizen of the Republic to-day is prouder of being an American than he is of being a native of any State of the Union. This is a far look ahead, no doubt, but patriotism is an expansive quality, and men to-day are as patriotic in regard to an entire continent as the ancients were about their respective cities and provinces. The time is coming when even race patriotism will give place to the citizenship of the world.

While the decisions of the council would necessarily be restricted to such questions as arose between the members of the race, its influence, and in extreme cases its recommendations, if unanimously made, could not fail to be of weighty import. We can imagine such a tribunal, for instance, unanimously saying a word upon occasion which would settle the most important subject within our horizon of to-day. Is it a very improbable idea that it might hold and obtain the unanimous approval of the powers represented in so holding that the peace of the world, in which the industrial English-speaking race is most deeply concerned, is a question which other nations cannot be allowed wholly to determine for themselves? The commanding position of our race will place upon it correspondingly great offices. United as described, it would wield such overwhelming power that resistance would be useless. Its verdict could never be questioned; its word would be law. I believe that it is by our race, and through such means, that war is most probably to be driven from the world which it disgraces, and the reign of peace established among men forever.

In the pursuit of an end so noble, the English-speaking race, wherever situated, can confidently be appealed to; its realization would be a service to mankind which justified labor, expenditure, and even risk. The feeble beginnings of the federation of Europe are already seen in the Triple Alliance. It may fail because not so overwhelmingly strong as to render impotent all efforts to cope with it, and all depends upon this; but the idea is there, for three nations have declared themselves banded together, not for the purpose of aggression, defensively, not offensively, and only to keep the peace and to punish the peace-breaker. We have nothing to do here with the merits of the controversy which called it forth, but what this Alliance aims to do for the three countries concerned for a few years, the true federation of the English-speaking race would be able to do permanently for the world. The duty is to be ours, if we coöperate, because ours is the only race of which the slightest hope can be entertained that it is soon to become so much stronger than any other race, or probable combination of races, as united to be omnipotent.

A race alliance will hasten the day in the coming of which I have implicit faith, when our race will be quite able to say — and will therefore as a duty say — to any powers that threaten to begin the murder of human beings, in the name of war, under any pretence:

Hold! I command you both; the one that stirs makes me his foe.
Unfold to me the cause of the quarrel, and I will judge betwixt you.[15]

If ever the parent-land and all her children unite in speaking these words, it need not be feared that a shot will be fired or a sword drawn. The writ of that race union will run the circle round and insure peace. We should thus have the Kriegsverein with power so overwhelming that its exercise would never be necessary. The Zollverein is something so much lower, being only a question of trade, that it scarcely deserves mention in comparison; but even the Zollverein will come of itself in its own good time, when the various members have had time to test and learn their respective capacities — what they can produce best at home, and what they must continue to purchase abroad. Protective tariffs are in their

---

[15] This seems to be a confused memory of a celebrated passage from the play by Home, *Douglas* (1757), once thought to rival Shakespearean tragedy. The lines should read:
"Hold, I command you both. The man that stirs
Makes me his foe." (Act IV, scene 2, lines 385–386.)

very nature experimental and temporary devices. These require little attention from the true federationist; indeed, the less they receive the sooner they will pass away. All the forces at work tend to equilibrium of cost throughout the world, and hence the reduction and final abolition of protective duties as no longer necessary.

It is obvious that such an alliance of the race is dependent upon a union of hearts, and that force or pressure would only defeat it. No more seeds of lifelong bitterness should be sown. The younger members of the race should remember what is due to the parent; the parent should seek to retain their love and reverence by being "to their faults a little blind and to their virtues very kind," [16] freely according to each, when maturity arrives, the same independent existence and the same exclusive management of its own affairs as she claims for herself, and rather than relinquish which she would sink under the sea. Each member must be free to manage his own home as he thinks proper without incurring hostile criticism or parental interference. All must be equal — allies, not dependents.

Fate has given to Britain a great progeny and a great past. Her future promises to be no less great and prolific. Many may be the members of the family council of all the English-speaking nations, each complete in itself, which I have predicted as sure to come sooner or later; but, however numerous the children, there can never be but one mother, and that mother, great, honored, and beloved by all her offspring, — as I pray she is to be, — "this Sceptered Isle," [17] my native land. God bless her!

[16] Quoted inaccurately from Matthew Prior, "An English Padlock," line 79.

[17] *Richard II*, Act II, scene 1, line 35.

THE JOHN HARVARD LIBRARY

*The intent of
Waldron Phoenix Belknap, Jr.,
as expressed in an early will, was for
Harvard College to use the income from a
permanent trust fund he set up, for "editing and
publishing rare, inaccessible, or hitherto unpublished
source material of interest in connection with the
history, literature, art (including minor and useful
art), commerce, customs, and manners or way of
life of the Colonial and Federal Periods of the United
States . . . In all cases the emphasis shall be on the
presentation of the basic material." A later testament
broadened this statement, but Mr. Belknap's interests remained constant until his death.*

*In linking the name of the first benefactor of
Harvard College with the purpose of this later,
generous-minded believer in American culture the
John Harvard Library seeks to emphasize the importance of Mr. Belknap's purpose. The John Harvard
Library of the Belknap Press of Harvard University
Press exists to make books and documents
about the American past more readily
available to scholars and the
general reader.*